BEYOND
COUNTERCULTURE

BEYOND COUNTERCULTURE
the Community of Mateel

Jentri Anders

Washington State University Press
Pullman, Washington
1990

Washington State University Press, Pullman, Washington 99164-5910

Copyright 1990 by the Board of Regents of Washington State University

All Rights Reserved

Printed and bound in the United States of America

First published 1990

00 99 98 97 96 95 94 93 92 91   1 2 3 4 5 6 7 8 9 10

No part of this book may be reproduced or transmitted in any form or by any means, electronic or mechanical, including recording, photocopying, or by any information storage or retrieval system, without permission in writing from the publisher.

Library of Congress Cataloging-in-Publication Data

Anders, Jentri, 1942-
Beyond counterculture : The community of Mateel / Jentri Anders
p. cm.
Notes: p.

ISBN 0-87422-061-0
ISBN 0-87422-060-2 (paperback)

Cover design: Sharon White

Contents

Foreword by John Bodley   vii

Introduction   ix

Chapter One   Who are the Mateelians?   1
Chapter Two   Mateel: The Unit of Study   21
Chapter Three   Ecotopia   35
Chapter Four   Amerika   47
Chapter Five   The Primitive Model   61
Chapter Six   Worldview   69
Chapter Seven   Political Behavior   119
Chapter Eight   Economic Behavior   159
Chapter Nine   Social Interaction   195
Chapter Ten   Kinship   221

Conclusion   279

Appendix One   Note on Methodology   301
Appendix Two   Song of Twelve   307
Appendix Three   Note on Mateelian Names   315

Notes   317

Foreword

This book was at least partly inspired by Jentri Anders's reading of my earlier work, *Anthropology and Contemporary Problems* (1976, 1985) in which I contrasted the ills created by large-scale industrial civilization with relatively balanced adaptations enjoyed by small-scale, self-sufficient, tribal cultures. I noted that the "counterculture" communities that were then appearing were in fact experimental attempts to merge the best features of small-scale culture with the most positive features of industrial technology. At that time, little reliable information was available to show how such communities might arise or how they actually worked. I was delighted when Jentri came to Washington State University in 1980 with a proposal for a dissertation in anthropology that would be just the kind of study that was needed. Her work is unique in two important respects. While there have been many studies on communes, and much has been written about the counterculture, this book is the only major anthropological study of a regional countercultural community with thousands of members. Furthermore, the research was carried out by an insider, who was a participating member of the community for nearly fifteen years and is still a "native."

    Jentri went into the field as a trained anthropologist with an M.A. in anthropology from Berkeley. After some ten years of field experience she returned to graduate school for more course work and library research, and still took time for more formal field work in Mateel. This is real participant observation, even beyond the tradition of Malinowski, yet there is no loss of objectivity. This total immersion in the field experience makes for remarkable insights into the native mind and provides an unusually rich data base.

    The significance of the research lies in its basic concern with exploring cultural solutions to some of the most intractable problems of our time: resource depletion, environmental deterioration, and a wide range of socioeconomic ills. These issues are even more critical today than when Mateel began to form in the early 1970s. Anders describes a cultural system that indeed responds to many of these problems, and she considers how such a culture can be created. Her emphasis on ideology, individual consciousness, and communication as critical elements in the process of creating a new culture, reflects the views of the Mateel culture itself, and represents an important challenge to the materialist emphasis which is so prevalent in contemporary anthropological theory. Some readers may be disturbed by the book's emphasis on the role of mind-altering drugs in the genesis of Mateel; however, it should be remembered that this is the view from Mateel culture, and it describes the culture at a particular point in time. There clearly can be many pathways out of our present dilemma, but they will require major change.

I am pleased to report that the dissertation version of this book was selected as the 1986 Washington State University Outstanding Dissertation and was a nominee for a Council of Graduate Schools/ University Microfilms International Dissertation Award. In condensed form, it won first place in the graduate student paper competition at the 1986 Northwest Anthropological Conference.

John H. Bodley
Pullman, Washington
1990

Introduction

The major theoretical questions addressed by the science of anthropology are "what causes culture," and "why is this culture like it is." However, scientists disagree in the way they arrive at answers to these questions; some have stressed the intellect, others the physical world. Marvin Harris's encyclopedic work, *The Rise of Anthropological Theory*,[1] sees a dichotomy between those who favor "ideology" as a cause for culture and those, like himself, who emphasize material factors.[2] Ideological elements include language, value system, religion, philosophy, worldview, art, and all subjective experience, that is, phenomena that can only be studied by asking subjects what they think. The current anthropological jargon for these ideological elements is the term *emic*.

Material factors include all of those things that anthropologists are able to observe without resorting to an informant's interpretation—technology, resources, environment, economic strategies, and biological data. The term applied to material factors collectively is *etic*. Marvin Harris asserts, without qualification, that etic factors cause emic factors. For him, etic (materialistic) factors are constants; those things considered emic (ideological) are variables. Harris specifically dismisses counterculture as a possible source for serious cultural change, because it emphasizes the emic. This characteristic, he maintains, leads to an apolitical, ineffective outlook.[3] Sociologist Bennett Berger takes Harris's materialist position and applies it to American counterculture with his own concept of "ideological work" in which people rationalize practical necessities into self-serving ideologies.[4] Neither Harris nor Berger base their views of counterculture on ethnography as it is defined traditionally by anthropologists. Harris relies on Carlos Castaneda's *Teachings of*

Don Juan as if it were the definitive ideological basis for American counterculture.[5] Berger spent some weekends at a commune within convenient commuting distance from San Francisco and calls it participant observation.

The theoretical position for this book is a contrasting and decidedly less value-laden approach than either Harris or Berger have offered, one in which it is more important to understand the relationship between economic necessity and ideology than it is to establish which "came first." This approach derives directly from the work of Gregory Bateson, who viewed culture as a vast, complex communication system susceptible to the rules of general systems theory. Cultural systems display positive and negative feedbacks, deviation amplification, cybernetic control mechanisms, in exactly the same way that ecosystems, such as a redwood tree or a human mind does. Within all such biological systems, cause is circular:

> Any change in any part of the circle can be regarded as a *cause* for any change at a later time in any variable anywhere in the circle.[6]

If we accept this view, it is as possible for change to come from an ideological component as from one that is materialistic. In fact, one kind of change cannot happen without the other.

In some situations, particularly within Western societies, which so highly value individuality, cultural change can spring from subjective experience, which influences the individual and, eventually, the collective worldview. With particular reference to Mateel, ideals generated from similar individual experiences are hammered into the group worldview through intense, personal interaction in the context of a shared environment.

Forces that created Mateel relate to the present state of the global environment in two ways:

1. the sociological trends that influence the environment negatively are the same ones against which Mateelians reacted when they created their community

2. the degree of their success suggests that lessons can be learned from this community about making the changes necessary to rescue our natural environment.

Chapters one through five introduce the social side of environmental degradation and the community of Mateel; these chapters also contain descriptions of three hypothetical models to which Mateel will be compared. The remaining six chapters analyze and describe Mateel's cultural system, comparing various components of it to three models.

Friends gather for a marriage ceremony under a parachute at the community school in Mateel.

Chapter One

Who Are the Mateelians?

Man, if you ain't scaaaared, you ain't rite!

—*Taj Mahal*

The context for this book is crisis. From the melting of the earth's polar ice caps to the prospect of nuclear war, from the alienation of individuals from society to increases in child abuse, symptoms of crisis appear at every hand. In the course of recent evolution, human beings have become isolated from nature by a barrier of culturally determined meanings. The species has responded sluggishly, if at all, to critical information that points to the destruction of their natural environment. In this respect, *Homo sapiens* is unprecedented in the biological world.

In a period of time breathtakingly short in evolutionary terms, this one species has caused the extinction of hundreds of others and has turned forests into deserts, islands into craters, rain into an acid solution, rivers and oceans into chemical cesspools, and has rearranged the molecular structure of the atmosphere itself. So far as is known, no other form of life has ever destroyed its environment on such a massive scale.

Many writers in the field of ecology are convinced that "human impact on the environment increases with economic and technological scale."[1] Others argue that the philosophical alienation of people from nature has short-circuited the reciprocal flow of information that might have prevented the species from becoming out of balance with its resources.[2] Anthropologist John Bodley declares that ". . . if civilization is considered a patient, it will now either get better or die."[3]

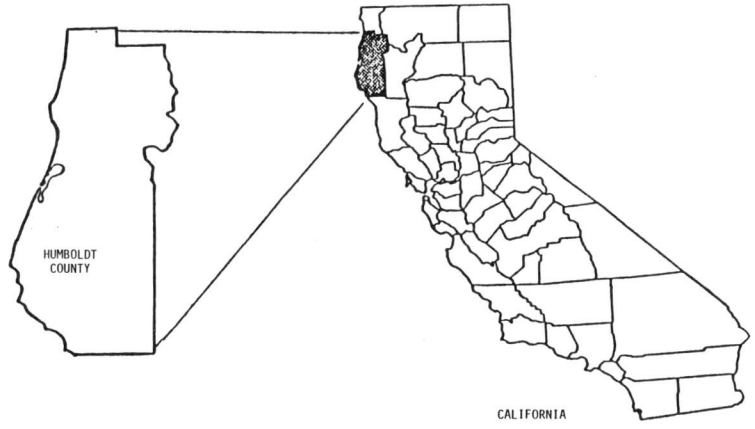

Figure One. Humboldt County, California

This book is about a community trying to "get better." We will call the community *Mateel*. The cultural system of Mateel will be described and analyzed in order to determine whether or not anything can be learned from it about planning a route out of our present environmental crisis. Comparisons will be made with three other models of society: 1) a hypothetical society called "Ecotopia" based on the writings of ecologically oriented futurists; 2) industrial society in its negative aspect, which will be called "Amerika"; and 3) a generalized model of primitive society, called "primitive."

The word Mateel refers to a community, its cultural system, and to the space it occupies. That space is a geographic area in Humboldt County, northern California (Figure One), roughly approximating the upper watersheds of the Mattole and Eel rivers (Figure Two). The word Mateel was derived from the combination of the names of

Who are the Mateelians? 3

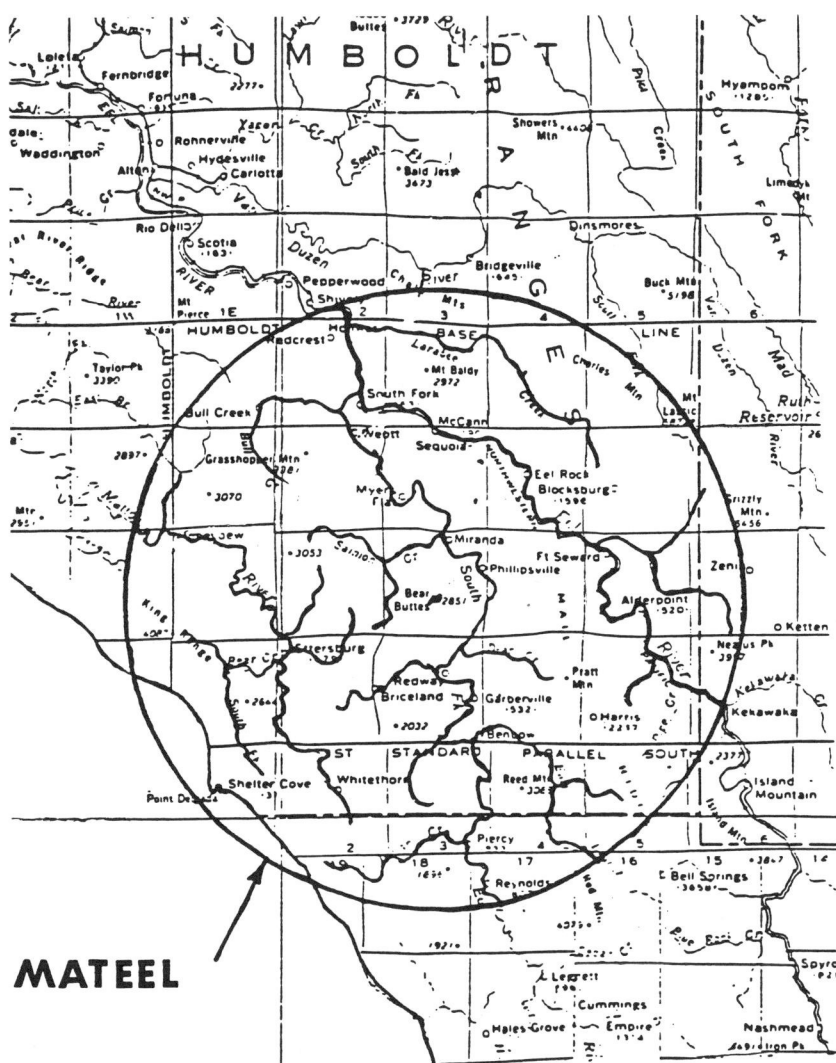

Figure Two. Mateel. The Circle is arbitrarily drawn with Bear Buttes at the center.

these two rivers. The social entity is more difficult to define than its physical location. For the present, consider it a cultural system—that is, an arrangement of meanings and behavior accepted generally by some of the individuals residing in the defined geographic area. The degree to which individuals are considered members of the community depends on the extent to which they subscribe to the Mateelian cultural values. At first, this interim definition may seem ambiguous. Nevertheless, the cultural system is best described by leaving precise social boundaries unmarked, at least at the beginning. It is a social network that represents the continuation of the 1960s movement Theodore Roszak called the "counter-culture."[4]

The Environmental Crisis

William Catton, in *Overshoot: The Ecological Basis of Revolutionary Change*, provides a concise description of the present situation regarding humans and the natural environment; he calls it a "predicament."[5] Regardless of whether this analysis is accepted or whether our situation is a "crisis," as John Bodley declares, the circumstances are the same.[6]

> Human beings, in two million years of cultural evolution, have several times succeeded in taking over additional portions of the earth's total life-supporting capacity at the expense of other creatures. Each time, the human population increased. But humanity has now learned to rely on a technology that augments human carrying capacity in a necessarily temporary way—as temporary as the extension of life by eating seeds needed to grow next year's food.[7]

John Bennett believes that the development of agriculture and the accompanying growth of civilization were early examples of technological shifts leading the "ecological transition" to an unbalanced state.[8] He views increasing environmental damage as inevitable, but acknowledges that pre-agricultural human populations managed to maintain a balance with resources for periods of thousands of years.[9] Others have argued that primitive societies in the modern era tend to live in balance with their resources, exceeding that balance only when they come into contact with civilization.[10] A similar technological shift causing population growth and environmental damage was the development of science and its applied manifestation, industrialization.

Because industrialization is now a global phenomenon capable of causing the extinction of humans, and other species as well, studying its history is not a mere academic enterprise.[11] For unless we understand the origins of the potential catastrophe with which we are faced, we stand little chance of preventing its occurrence. While it is true, as complacent defeatists assert, that the impersonal "forces of Nature" will restore balance through natural processes such as famine, disease, and intraspecies violence, most of us recognize that these are not acceptable solutions. Intraspecies violence among human beings often takes the form of war; in modern times that may mean a nuclear conflagration. "Balance," after a nuclear war, might well mean a global ecosystem dominated by radiation-resistant cockroaches.

What kind of "balance" could be restored after the loss of the earth's ozone layer? Most of us cannot help feeling a certain whimsical attachment to those creatures, human and non-human alike, that would suffer so profoundly first. Those who place faith in modern technology's ability to solve such large problems fail to recognize its reliance on increasingly scarce nonrenewable energy sources.[12] Catton characterizes such approaches as simply "stealing from the future."[13]

Because of the diminishing returns involved in tapping hard-to-get energy sources, such as off-shore oil, their exploitation represents a regression, not an advance.[14] Like Bodley, many analysts believe that the way out of our dilemma requires "nothing less than a complete cultural transformation."[15]

To date, most actions taken to meet the environmental crisis have concentrated on cleaning up polluted areas, or on stop gap measures, such as building fuel-efficient automobiles to conserve petroleum. These strategies are limited in scope and stand in sharp contrast to strategies that rely on education and serious social change. Traditionally, when attempts have been made to alter public attitudes, environmentalists have presented their arguments in apologetic, defensive ways. For example, when Jerry Brown was elected governor of California in 1976, his platform incorporated the phrase "lowered expectations" from E. F. Schumacher's 1973 book titled *Small is Beautiful*.[16] This approach, though aimed in the right direction, illustrates a basic mistake in cultural planning, an exercise in "how not to do it." Brown could have called his platform plank *raised expectations* and stipulated that raised environmental and social expectations require changed material expectations, most of which would lead to improved living standards.

Alvin Toffler's use of the word *ascetic* to describe the voluntary simplicity movement reflects a similar culturally determined bias in favor of consumption.[17] Those aspects of countercultural life called ascetic by mainstream Americans, such as vegetarianism, living in isolation, using limited amounts of electricity, or abandoning modern plumbing, are not perceived in the same way by participants. They are freely chosen by individuals in the context of their raised social and spiritual expectations. Any discomfort resulting from these choices is considered to be more than compensated for by non-material rewards of a simpler lifestyle.

One example of a situation that could have had a cultural, rather than a technological, solution occurred in the late 1970s when U.S. Congressman from Texas James Mattox showed up for work one day in a blue, short-sleeved cotton shirt and no tie. He had adapted to Washington, D.C.'s summer heat and was trying to comply with President Carter's order to raise settings on air conditioning units in view of an energy shortage. Speaker Tip O'Neill asked Mattox to go home and return to the House of Representatives properly dressed. Mattox refused and tried to speak, but O'Neill would not recognize him. Mattox later explained to newsmen that wearing a coat and tie in the summer heat was "silly" and "archaic," a tradition that should be abandoned. Electric fans were subsequently installed in the House to supplement air conditioning, illustrating the triumph of a technological solution over a cultural one.[18]

Few politicians, other than former California Governor Jerry Brown, have had the courage to say that Americans must alter their behavior if they are to rescue the global environment.[19] Cultural changes suggested by ecologists are routinely deleted from political documents, along with passages describing basic ecological relationships. No one suggests lowering the American standard of living because uttering such statements is assumed to be a form of political suicide. Politicians and planners alike, assume that Americans cannot be asked to live on what they define as less; they are equally unwilling to change their definition of what less might be. It is therefore important to document a coherent cultural system in which pathological obsessions with technology and growth are replaced by fulfilling, expressive behavior, social and spiritual values, and increasing individual and collective sanity. Mateel is becoming such a community.

Mateel: What It Is

Hypothetical models for cultural change abound.[20] One that is particularly relevant to Mateel is G. Rattray Taylor's "paraprimitive solution."[21] Taylor looks to primitive societies as models because they are, in terms of ecological balance, relatively stable. To arrive at the paraprimitive solution he combines the best elements of industrial civilization with the best elements of primitive cultures to create a stable society in balance with its resources. The Mateelian community is an embryonic form of Taylor's paraprimitive solution. It is an unplanned social experiment that has, while reacting to the problems of modern industrialized society, inadvertently opted for many paraprimitive problem-solving strategies. In the process of implementing these strategies, residents have begun to accept values implicit in them. A better source of primary data on efforts to adopt paraprimitive values and strategies would be difficult to find.

Mateel had its origins in the counterculture movement of the 1960s and early 1970s. In fact, the vast majority of the Mateel community's original inhabitants were dropouts who were once a part of the counterculture. Central characteristics Mateelians share with other counterculture movements are: a discontent with mainstream American society and a strong desire to avoid what society held for them. Their actions should be interpreted as efforts "counter" to those aspects of modern, industrialized American society they consider dehumanizing, ecologically unsound, and alienating.[22]

It would be a mistake, however, to depict Mateelian culture as it evolved in the 1980s simply as an effort to counteract negative elements found in a way of life that had been left behind. What began as a movement of exiles has evolved, *through* the reversals that shaped countercultural thought, into a series of new approaches to old problems. These approaches combine elements taken from the mainstream

American past with ideas borrowed from other cultures, and solutions that can only be described as futurist thinking.

A study of Mateelian life histories indicates that many members of the community are refugees from technocracy; they came to Mateel to escape from something. Some are fugitives, fleeing real or imagined persecution. Some are Vietnam veterans unable to cope with post-war America; some are wives fleeing the oppression of traditional marriages; others are former urban residents escaping what they believe to be the death of America's cities. Mateel also contains former drug abusers escaping social networks that prevented their "drying out," ex-convicts, homosexuals, and spiritual seekers fleeing the moral and aesthetic bankruptcy of mainstream America.

The earliest Mateelians were more often refugees than were later arrivals, who had less extreme reasons for immigration, and who moved into the community after an alternative social system had been established. Many of these later arrivals, professionals who were unwilling to assume the economic risk taken by the first Mateelians, came into the area after the population base was sufficiently large to support them. Still, the refugee experience for most emigrants has proven to be definitive, and to have exacerbated emotional discontinuity and the physical isolation of dropping out. Many mainstream locals reacted to the arrival of these cultural refugees just like similar populations the world over react: with suspicion, fear, avoidance, and violence. This negative experience with members of the local community has influenced the Mateelian collective self-image and underlies much of the interaction between the two groups.

It is easy to read into the Mateelian experience a yearning to recapture the past. But insofar as this is a valid inference, the yearned-for past is idealized and reflects a variety of environmental and social concerns that are characteristic of the present.

Many Mateelian feminists abhor social aspects of the historical past, yet they take pride in performing work similar to that done by American pioneers, male or female, and in returning to traditional childbearing practices, with women in charge of the process. Mateelian images of the past suggest that it was a place where families could support themselves by virtue of their labor on small pieces of land.

However, economic units that work small pieces of land in the Mateelian present may take many forms. They may be nuclear, extended, communal, matriarchal, or patriarchal families, or other social arrangements not necessarily sanctioned legally. It could easily be said that Mateelians yearn as much for the future they are engaged in creating as they do for an idealized past.

Mateel: What It Isn't

The most negative argument used to undermine what is being done in communities like Mateel is the assertion that inhabitants want to reverse the course of history. Alvin Toffler's description of "first wave reversionists" in his book *The Third Wave* is typical of such views.[23] He complains that reversionist groups deter progress and are impediments to change because the public confuses their vision with that possessed by advocates of alternative technology. He sees reversionists as a "small vocal fringe of romantic extremists hostile to all but the most primitive First Wave technologies, who seem to favor a return to medieval crafts and labor. . . ."[24] Since Toffler does not expand this discussion, we must assume that he is confused about the extent to which countercultural groups are proponents of hand labor and craftsmanship. In Mateel, as elsewhere, these preferences are usually combined with an acceptance of both alternative energy sources and appropriate technology in general.

Toffler, like many Americans, does not sufficiently grasp the connection between social systems and levels of technology. Indeed, he seems to believe that technology is either present or absent, not something that evolves as it moves from culture to culture. Many social changes called for by paraprimitive advocates are identical to reversionist trends that Toffler criticizes:

> In extreme form [First Wave reversionist] policies would eliminate most technology, restrict mobility, cause cities to shrivel and die, and impose an ascetic culture in the name of conservation.[25]

However, advocates of paraprimitive solutions also call for a technological advance nearly identical to that outlined by Toffler, that is, for ". . . a new, more intelligent, sustainable, and scientifically based energy system."[26] The difference is that paraprimitive strategists realize that such a change, by itself, is not sufficient. They believe that most modern technology, described by Toffler as *Second Wave* energy systems, should be abolished. Restricted mobility is a part of their program because the amount of travel to which most Americans have become accustomed is unnecessary and wasteful. Advocates of paraprimitive solutions argue that cities should become smaller because they are either too large, like New York, or they are located inappropriately, far away from important water resources, like Los Angeles. These futurists hope to bring about the creation of a new culture in which individuals find spiritual and psychological rewards as preservationists and conservers, not as wasteful consumers. Unfortunately many Americans have become so wasteful that they perceive of such approaches as being ascetic.

These changes necessarily accompany the acceptance of more efficient ways to use energy; they are characteristic of cultures that predate organized agriculture, that is societies in which most members produced what they consumed.[27]

Mateelians, however, are not simply reversionists who want to exclude all new technologies. The locally owned and run alternative energy store in Garberville, for instance, sells more solar panels for domestic use than any retail store in the country.[28] Computers were also high on the list of items purchased by Mateelians when the marijuana boom gave them the resources to invest in this technology. Using solar-generated electricity, many Mateelians have found appropriate uses for home computers—so much so that at least one of the alternative schools is equipped with several computers for student use. Far from being reversionists, Mateelians are constantly in search of non-polluting, low-energy technology to combine with their labor-intensive strategies and high-quality crafts.

There are other labels that clearly do not apply to Mateel. First, it is not a utopia. An examination of the history of utopian movements over the past century reveals that most were remarkably inflexible.[29] As aspiring anarchists, Mateelians cannot tolerate inflexibility, preferring to organize themselves by a process somewhat akin to spontaneous combustion.

Second, Mateel is not simply an extension of modern America. The cultural discontinuity experienced by individuals is real and has become collective. Mateelian cultural assumptions are fundamentally different than those of most modern Americans and are unlike those of any ethnic group living in the United States. The American mainstream and Mateelian systems lie at "opposite and incompatible poles," like primitive societies that "are so unique that they can only minimally interact with states and still retain their full identity."[30]

Third, the Mateelian community is not analogous to such subcultural groups as the Amish, because Mateelian society is minimally structured and still in flux, rather than being stabilized at a particular stage of development. The hierarchical organization of groups like the Amish, as well their patriarchal nature, is an anathema to Mateelians in general and feminists in particular.

Fourth, Mateel is a countercultural community that has evolved beyond the counterculture movement in general. It is not a communal movement, although communes do exist within the community and many individuals were, at one time, members of communes. In spite of attempts by the news media to present Mateel as such, it is not a fad. Traits that characterize communities like Mateel, such as public nudity, the use of hot tubs, or the wearing of "country fashions" often show up in other places through a kind of social osmosis and often become cliches. In Mateel, however, such traits are integral components of a dynamic culture.[31]

Mateel is not a primitive tribe, as some of its members would like it to be. Mateelians retain all of the information from their lives in mainstream American society. Their sophistication in understanding global matters alone differentiates them from primitive peoples they might idealistically seek to emulate. Hugh Gardner in his book, *The Children of Prosperity: Thirteen Modern American Communes*, suggests that "the protracted leisure and educational opportunities" of the early members of the counterculture "brought them into contact with many different cultures and a vast array of alternative models for arranging their lives."[32] This aspect of the counterculture was a force in shaping Mateelian social and technological experimentation. The conscious examination and evaluation of ideas drawn from other cultures is an obvious feature, especially when the counterculture is viewed from the community level, rather than as an entire movement.

Two cultural models Mateelians frequently use are Eastern civilizations and tribal societies. Philosophy and ceremonialism are drawn from both, but social organization, kinship, economics, and political structure appear to be more influenced by the tribal model. To trained anthropologists, the tribal model used might appear overly romanticized or even inaccurate. Yet, the apparent equality found within groups like the Bushmen or Shoshoni is often cited in relationships where hierarchy might be an issue. The "Cheyenne" attitude toward death informs Mateelian funeral practices; drumming, dancing, and singing from Yoruba and Sufi traditions is widespread; consensus and decision making are modeled after Plains Indians' tribal gatherings.[33]

The use of primitive models in social organization has resulted in the incorporation of many tribal society traits, bits and pieces taken from various cultures that do not neatly fit together to form a coherent system. In fact, the disparate nature of these usages is sometimes a source of tension within Mateel. For instance, the resistance to any appearance of personal ambition to dominate the group (a power or ego trip) is clear evidence of an emphasis on group equality. The opposing need for leadership in cooperative ventures, combined with a traditional hostility to people adopting leadership roles has often resulted in solutions to immediate problems being delayed. On the other hand, this fear of hierarchy has forced the development of a society based on families and small groups, rather than on established structures and centralized leadership. Given these anarchic tendencies, the Mateelians have generated their culture painfully and in spite of themselves.

Changing Culture in Mateel

If the changing of cultural attitudes is considered to be the best long-term approach to solving the environmental dilemma caused by industrialization, then the next challenge to our democracy is how to bring it about without coercion. The real question is, where does change come from in culture? The proposition explored in this book is that cultural change must emanate from the *abstract realm* of ideas as readily as from the *real world* of economic motivation. John

Bodley declares that we need "a complete cultural transformation";[34] educator Lewis Perelman goes further, calling for ". . . a profound and far-reaching transformation, not only of human society but of human consciousness as well."[35]

Consciousness is a word that is often used by Mateelians; after all, their community was generated almost exclusively from the interaction of individuals who were trying to implement what Perelman called "profound and far-reaching transformation" and who were actively engaged in reprograming their own internal reality. One might say that the alteration of culture through the transformation of personal worldviews continues to be tested in Mateel. Mateel is an ideal place to study intentional, self-directed reprograming as a cultural phenomenon, because the importance of consciousness is the basic tenet of the culture.

The speed and comprehensiveness of change in Mateel is remarkable. In fewer than twenty years, distinctive cultural patterns have developed based on the principles of harmony with the environment, local self sufficiency, social equality, expectations for less material consumption, and personal responsibility for the implementation of these ideals. These cultural patterns are conspicuously represented by a tendency to reject public utilities, an emphasis on alternative energy sources, the use of natural and holistic healing and preventative medicine, home production of food, recycling, owner-built homes, alternative service organizations, alternative schools, consumer cooperatives, natural childbirth and midwifery, tolerance for social diversity, redefinition of social roles, and environmental priorities in resource use. Radical experiments in kinship, marriage, family and political organization, and ownership of property abound, revealing a willingness to endure emotional pain to create something new.

These patterns are notable because they involved no formal planning, no special development programs, and they occurred in a short period of time. Three interacting components account for this accelerated process of social change:

1. isolation from mainstream culture in the early stages of cultural development
2. a personal and direct interaction among individuals

3. the use of mind-altering substances. Exploring these three factors in more detail will provide historical context and will explain how change could occur with such rapidity.

All serious researchers are agreed that the hallucinogenic experience played a crucial role in the emergence of the counterculture. In Mateel, marijuana's significance has been essentially the same as the psychedelics. One experience might be seen as more acute than the other, but both point in the same philosophical direction. The hallucinogenic and marijuana experiences are, among other things, temporary suspensions of the conscious and unconscious cultural assumptions that form a person's model of reality. Once these assumptions are suspended, the degree to which behavior is a function of culture becomes clear; that is, personal actions can be seen as having been directly structured by what one has learned. Humphrey Osmond, a clinical researcher who works with psychedelics, observed that:

> Once our mold for world-making is formed it most strongly resists change. The psychedelics allow us, for a little while, to divest ourselves of these acquired assumptions and to see the universe again with an innocent eye.[36]

For a brief moment, countercultural people, many of whom were already questioning social values, caught a glimpse of a world-before-assumptions, an experience that can be called *culturelessness*. The next move was obvious to those who dropped out: to change the world, they must first change their own culture-based internal programming, what the counterculture calls "consciousness." If enough people do that, culture will change. As one researcher put it:

> The overwhelming significance of the psychedelic drug use is the erosion of the old social order in the mind of the user; the breakdown of society's conventional value system, the dislocation of users from the life plans and career tracks marked out for them, and the consequent exodus in search of new worlds, new fulfillments, new selves.[37]

This motif for changing the world by changing the way we communicate with ourselves and others has become a persistent and repeated theme in Mateelian culture. The expression "you make your own reality" has the status of an adage and the complaints of children and adults are frequently met with this truism. In Berkeley in the late 1960s the graffiti "off the pigs" was frequently altered to read "off the pig in you." The concept expressed by this change, which was and still is anathema to conventional revolutionaries, has been cited by many Mateelians as their prime motivation in life; to "off the pig" in themselves as a means of eliminating warfare from the repertoire of human activity. It is partly this tenet, that social change must start with the individual, that has enabled cultural evolution to take place so rapidly in Mateel.

Assuming that enculturation, the process of learning one's culture, is life long, the cultureless experience and the altered programming derived from it may be viewed as a discontinuity. This discontinuity at mental and spiritual levels, took a physical form for those who moved to Mateel. Mateelians often describe some experience that, usually in combination with the use of a hallucinogen, led them to break consciously with mainstream America. But even in America, one "puts one's money where one's mouth is" in order to be taken seriously. Mateelians retained this single American ideal. The decision to drop out of the mainstream was a physical action. It depended on whether or not an individual was willing to face the likelihood of having a reduced, unlikely, or unpredictable, source of income.

The first step in rejecting what Mateelians saw as American hypocrisy was to disconnect themselves from the economic system, a process that meant facing unforeseen consequences. Those most affected by this discontinuity were people who saw the change as a struggle to accept a fundamental truth or a way to retain their own sanity. As a result, they tried to remove themselves from the influence of mainstream culture, which was seen in varying shades of evil. For some, it was a political decision against *The System*; for others, it was a recognition that if they remained in mainstream culture, they might not survive as sane individuals. Some dropouts became nomads and traveled the world, often coming back to Mateel for what was called a "social hit," meaning interaction. Others looked for more sedentary isolation from the mainstream culture. Northern California was one of the places that offered this isolation.

A consistent pattern in the life histories of Mateelians is a period of individual isolation. It occurs in the lives of most people after they have left mainstream culture and before they have become, actively or passively, part of the Mateel community. Many people remain in this phase for a long time, living like hermits, denying relationships to the larger community, and failing to perceive that their simple presence is a factor in the life of the community. This individual withdrawal is also part of a broader pattern of isolation that contributes to the speed of change in Mateel. It provides a period during which discontinuity is incorporated into the private system of meanings, a process resembling closely Anthony Wallace's description of "mazeway resynthesis,"[38] a subject covered in a later chapter.

Most people soon make enough progress with their individual reprograming to seek social contact. When they do begin their social reentry, they find waiting for them a dynamic society constantly being created by others who have undergone experiences similar to their own.

Among the factors insulating Mateelian culture from the rest of the world are its physical isolation and its economy, both of which restrict movement. Geographically, there is distance. Mateel is located 200 miles from San Francisco, the nearest large city, and eighty miles from Eureka, the nearest small city. Most Mateelians live on privately maintained dirt access roads, at least a half-mile and up to twenty miles off county-maintained, paved roads. Given a climate characterized by torrential winter rain, these dirt roads can become impassable. People who define themselves by owning a "clean machine" are automatically weeded out by the condition of Mateel's roads. Many roads are deliberately maintained in a state of disrepair for just this reason.

When poverty caused by the economic break with mainstream culture was added to distance and bad roads, Mateelians were effectively isolated from frequent interactions with non-Mateelians. This "forty miles of bad road" form of isolation is still true in many parts of Mateel. The positive effect of seclusion is that Mateelians have become dependent on one another. The needs they share, along with their acceptance of bad roads and weather, encourages accelerated cultural evolution.

A second factor contributing to the isolation of Mateelian society from mainstream America is the lack of electricity, which translates into an absence of radios and television sets. Whereas Mateelians today frequently have solar panels or water wheels to generate electricity, most did not during the period when alternative cultural patterns were being established. Even for those willing to defy the general Mateelian disapproval of the news media, there were few means to do so. Newspapers are not delivered. People seldom went to town. Mailboxes are located in town or on county roads, usually miles away from residences. Contact by telephone is even more limited, a fact that hampers interaction, but increases the probability that, when it does take place, it is face to face. The number of long-distance telephone calls Mateelians make is still limited by the distance from home to the nearest pay phone and by the inconvenience of having a conversation while standing in the rain, heat, cold, or being pestered by mosquitoes and the dust from trucks rolling by on county roads.

One member of the community who had been a "hopeless news addict" described how, after three years with no electricity, she happened to go to town one day and learned that Richard Nixon had resigned as president of the United States. Hearing that his speech would be broadcast that night, she drove to the top of a nearby ridge to increase the reception of her car's radio, and then listened to Nixon's remarks through the static.

A third factor contributing to isolation is the way cultural differences are perceived by both Mateelians and non-Mateelians. Cross-cultural contact is, to some degree, mutually avoided. Interaction across cultural lines has ranged, at various points in the history of Mateel, from violence to simple avoidance to active cooperation on projects of mutual interest. Individuals from both groups vary widely in the degree to which they seek and can tolerate cross-cultural contact. There are cases where individual cross-cultural relationships have been so cordial as to approach fictive kinship. However, as a general rule, the two groups recognize their differences and seek social interaction from within their own cultural systems. Still, distinctions between the two culture systems have become blurred by the addition of a late-coming professional class, by more recent arrivals motivated exclusively by the marijuana industry, and by the emergence of politically motivated "bridge-builders." Other factors, such as the California attorney general's "Campaign Against Marijuana Planting" (CAMP), have served to highlight cultural differences and to cause each group to solidify its position. This picture has not changed in fifteen years. It has only become more complex.

A phenomenon known as *interactional strategy* is the final element contributing to the acceleration of Mateelian cultural evolution; it will also form the basis for a subsequent chapter in this book.[39] For now, it is sufficient to say that discontinuity and isolation have spawned alternative means for evaluating one's self, others, and society in general. These criteria include a repugnance for social posturing, negative sanctions against what is seen as dishonesty, and positive acceptance of what is considered forthrightness in personal relations. The result is greater personal flexibility and an openness to social experimentation that cannot be found in most mainstream forms of communication.

Interaction is more likely to be of a personal nature among Mateelians than among mainstream Americans for several reasons: 1) the bonding brought about by the use of hallucinogens and marijuana—the experience itself and the fact that the use of these substances automatically makes one an outcast from mainstream America; 2) the fact that Mateelians, like primitive peoples, must cooperate to accomplish so many things that are provided to mainstream Americans by the state; 3) the sedentary orientation of Mateelians, in contrast to the mobile orientation of mainstream Americans, and; 4) the small scale of their community.

The intensity and openness of interaction promote the rapid spread of innovation from the intrapersonal level to the entire culture. The discontinuity experience and the interaction generated by it give Mateelians an advantage by allowing them individually and collectively to bypass the assumptions of mainstream American culture in order to experiment and adapt themselves to the world in new ways.

Jill, Spirit, and Loretta sing "Too Many Men on My Mind" and "I've Got None at All" in the Laundromat scene from *Vibram Soul*.

Chapter Two

Mateel: The Unit of Study

Gonna get back on the land and try and set my soul free....
—Joni Mitchell

One environmental aspect unfamiliar to persons new to the community is not necessarily the physical setting, but its isolation. In the play, *Vibram Soul*, a recent arrival from New York City complains:

> I shoulda stayed in the city. At least in the city, there were millions of people. Sure, I was alone, but I was alone with millions of people. Here, I'm alone by myself.

He is answered by his land partner who has made the adjustment:

> Oh, Larry, you're not by yourself. You got friends that love you, Larry. You have a piece of land with a nice little house. And lookit where you're living, Larry, lookit those gracious, rolling hills, that vast expansive sky. Breathe in those negative ions, Larry. You know what it is? You're depressed. When I'm depressed like you, Larry, I just take a walk . . . until I find a tree that's just right and I sit . . . until I feel at peace again.

Adaptation to isolation is considered a profound learning experience by many members of the community, most of whom grew up in large cities. The three most frequently mentioned places of origin are New York, Los Angeles, and the San Francisco Bay Area.

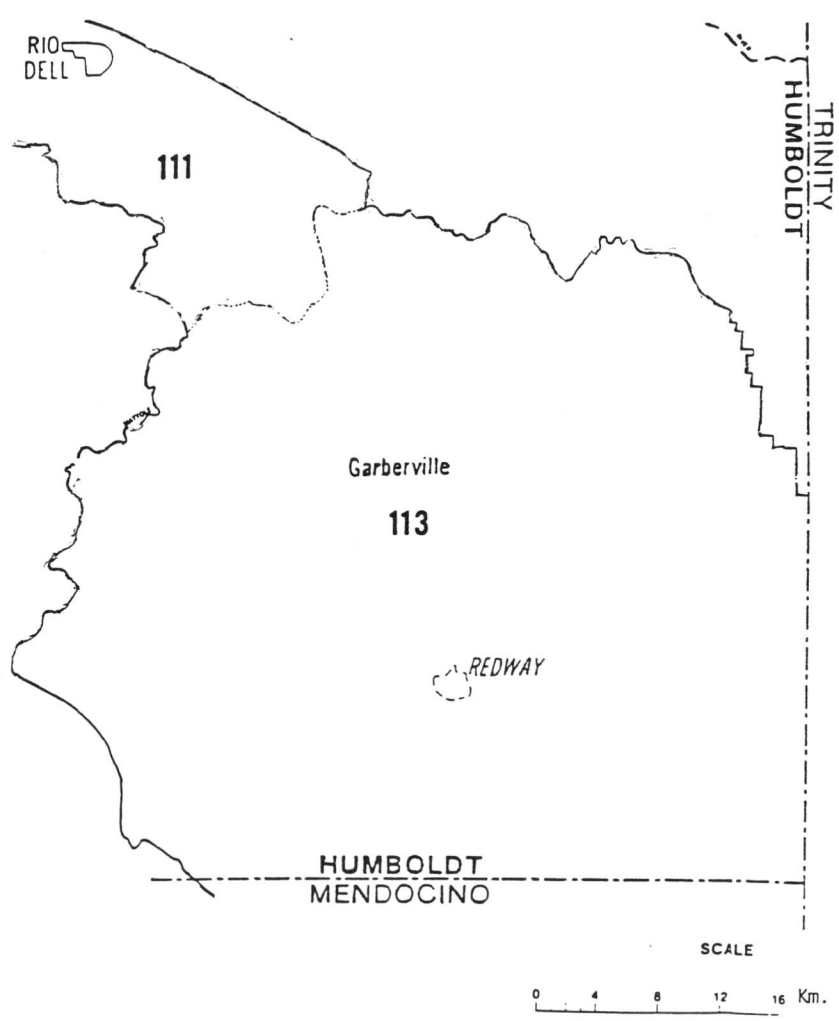

Figure Three. Garberville Census District.

Only a handful of people who come to Mateel have experienced rural life complete with gardens, domestic animals, and long rides on school busses.

The natural environment shapes Mateelian daily life. Coping with rain, drought, and limited resources sometimes proves to be more than many can handle. Some who make the attempt fail; they return to living with central heating, unlimited electricity, paved roads, indoor toilets, and telephones. Marriages are occasionally dissolved when one partner makes the urban-to-rural transition and the other does not. When Mateelians ask "How long have you been here?" they are really asking "Have you paid your dues, have you survived a winter and a summer?" and, ultimately, "Are you one of us?"

The transition from an urban to a rural life style is eased by the fact that Mateel is not an especially harsh environment. In January, for instance, the mean temperature in Eureka, eighty miles north of Garberville on the coast, is 47.3 degrees. Inland areas experience lower mean temperatures, with elevation being the major variable. The highest elevation in Mateel is 4,087 feet at Kings Peak on the coast. Snow may become a problem for a week or two in the higher elevations, but it rarely stays on the ground for long in the valleys or on the low ridges. In August or September, temperatures may go over 102 degrees for as much as a week at a time. Winter fogs lower average valley temperatures and frost is on the ground more often and for longer periods of time in these areas, but shade from the mountains makes the summers cooler. The forest also mitigates the harsher effects of seasonal climatic change; life under the redwood trees is uncomfortably damp in the winter but less prone to frost and is pleasantly cool on hot summer days.

The most difficult regional climatic factor to accept is the pattern of precipitation. From October to April, the King Range, the mountain backbone of Mateel, receives as much as 200 inches of rainfall at higher elevations. That statistic, however, cannot convey the full effect that rain has on the residents. Although emergency flood conditions only occur about once a decade in southern Humboldt County, violent winter storms routinely alternate with weeks of pervasive gray dampness. During these periods, wood stoves may be kept burning more to fight mold, mildew and rot than to raise room temperatures. A common piece of advice offered to newcomers is "when in doubt, assume rain." The unrelenting chill and humidity often produce a chronic, low-level bronchial infection that Mateelians fondly call the "Humboldt Hack."

Persistent winter rain makes attention to roofing a matter of paramount importance. Even the most expert shingling jobs leak during the worst winters. Owner-built homes and outbuildings converted to dwellings are often unable to withstand the punishment meted out by winter storms, giving owners cause to wear rain gear indoors as well as out. Watching one's possessions succumb to mold, mildew, corrosion, and direct water damage, while placing every available container under roof leaks and struggling endlessly with the Humboldt Hack, is an exercise in what Mateelians call "learning detachment from the material plane."

The rain destroys dirt roads cut by bulldozers on steep hillsides. During storms, it makes necessary the maintenance by hand of drainage ditches. Keeping small children dry in wet weather is difficult, given the predominant form of plumbing (pit privies or compost toilets located outside and at some distance from the main houses). The juvenile need for mobility, much a part of Mateelian child-rearing philosophy, presents some of its most serious problems on rainy days.

In summer, precipitation is not a problem; lack of rainfall is. Drought ensues; springs and streams begin to dry up. The maintenance of water systems becomes a central concern, since a break anywhere in a plastic waterline can drain a storage tank in a few hours. Land partners, or neighbors on the same network, must coordinate water use, a frequent cause of conflict in Mateel. One characteristic of most Mateelian gravity flow systems is that uphill and downhill outlets cannot be used simultaneously because water always exits at the open valve at the lowest elevation. With uphill and downhill orchards, frequent watering of gardens, and household needs, the coordination required within a family is difficult enough. For land partners or neighbors sharing watering systems, living without telephones and perhaps on different roads, it may be nearly impossible.

Drought, in combination with the lack of telephone service, extreme distance from fire-fighting equipment, and bad roads make forest fires a continuing nightmare. Blazes are started by inexperienced or simply careless people, residents and tourists, by spontaneous combustion, bottle bottoms left in grass, spark-producing machinery, propane leaks, and the lightning that accompanies rainless August and September storms. More frightening to contemplate, however, are the fires started deliberately as a result of cross-cultural conflict between Mateelians and "locals," by feuding neighbors, or by non-residents who come to Mateel for the marijuana harvest. Fear of summer fires has spawned volunteer fire departments in several isolated areas of Mateel and has caused many residents to accept citizen-band radios as appropriate technology.

Naturally occurring asbestos in the streams that run past serpentine rock is a health problem in some parts of Mateel. No one is sure exactly what added dangers lie in the universal use of PVC pipe for water systems. Although most areas of Mateel have been heavily logged, and some logging continues, the environmental damage caused by this activity is not as obvious as in other parts of northern California. Most logging was completed in the 1960s, more than twenty-five years ago; secondary growth forests of oak and madrone have covered most of the scars. To people raised in urban environments and who were unfamiliar with the original look of the land, the wilderness they found in Humboldt County appeared almost pristine at first. However, years of intimate contact with the countryside has made Mateelians aware of gigantic fir stumps, the remnants of the area's primary growth, the silted streams that no longer support salmon, and the erosion caused by clear-cutting and road building. It was only because the land was so damaged that countercultural dropouts could afford to settle on it. The transitional nature of the countryside has had a profound effect on Mateelians in another way; had they moved to a pristine area, their intense environmentalism might never have evolved.

Steep terrain limits access to Mateel by road and restricts the number of housing sites that are available. It also means that erosion caused by clear-cut logging and road building is a major environmental problem. Steep hillsides turn gardening and construction into athletic enterprises, keeping Mateelians in fine physical shape. Negative environmental factors include the presence of poison oak (a secondary growth plant that invades areas where fir and redwood timber were clear-cut), yellow jackets, mosquitoes, mice, rabid animals in the summer, and scabies and lice in the winter. Rattlesnakes are found throughout Mateel, though they avoid contact with humans.

Positive environmental factors do not include the cliched moonlight on palm trees, but moonlight on fir trees is equally breathtaking. The air is generally clear; the worst pollution is apparent in early fall, during fire season, when forest fires as far as a hundred miles away can produce enough smoke to sting the eyes. The water from springs in the upper watersheds is assumed to be reasonably free of chemical and sewage pollution, although major tributaries of the Eel River and the main channel of the Mattole can become clogged with dead fish, soap suds, algae, and even oil slicks.

In spite of these problems, most Mateelians put the physical environment high on their list of reasons for remaining in the community. To urban eyes, the healing, logged-over hills are beautiful. Never mind the secondary growth and the absence of a virgin forest. Ridge-top houses enjoy constantly changing views of mountains, rivers, and fog that extend for as much as fifty miles. Hawks and ravens wheel and dive in the clear skies, and one never steps outside without seeing squirrels, rabbits, quail, or deer. In recent years, mountain lions have been seen well within the area, and the restocking of coastal areas with elk has been successful enough to cause residents to report threats to their gardens. River otters, bobcats, silver foxes, and small brown bear are also seen by sharper-eyed observers. Even though the land is damaged, it is not hard to imagine what it must have been like when Native Americans were the only people to occupy the area.

The name Mateel has only recently come into general use, having been coined by Deerhawk, a local poet and one of the earliest Mateelian settlers. The word "Mateel" first appeared in two poems he wrote in 1981; these works marked a turning point in the collective self-image, which up to that point had been based more on the experience of refugees-in-exile than on the community experience (see Appendix Two)[1]. The advent of a name was significant, representing for many the self-recognition of a collective entity and of the inseparable nature of that entity from the place where it was created. This remains true, even though the name is not universally accepted and is, in some cases, even disliked.

The Mateel community does not include everyone who resides in the area. Many people vehemently deny any association with the word "Mateel" (a term formally used in print nowhere but in this book). Many who reject association with the term are members of the local mainstream population who were in the area before the Mateelians arrived. Others, usually recent arrivals, simply do not understand the meaning of the name; they neither accept or reject it. Still others, those who are clearly Mateelians culturally, exclude themselves because of their distaste for labels, or because they recognize no entity beyond the individual. This aversion to collective self-identification, referred to here as the "we-are-not-here" syndrome, will become relevant in later chapters. Finally, a handful of people express distaste for the word Mateel on aesthetic grounds, objecting to its sound, but they do not oppose the general notion of a group name.

Shortly after the name's presentation at a Community Center-sponsored Summer Arts Festival, the building itself was renamed "Mateel Community Center." Another organization, one then being formed, took the name Mateel Community Credit Union. At least one local business, Mateel Sound, also adopted the designation. The credit union, seeking to expand its membership, dropped the word Mateel after only a year or so. The Board of Directors of the Mateel Community Center soon found itself in a peculiar position with regard to the name after the hall burned in an arson-set fire on Thanksgiving Day, 1983. In an effort to raise funds to supplement the insufficient insurance for rebuilding, by appealing to what is often called "the wider community" (the mainstream population), the board dropped the word "Mateel" from its organization's title. This action met with vociferous opposition from the general membership. The ensuing controversy prompted Deerhawk to specify that Mateel, in addition to describing a geographical area, referred to "a system of values, chief among which is respect for The Land" (from the transcript of a taped meeting of the general membership of the MCC).[2]

Prior to the name Mateel, Mateelians called themselves "hill people"; most still use the phrase in normal conversation, leaving it to others to describe them as "hippies." Theodore Roszak's term, "counter-culture," while accurate and descriptive of their life style, has never been widely accepted by Mateelians because of their bias against social scientists; the name also suggests that their movement was nothing more than a collective "reflex" reaction.[3] In contrast, the name Mateel seems particularly appropriate because it came from within the community and because Deerhawk's poem, "A Song of Twelve," so beautifully describes the Mateelian world view.

At present, the number of people living in the area in which Mateel exists appears to be growing. The general population of the Garberville census district more than doubled during the 1970s, rising from 5,026 to 11,010.(Figure 3)[4] Since the preceding ten years witnessed a drop in population from 7,440 in 1960 to 5,026 in 1970, it is reasonable to assume that this reversal in the 1970s reflects the influx of those who became the Mateel community, approximately 6,000 people.[5] Such measurements as the number of people waiting for boxes at the local post offices and the shortage of parking spaces in Garberville during winter months, a time when tourists are scarce, suggest that the permanent population of Mateel has continued to increase since the 1980 census. The present population is undoubtedly larger than it was in 1980, but how much this increase might be affected by the marijuana boom would be difficult to say. The rise in population after 1980 surely includes marijuana growers and workers, as well as retirees and professional people drawn by the potential need for services. In any case, the culture of southern Humboldt County is strongly influenced by the presence of the Mateelians. In fact, it is quite possible that Mateelians dominate the area numerically during the winter.

Geographically, Mateel includes the towns of Redway, Briceland, Whitethorn, Garberville, Phillipsville, Miranda, Harris, Alderpoint, Honeydew, Ettersberg, Petrolia, and Piercy. Mateelians are not distributed evenly throughout this area, but apparently comprise a majority of those who live in the hills surrounding the riverside towns. This fact is related to ecological succession. Clear-cutting of Douglas Fir and Coast Redwood left large tracts of eroding land, filled with poison oak, madrone, tan oak, manzanita and other secondary growth. The decline of the timber industry in the 1960s caused a population reduction, as loggers lost their jobs and abandoned the area.[6] Local ranchers who stayed discovered that logged-over land could be sold to people from the city who were anxious to try their hand at being self sufficient. These new residents formed the nucleus of what would become the Mateel community. Friends soon followed those first immigrants and bought adjacent land parcels. In order to make the minimal down payments and low monthly payments, others formed partnerships and purchased pieces of the newly subdivided real estate . The ultimate prices paid for these land bargains were measured in years spent packing in supplies and building materials, transporting water, heating it over portable stoves or camp fires, and camping out until sufficient improvements could be made.

Because Mateelians tended to concentrate their settlement in specific locales, it is possible to locate the core area of their cultural system in space. The result is a more accurate definition of the unit of study than has been the case with previous investigations of countercultural groups. Those persons who bought the most isolated, least valuable, least improved land are also the most distinct from mainstream Americans in other ways. Obviously, their decision to buy undesirable real estate was based on considerations directly counter to mainstream American cost/benefit analysis.

Six geographical locations, considered to be "core" areas of Mateelian culture, were chosen for concentrated study. Each comprises a social and ecological unit recognized by its members and the community at large. Five are watersheds; one is a ridge-top between two watersheds. Each area has a high ratio of Mateelian to non-Mateelian population. Rather than coining a word for these six cultural core areas, they will be called simply the *watersheds*, even though one is a ridge-top.

Because frequent, intense, and local interaction has been one result of physical isolation, these watershed groups have, in some ways, begun to resemble band organizations found in many primitive societies. This tendency is enhanced by the fact that, in the beginning, friends tended to hear about land deals from other friends and to settle near them. In other words, watersheds were often settled by people with similar interests. Aside from the Sinkyone and Mattole Indians who left plentiful evidence of their original occupancy, the core areas were first settled in a uniform way during the 1970s. The six watersheds are therefore areas where residents have been generating Mateelian culture for the longest period of time. Everything described as typically Mateelian is most true of these residents.

Starting late in the 1970s, the economic base of the area shifted increasingly to the cultivation of marijuana as a cash crop. Marijuana was originally grown by Mateelians for personal use and sold to supplement income derived from organic farming of vegetables and fruit, the sale of craft items, work in service industries, scavenging, and efforts to gain financial support from sources such as welfare, unemployment, pensions, and inheritances. A subsequent technological breakthrough resulting in a particularly strong strain of marijuana, and the switch to a species better adapted to the ecological conditions of Mateel, led to increased economic reliance on marijuana farming. Local mainstream Americans, especially those who were unemployed, also began cultivating marijuana. Unlike Mateelians, they generally did not plant small, scattered patches that had to be worked by hand, nor were they usually organic farmers. Instead, they followed agri-business practices, creating large fields that had to be worked with tractors, and used chemical fertilizers, pesticides, and herbicides. Market prices soared. News media, attracted by potential stories about "big growers" and "instant wealth," focused their attention on the Garberville area. Ensuing publicity attracted the attention of numerous non-resident growers and inspired another wave of immigration. The new "outsiders," primarily growers, tenant farmers, and farm workers, shattered the isolation that had characterized the earlier Mateel community.[7]

The economic boom had a profound effect on the Mateelian culture. It brought in its wake patterns of increased personal spending, local inflation, rising land prices, and the proliferation of locked gates as protection against crime. The boom also had as a side effect increased tension between the local mainstream population and the

Mateelians. Many mainstream residents who did not grow marijuana, while ignoring the fact that "locals" were involved in the industry, resented the increased and untaxed prosperity of the "hippies." They also resented the influx of questionable people, perhaps members of organized crime; this was a sentiment shared with most Mateelians. Mateelians, for their part, disliked non-Mateelian growing methods used by residents and non-residents alike. In spite of these problems, however, the influence of marijuana cultivation has not negatively affected Mateel's value system. In other words, increased economic activity reflects the presence of more buying power, but not a return to mainstream American behavior and consumption patterns.[8]

The establishment in 1984 of the Campaign Against Marijuana Planting (CAMP), a county, state, and federal police effort, brought in drug enforcement agencies that operated like military organizations found in many dictatorships. Their actions left them so open to charges of violating personal privacy, disturbing the peace, and disregarding civil rights that a federal judge imposed an injunction against the program. He described their behavior as exactly the type that the U.S. Constitution was designed to prevent.[9] As an unintended side effect, the CAMP program inspired the creation of the most coherent political organization that ever occurred among Mateelians. In fact, it counteracted the community disruption caused by the marijuana boom. To some degree, "locals" and "hippies" were provided opportunities to understand one another better because CAMP personnel, brought in from the outside, appeared indiscriminate in their harassment, assuming that all residents of southern Humboldt County were marijuana growers.

In the course of time, one of three things will happen with regard to marijuana cultivation in the area. 1) It will become a stable part of the region's economic base as the result of legalization. 2) It will return to its original position in the economy as the result of increased activity by law enforcement agencies and criminal elements. 3) The impact of the marijuana industry on Mateel will destroy community cohesiveness. If either of the first two cases proves to be true, then marijuana will have had only a transitory and superficial effect on Mateel. If the third possibility occurs, Mateel will cease to exist and future studies of it will reveal how a small culture was destroyed by contact with a larger, more powerful one.[10]

The Mateelian Culture System

Because Mateel exists within a larger, pluralistic, and heterogeneous mass culture, concepts used to define traditional societies, such as language, are of limited value. It is more useful to view Mateel as a system of communication that exists at a particular time and in a particular place.[11]

Individuals are considered a part of Mateelian culture to the degree that their mental processes operate on inputs from the Mateelian system. Mateelian culture is constantly being generated from the interaction of individuals with their families, their neighbors, and friends, rather than from participation in economic or political hierarchies. The most important level of organization above the one made up of family, neighbors, and friends is the watershed. Above the watershed level are the various Mateelian institutions.

These institutions form a part of the interface between Mateelian culture and mainstream America. They embody Mateelian philosophies, goals, and values that evolved at the heart of the culture. In recent years, the Mateel community has had an increasing influence on the various town populations in the area. But during the period from 1968 to 1980 most Mateelians lived in the hills.[12]

Although their institutions were based on values made explicit by rural residence, they were established in places where the largest number of Mateelians would have access to one another—in the towns. Because these relationships and organizations operated above the watershed level, they included some individuals who did not reside in the six core watersheds. These institutions were, nevertheless, important because they were created primarily by people from the core area and reflected their values.

It must be understood that the way Mateelians interact with the American mainstream is complex, highly idiosyncratic, and often undifferentiated. The assignment of any individual to either group, Mateelian or mainstream, is based on several criteria, including personal values, self definition, occupation, life goals, personal tastes, and world view; in many cases, the process would seem arbitrary. Yet, both mainstream and Mateelian individuals are usually able to recognize one another and orient themselves toward their chosen group.[13]

Because the population of southern Humboldt County fluctuates seasonally, with tourists and non-resident growers flocking to the area in summer, it is necessary to specify that only residents are included in the study. Residents are defined as individuals who came to Mateel for reasons other than marijuana cultivation, remained through at least one winter and were not deterred from permanent residence by that experience.

A Mateelian stream bed, badly eroded from the effects of logging in the area.

Chapter Three

Ecotopia

*We are stardust, we are golden and we got
to get ourselves back to the garden. . . .*

—*Joni Mitchell*

The word "Ecotopia" and the novel written by Ernest Callenbach with that title became popular about the time that the counterculture spawned numerous back-to-the-land movements like Mateel. Callenbach's work is based on the premise that northern California and the states of Oregon and Washington secede from the United States and create a separate nation based on ecological principles.[1]

Ecotopia was widely read in Mateel, but the extent to which it became a sourcebook is difficult to determine. At least one community member said, "Callenbach must have gotten his ideas by watching us."[2] Callenbach's hypothetical society was believable to many people because it went beyond a discussion of technical problems, such as pollution control and resource management, to address social questions such as: what kind of a society would be best suited to using "appropriate technology"? What kind of people would live in that society? How would they live and in what kinds of situations might they find themselves?

A body of literature already existed from which Callenbach could draw material for this exercise in "culture sculpture," and much has been written since. Most of this work has been based on a simple premise: the earth was once a balanced ecosystem and the cause of our present crisis began when human communities got out of equilibrium with available resources. As various groups outstripped the ability of their locales to provide food and shelter, they were forced to migrate or to rely on the importation of resources to stay alive. Increasingly, humanity turned to technological solutions to make up for resource deficits. During the interval of time we label history, this process accelerated at an increasing rate to the point where significant environmental imbalances are now seen at the global level. Whatever the cause—population pressure, inequities leading to overconsumption, or technological sophistication—it is clear that humanity has disrupted the mechanism that keeps populations in balance with their supporting resources.

Elements that control population growth are functions of how species interact with their environment. These species responses, or "feedbacks," are often quantifiable, taking the form of lowered reproduction rates, high rates of infant mortality, or increased death rates caused by disease—all of these factors come into play before more drastic responses, such as mass starvation.[3] In recent years, scientists have found evidence to suggest that feedbacks found in pre-civilized human groups were both physiological and social; the former expressed relationships such as the fat to muscle ratio and its effect on female fertility, or the way that physical exercise affects female reproductive hormones. As is the case within other species, aggression also plays a role in shaping human behavior. However, it appears that only civilized humanity has molded its aggression in the form of highly structured warfare.[4] And since human technological sophistication has now reached a point where it can destroy most life on the planet in a short time, a central problem addressed by Ecotopian writers is how to abandon environmental relationships that promote warlike activity.

Other frequently mentioned factors contributing to our present environmental crisis are: overconsumption, unequal distribution of natural resources and sources of energy, questionable technological progress, overpopulation, urbanization, and the rapid spread and unquestioning acceptance of Western values in general. Ecotopian writers approach these problems in various ways, focusing on different facets according to their expertise. Yet, the picture that emerges from their work is clear. Dramatic population growth and present patterns of resource consumption will be radically altered, whether or not we wish to make the necessary changes.[5] If we are fortunate and these events are not triggered by a global nuclear war, then most Ecotopian writers agree that one of three things will happen: 1) economic disparity between various human groups will increase; 2) pre-industrial societies will re-emerge; or 3) Ecotopia. In Ecotopia, poverty will be shared equally, labor will be concentrated in service industries, the crafts, and in enterprises that emphasize reuse and multiple use of resources. Efficiency will be stressed when allocating resources and ecological regulation will be put in place on a world-wide scale. This Ecotopia would be:

> . . . a relaxed place of efficiency and material simplicity. People would probably not work much of the time. Leisure and status . . . would be concerned with amassing . . . intangible commodities; education, recreation by walking and observing, festivals, arts, crafts, skills and services of all kinds. . . . Appreciation of nature, and perhaps, religion would return to such concerns.[6]

Writers have filled in this picture considerably. Among the more comprehensive efforts is Gorden Rattray Taylor's work *Rethink: A Paraprimitive Solution*, which contains a description of a hypothetical society created from appropriate technology, modern social patterns, and primitive social characteristics.[7] In general, Taylor's paraprimitive society is based on: localization of the economy; reduction in the size of cities; regulation of technological innovation—perhaps through the use of computers; reduction in the amount of physical mobility; and decentralization of authority and political power. Among areas of significant change he lists: 1) more personal relationships, including those classified as economic and administrative; 2) "mixed motives" in economic behavior (planning based on economic and non-economic elements) and; 3) a proliferation of meaningful activity such as work.

His vision of a paraprimitive community suggests that it would be populated by men and women who insist on breathing clean air and drinking clean water. It would be a place where slums, junkyards, and factories have been eliminated and noise and the use of internal combustion engines would be limited. Villages and small towns would thrive. Inside his factories long production lines and repetitive jobs will have been replaced by a system where groups of people make complete products at their own pace, working at different times of the day. These changes would come about because of altered attitudes toward personnel relations, legal and administrative arrangements, economic and tax structures, education, and the atmosphere of home life.

Taylor, unlike some other writers, sees the necessary changes occurring because they reflect the character of his hypothetical society's population, not because it was determined by social structure or technology. "It is precisely the creation of a sensible populace which constitutes the problem."[8] Taylor stresses the changes that must take place within individual personalities before society can achieve this goal:

> I am looking for a Utopia which is flexible, which can evolve and adapt to changing circumstances. Such a Utopia is only possible on the basis of modifying personality. Then, in proportion to the extent to which people change their attitudes, political and social changes can also be made to confirm and support such shifts.[9]

The personality capable of accepting this transition is, according to Taylor, one that is balanced between "matrist" and "patrist" values, between "hard" and "soft" ego types. Taylor would replace hard-ego-striving-for-success attitudes with soft-ego-sense-of-being-a-part-of-the-community outlooks. In general, he would shift from modern society's more-inhibited patrist frame of mind to a less-inhibited matrist worldview. He would restore individual identity, a sense of mastery and self-determination to work, and he would encourage maturity by adopting measures such as adolescent-to-adult rites of passage, a memorable feature of the pre-Ecotopian society. Anarchy, which Taylor defines as true democracy, is the form of government best suited to this personality type.[10]

A recurring theme in Ecotopian writing is the decentralization of politics, economics, and population density. The best Ecotopian social unit is viewed as a small community, the advantages of which are economic efficiency, social cohesion, and mental health. Such communities would include industrial productive units as integral parts of their structure,[11] thus eliminating energy-wasting, pollution-producing, long-distance commutes on freeways. Taylor would have no population concentrations over 100,000.[12] Others set optimum city sizes at 250,000.[13] Jay Forrester declares that we should consider "confining the cities" and "curtailing the goals of urban areas."[14] Most writers call for community diversity: each city or town should be as self-sufficient as possible, but each should specialize in activities and pursue interests that are beyond self-sufficiency.[15] Small communities are seen as better able to provide social rewards that offset lowered consumption.[16] Phillip Slater believes that small, stable social units are more conducive to achieving balanced personalities than are suburban networks, which encourage bifurcation of personality:

> In small, stable communities, you can pick your closest friends, but not your total social environment. Everyone knows everyone and must interact with everyone to some extent. This guarantees a certain balance of interpersonal styles and expressive patterns. Everyone is obliged to have a balanced interpersonal diet as it were.[17]

These towns and small cities would house populations that were relatively static; general mobility that wastes energy would be reduced.[18] Further, increased social stability would raise general levels of mental health and re-establish the interdependence of community members.[19]

Ecotopian politics would be based on public involvement and wisdom.[20] The existence of small-scale communities would increase lateral channels of communication, and promote participatory democracy.[21] Government legislative activity would be reduced because social control would be based on community values and public opinion, rather than on authority.[22] Population growth would be stabilized by conscious regulation and real incentives.[23] Schools, hospitals, and welfare systems would be run by communities.[24] Under such circumstances, leaders would be more diverse, less authoritarian, and their decisions would be made at appropriate levels and with less confrontation.[25]

The themes of stability and decentralization would extend to Ecotopian economics, as well. The economy, it goes without saying, would be based on a philosophy of no growth and no war.[26] As

Toffler declares, "the goal is a system under which no output is produced that is not an input for another production process downstream."[27] Decentralizing industry so that it serves local needs would cause a direct interchange between the forces of demand and supply.[28] Businesses would be small or collective.[29] Farms would be small, individual holdings. Their owners would seek to expand food production for local use.[30] A constant supply of capital would be the norm.[31] The negative psychological influence of economic competition would be reduced.[32] The feasibility of new projects would be judged on the basis of energy consumption and availability, not profit.[33]

In the area of resource management, the goal would be minimal consumption.[34] E. N. Anderson, for instance, calls for world-wide regulation of resource use.[35] The pathological obsession with consumption would be reduced by replacing consumer goods with social rewards.[36] What goods remained would be distributed equitably.[37] They would be of high quality and built to be repaired and to last;[38] "planned obsolescence" would be eliminated.[39] The tax structure could be modified to discourage the production of useless goods, as well as to decrease urban population density.[40]

The work force in Ecotopia would be large, since many tasks previously accomplished by consuming non-renewable energy sources would now require more labor intensive methods.[41] Services, such as health care, would employ large numbers of people.[42] Artists and artisans would be paid and non-financial incentives, such as more leisure time, status, and education would combine with financial incentives.[43] Toffler sees more flexible hours and job sharing as replacing wages as the main criterion for choosing employment.[44] Day-care centers and reproductive leaves would certainly be commonplace in this new society.

Technology would be geared toward renewable energy sources such as solar, wind, and water power.[45] To achieve minimal pollution, the number of automobiles would be reduced, or they would be replaced by mass transit.[46] New forms of communication would encourage participatory democracy.[47] As time passed, technological innovation would be evaluated in terms of its ability to expand human potential.[48]

The potential impact of such changes on family and home life is often overlooked by Ecotopian futurists who focus on technology, politics, and economics. Fictional situations that incorporate assumptions about how families might function are, however, presented by some writers. Alvin Toffler, for instance, believes that home computers as a technological innovation might lead to work-at-home families and the re-establishment, on a more compassionate basis, of child labor.[49] In Toffler's "electronic cottage," the family could take a variety of forms.[50] The assumption is, of course, that the surrounding culture would display tolerance for such diversity. Families might be non-nuclear, child-free, or less child-oriented. They could be economic units in which all members shared all types of work. Reasons for choosing mates would change as a natural result of this reestablished economic function of the family, with work-related abilities high on the list, as they are in many primitive societies.

Paul Ehrlich, whose main interest seems to be the family as it affects population growth, calls for a redefinition of marriage to include the idea of planning for wanted children only.[51] He suggests better ego support for both sexes, replacing the ego rewards that derive from reproductive activities. This attitude implies sexual equality in employment, since it is difficult to imagine other substitutes for female ego supports provided by childbearing. In other words, sexual equality would become a part of the Ecotopian social scene, though it is not discussed in detail by Ecotopian writers other than Ernest Callenbach.[52]

Most Ecotopian writers recognize how personal values and philosophies are important to the creation of Ecotopia. It is obvious that none of the changes described so far could be achieved without significant alterations to our Western values. The list of changes is long. Establishing the "concept of enoughness," to use Toffler's phrase, would be a starting point.[53] What Slater calls the "pathology of consumption" would have to be replaced by an interest in art, science, nature, and interaction with other people.[54] Status in the new society would be based on function in the community rather than on the accumulation of possessions.[55] The present "blind faith" in marketplace economic forces as a positive good would cease to exist.[56] The values of self-determination and craftsmanship would be restored to work by re-establishing quality as a criterion for consumption.[57] The concept of freedom would be subject to environmental limitations.[58] Individual and community interests would not be seen as mutually exclusive.[59]

Ecotopia as an ideal is best summarized by saying that it would be a place inhabited by people who value small, cohesive, largely self-sufficient, non-polluted, slowly changing communities and who find in their environment rewarding substitutes for large, atomized, economically dependent, polluted, constantly changing networks of suburbs and slums populated by individuals living in isolation from one another.

How this value system is to be achieved, many writers argue, is through the creation of a new archetypal personality by means of education and religion.[60] Gregory Bateson labels the process "deuterolearning," or learning to learn under changing circumstances. Educator Lewis Perelman describes an educational system based on deuterolearning that would encourage cyclical and processional thinking and would "cultivate" rather than "input" education.[61] Phillip Slater's call for education that is oriented to relational thinking and language is similar.[62]

Many writers see the characteristic Western personality as adolescent; they contrast it to the mature Ecotopian ideal with its strong personal identity, clear aims and values, its pride in individual and group achievement, and its emphasis on self-discipline and self-realization.[63]

Ecotopian writers disagree on religion's place in society and its role as an agent of change. On the one hand "there is no custodian of the long-term goals unless it be the religious institutions."[64] On the other, "Christianity is a religion of exponential growth."[65] The latter view, best presented by Lynn White, Jr., has been a controversial one among Ecotopian thinkers.[66] Anthropologists generally agree with the materialist position that religions have always supported economics in cultural causation.[67] Yet, the bulk of Ecotopian writers place emphasis on changing values, thought processes, epistemology, and folklore in order to create their image of a new society. In short, they incorporate all of the things that Marvin Harris dismisses as "ideology" and sees as unlikely to be of assistance in changing culture.

One area of potential confusion is whether the discussion is about religious thought or religious institutions. Many organized religions in Western industrial nations accept social philosophies that foster industrial growth. Gregory Bateson places "certain wrong values of Occidental culture" on an equal plane with technology and population growth as causes of the environmental crisis. At the same time, he implies that Eastern philosophies are not based on the same misconceptions.[68]

In contrast, E. N. Anderson includes Eastern cultures in his condemnation of industrialization, citing rampant pollution and overconsumption in Japan.[69] However, Buddhism's failure to protect Japan from industrialization in spite of the religion's non-exploitative approach to the environment, is undoubtedly related to a wider process of secularization of religion, which generally accompanies industrialization. The same may be said of other Eastern philosophies. It is not that the values of these religions are compatible with industrialization in the same way that Judeo-Christian values are, but that religions in general no longer have the moral force they once had because industrialization has secularized society.

Another factor to be considered is the transitional state of Eastern culture, which experienced its industry caused environmental deterioration later than the West. E. T. Hall describes Japan's transition from Eastern to Western values as having contributed to some strange cultural contrasts.[70] Another way to understand this dilemma is contained in Robert Redfield's notions of the *great* and the *little* traditions in religion.[71] It may be that those Eastern values, believed by some Westerners to be environmentally sound, are found only in the *great* tradition carried on by philosophers and priests, not within the *little* tradition understood by lords, farmers, peasants, and warriors. These values, written, practiced, and preserved by priests and monks, are highly visible to students from the West who seek models, but are not relevant to the lives of the Eastern majority that appears to welcome industrialization eagerly.

Randers and Meadows and Forrester see organized religion as the only viable vehicle for modifying values.[72] They call on churches to initiate the necessary changes. Odum, who uses religious metaphors such as the "false god of the automobile" throughout his work, toys with creating an ecologically sound religion from existing religious concepts. He equates angels and devils with "order" and "chaos" respectively, defines sin as "excess power dissipation," prophets as "energy regulators," and the soul as a "level of special complexity of the unit system."[73] Those who believe that organized religion can help to bring about Ecotopia, understand that: 1) it must incorporate ecological principles, as Eastern and primitive philosophies do and; 2) it must be integrated with the rest of Ecotopian culture.[74]

If the only way to attack non-ecological values is through organized religion, the question then becomes one of worldview, a dilemma compounded by the structure of thought, language, epistemology, and institution. The importance of a worldview to bringing about Ecotopian change is expressed by several writers. Phillip Slater observes that ". . . the drying up of the technological impulse depends in part on the diffusion of uncharacteristic thought patterns. . . ."[75]

Kenneth Watt and his co-authors begin their work *The Titanic Effect: Planning for the Unthinkable* with a worldview incorporating ecology and systems analysis.[76] Their framework includes visions, the future, and ecosystemics, or recognition of humans as a part of the global ecosystem. The scientific nature of the Western worldview is thought by many Ecotopian writers to separate humans from the global ecosystem, treating them as if they were outside the balance that includes all other species. Paul Shepard goes so far as to say that Western thought is "anti-ecological"[77] in its separation of humanity from nature. Perelman states that:

> . . . ecological consciousness is a holistic vision of ongoing worldwide life processes in synergetic combination. . . . It is . . . the proper recognition of the role and performance of the individual mind within the context of the comprehensive global mind."[78]

Anderson also speaks to the separation, observing that a "revival of commitment . . . to the human and non-human world will be a cause and effect of Ecotopian development."[79]

A second idea important to the Ecotopian worldview relates to the way we understand time. Kenneth Watt and his coauthors would expand the Ecotopian concept of time to include more of the future.[80] The Western idea of time is both linear and compartmentalized. Slater contrasts the "mañana" mentality of Latin cultures to the Anglo-Saxon obsession with getting things done. He makes it clear that they get things done, but questions whether they need doing.[81] In this view, he is supported by anthropologist Edward T. Hall and his comparisons of American, Latin American, and other cultural perceptions of time.[82]

Advocates of Ecotopia seek to create a balanced, self-controlling system (a homeostatic system) in which relationships have been re-established between production and resources.[83] The level of organization at which these relationships operate, whether they are put in place by individuals, or by the operations of planning boards or religious institutions, is not an area of agreement. As in most ecosystems, the maintenance of equilibrium in Ecotopia would depend on diversity, the individual, the immediate community, and on equal participation of those living throughout the system. The goal is not simply to implement changes that will reduce the effect of humanity on the environment, but to create a culture that is self-correcting and sympathetic to nature's balance.

Owner-built cabin with a screened porch that is covered with plastic for winter-time use.

Chapter Four

Amerika

...feel myself a cog in something turnin'....

—Joni Mitchell

Technocracy is the form of culture that now determines the destiny of this planet. It transcends national borders, ethnic boundaries, and supercedes obsolete political and economic distinctions between communism and capitalism. Its vast scale makes technocracy inaccessible to any sort of control or comprehensive evaluation, and so it is examined bit by bit, by each of the social sciences in isolation. Anthropologists, who are comfortable studying social entities small enough to be viewed holistically, generally quail before the complexity of undertaking an assessment of technocracy, though that tendency is fast disappearing.

Technocracy is relevant to the birth of Mateel in that the community came into being as a reaction to it; technocracy also set Mateel on its evolutionary trajectory. Although much can be learned by comparing Mateel to the culture from which it sprang, American society is much too complex for an ethnographic model to be developed that could be compared to a Mateel. America contains too many subcultures, too many divergent groups, too many rapid changes occurring in too many different parts of its infrastructure for a comprehensive paradigm to be made. The one presented in this chapter is like the Ecotopian model discussed in chapter three. It is constituted on a higher level of abstraction than ethnographic models traditionally used in cross-cultural comparisons. Like the Ecotopian model, it is abstracted from the work of other researchers.

This departure from strict ethnological tradition is justified by the significance of the problem being discussed. Anthropology can no longer be put off by complexity; instead, it must address the problems of industrial culture in ways that will encourage intelligent change. The model of American culture developed here, then, should be seen as a step in that direction. It is not a model of America's culture in its entirety, only that part to which the counterculture has reacted. It is that part of American culture to which the majority of Americans aspire, no matter what their ethnic identity, and which, by comparison, increases our understanding of Mateel.

It is likely that only America could have given rise to Mateel; in other words, Mateel is an American product. But little can be learned from an analysis at this level. It is only by examining what is different about the Mateelian cultural system that information useful to thinking about our future can be obtained. The contrasting model does imply that industrial civilization, of which America is an extreme example, is a maladaptive trend in human evolution and in considerable need of correction. For convenience, this model will be called "Amerika," using Franz Kafka's spelling as a reminder that it is a model of a part of American culture, not the whole.[1] Throughout, Amerika will be spelled with a "k" when referring to the model and with a "c" when referring to American culture in general, or when paraphrasing the work of other researchers. No claims are made as to the degree to which Amerika coincides with America. That question is beyond the scope of this book.

Industrial Civilization

Like cancers, technocracies grow constantly. Although birthrates in most industrialized nations are lower than in developing countries, the net effect of industrialization is to increase population. This occurred when the first cultures began to industrialize and it is true today when tribal populations come into contact with industrial states.[2] It happens because traditional population control mechanisms are disrupted, because the state encourages population growth, and because modern technology lowers mortality rates.[3]

The most basic reason for eliminating overpopulation is that there are simply too many people and not enough food. To this may be added "quality of life" issues, such as overcrowded cities, schools, and freeways. Even in developed countries that have undergone demographic expansion, population density is at least a menacing quality-of-life problem.[4] Population growth might be viewed as a "biological success" except for the fact that it depends on nonrenewable sources of energy.[5] Another criterion for assessing potential overpopulation is per capita consumption that leads to resource depletion. Overconsumption goes hand in hand with industrialization.[6]

If there is one thing industrial civilizations, including Amerika, are not, it is self-corrective. Ecosystemically, they are characterized by a lack of immediate feedback from the environment to the human component. Technological changes accelerate in a geometric fashion, with each new change feeding back positively to accelerate the rate of change.[7] However, compensatory change in response to negative feedback from the environment is slow, a condition one observer sees as "incredibly maladaptive."[8] This situation serves to maintain the industrial system in a "runaway" state rather than one in homeostasis, or dynamic equilibrium. The opposing forces of stability and change, rather than serving to balance one another, are associated with different components of the cultural system. Change is given free rein in the technological component, but is resisted in the social component; therefore, the latter occurs at a much slower rate.[9] In other words, things are invented faster than they can be assimilated and adapted by social institutions.

This tendency toward imbalance within technological societies is placed into a long-term biological perspective by Bateson, who observes that any system that does not control the potential positive gain of one variable at the expense of others is inherently unstable. The evolution of the human mind to a point where ecosystemic balances could be circumvented and disrupted by the selection of variables that maximize human purposes was already a source of instability when modern technology became a part of human history.

Money and power had been the maximized variables in the civilized social system. The addition of modern technology to the civilized human construct vastly expanded the instability of the global ecosystem.[10]

The most fundamental characteristics of civilization are social inequality and extreme specialization of labor.[11] Inequality here does not mean social stratification alone, but unequal access to industrial resources or, as Karl Marx would have put it, to "the means of production." This kind of inequity is found primarily in advanced industrial societies and Amerika is no exception.[12] The situation is not caused by frustrated aspirations, as the Amerikan middle class often believes, but is rather a fundamental economic and experiential condition. Gerald Berreman, who has written extensively on social inequality, maintains that:

> Social inequality as it is presently constituted in the world is the root of the most immediate, fundamental, and fateful threats facing humankind.[13]

He blames social inequality for:

> ... hunger even when there is plenty, for high mortality, high fertility, and low life expectancy, for low levels of education, literacy, political participation, and other measures of the quality of life.[14]

Ultimately, social inequality will be the cause of "overt, perhaps catastrophic, conflict."[15] A dangerous characteristic of social inequality is the fact that it deprives the cultural system of input from those individuals first affected by the symptoms of crisis. Consumers faced with goods and services of decreasing quality have no avenues of communication open to those at the top stratum who make basic decisions about products or services.[16] Social inequality also prevents workers with suggestions about production from communicating with management.[17] Inequality is related to shoddy goods and poor service in that it reinforces competition. Ego-involvement with the job, rather than responsibility for it, implies that people are reluctant to admit and correct mistakes.[18]

The unequal distribution of consumer goods is the "cause maintaining factor" in growth-based industrial economies. The assumption in such economies is that if there is no demand for a good or service, that demand may be created in order to sustain the growth of the supplier.[19] This economic growth/consumption syndrome convinces the lower classes that they are moving up, even though their status remains the same.[20] In order to maintain an artificial demand for goods, producers constantly change the products available, using advertising to manipulate their value as status symbols, with the result that everyone must buy constantly in an attempt to keep their lexicon of status symbols current. Status symbols laboriously attained last year are passé this year, and an indicator of one's low position. The automotive and fashion industries are especially adept at using this tactic.

The distinction between social control based on values and public opinion, what sociologists call "internal control," and social control based on authority, what they call "external" control, was mentioned in chapter three. These concepts become relevant again in this discussion because external control is another function of inequality.[21] The problem with external controls is that they are much less effective and more unpleasant than internal controls. The larger and more unequal a society, the more totalitarian it must become to maintain control and sustain inequality. External forms of domination include thought control, in addition to threats and physical coercion. In modern civilizations television has replaced religion in helping to perform this function.[22]

Specialization of labor is an important aspect of civilization in that it forms the basis for the market economy, unequal concentration of wealth, political centralization, and the conflict between the interests of society and those of the individual or corporation. All of these are positive feedbacks into the runaway economic system.[23] In recent times, extreme specialization has caused such symptoms to be treated as causes, thus hindering a holistic approach to environmental problems without which no solution can be expected.[24] Factory workers, whose specialization is a tiny part of the production of a single product to which they have no other relationship, form one of the bases of the alienation of people from work.[25] These two factors, inequality and specialization, perpetuate continuing overconsumption and the ongoing absence of long-term changes. Additional characteristics of industrial economics are unemployment, market saturation, inflation, union and management price-fixing, planned obsolescence, and excessive use of resources. Economic planning is short range, elitist, and obsessed with economic values.[26]

The sheer size of industrial societies weakens social ties, causing problems in personal relationships that then tend to feed growth and consumption. Cartoonist Jules Feiffer captured the essence of this dynamic in eight frames. A housewife laments, "I can't stand my job. I go shopping. I quarrel with my daughter. I go shopping. My husband stays out all night. I go shopping. Four years of psychotherapy and what have I learned? The answer to misery is a sale."[27]

Taylor contrasts modern civilization with life in Europe before the industrial revolution:

> We are talking about changes that render whole patterns of life meaningless, which disturb value systems, create alienation, make life boring or frustrating or not worth living, raise crime, suicide, and alcoholism rates, and much more. We are talking about disacculturation and doing to ourselves what we have already done to many primitive peoples, plunging them into a technological world for which their institutions and values were unfitted.[28]

This weakening of social ties may be the source of the instability that characterizes both the social system and the individual. Instability may be seen in the cycles of inflation, recession, employment, crime and violence, and in the presence of subcultures that promote delinquency, violence, and retreatism.[29]

The mobility, scale, and instability of mass societies are seen by many as detriments to mental health. George Pettitt decries the lack of concern for children:

> ... in size, lack of unity, lack of interest in integration, and technological instability [American civilization] presents, more than anything else, a test of the adaptive powers of the hominid child.[30]

He cites as examples of this lack of concern, the loss of the extended family, the proliferation of unwanted children due to attitudes toward sex and abortion, the irrelevance of education to life, the failure to recognize the importance of peer groups, and the lack of job training or apprenticeships for the young.[31]

Slater's contrast between the emotional holism of small, stable communities and the fragmentation of the personality that is found in suburban "networks" was mentioned in chapter three. He is a proponent of the view that the scale and high mobility of American society results in widespread mental pathology and maintains that the schizoid personality is typical of industrial societies.[32] Contrasting the "colliding idea systems" of the "old culture" and the "new culture" in America, Slater insists that "the pathology of the old culture is accelerating," a process that can only be reversed by the elimination of the nation's growth/consumption obsession.[33]

The industrial personality has been defined by aimlessness and futility, while a "pathetic search for originality" and "short-term entertainment" are prime motivations.[34] One thinks of the "Cabbage Patch Doll" fad of the early eighties, wherein the "pathetic search for originality" was exploited by toy companies who provided each doll with its "own" adoption papers, name, and dress. So entrenched was this fad that riots actually broke out in department stores before the Christmas of 1983, when the dolls were found to be in short supply.[35]

The connection between overconsumption and social instability is a good example of the way in which mass culture is tied to environmental degradation. The growth economy, feeding on the constantly changing desires of mass culture, encourages consumption, which results in the overuse of resources with consequent environmental degradation. Overconsumption is a unique characteristic of industrial civilizations and defines them as "major economic, social and ideological systems [that are] are geared to nonsustainable levels of resource consumption."[36] People living in large-scale societies tend to seek unattainable rewards and, as in the Ffeiffer cartoon, attempt to substitute material compensation for social recognition.[37] In other words, industrial civilizations fail to provide adequately for the emotional needs of individuals.[38] Some critics see a connection between alienation, implied by the denial of death, on the one hand, and overconsumption on the other.[39] In other words, overconsumption is an attempt to compensate psychologically for the loss of those things that formerly provided social and emotional stability to the individual. The way these social factors are related to environmental deterioration in Amerika is that people overconsume to ease the pain of social disruption and the loss of spiritual values. In other words, overconsumption drives the economic machine that is destroying the environment.

Western Values

Many Ecotopian writers see industrial civilization as a logical historical outgrowth of Western values.[40] They cite a number of reasons for coming to this conclusion: 1) the belief in unlimited growth; 2) the importance of individuality; 3) faith in science, technology, and dualism—the idea that humans are unique among species, separate from nature and not subject to natural law. Science, or the scientific worldview, has been cited by many Ecotopian writers as being crucial to understanding the philosophical causes of the environmental crisis. These writers suggest, not only that it is the application of science (modern technology) that is to blame, but that the values accompanying it, continue to form the basis for action in most modern societies.

Others suggest that the Western religious tradition based on Judaism and Christianity is responsible for the growth of this dualism.[41] Paul Shepard's essay on Western dualism starts with Aristotle, tracing the humans-as-separate-from-nature through Western philosophy as interpreted by Thomas Aquinas, through Francis Bacon, Thomas Hobbes, René Descartes, Georg Hegel, and Karl Marx. If the human separation from nature had not become so much a part of Western thought by the nineteenth century, according to Shepard, Darwin's theories might have been a force to integrate humanity with nature. Instead, Darwin's ideas were incorporated into the existing paradigm, thus condoning further environmental exploitation. Shepard sees the result as a "pathology of isolation and fear," which is manipulated (presumably by those who stand to profit from the status quo) to urge more consumption, productivity, and growth.[42] Bateson, too, starts his list of Occidental "wrong values" with an example of "it's us against the environment."[43] If the industrial society is characterized by the separation of humanity from nature, belief in unlimited growth, and faith in the power of science and technology, then Amerika represents an extreme manifestation of this worldview.

One reason why Amerika represents Western values so well, lies in a history that orients it away from tradition and toward change. With the exception of Native Americans, the nation's creators were immigrants who, by definition, cut themselves off to some degree from old thought patterns and influences of the past.[44] Another historical circumstance, which the United States shares with other former colonies, is the fact that when the colonists arrived they found what seemed to them to be a land of unlimited resources. Because of technological differences between new arrivals and native populations, the land seemed to the European eye unused and crying out for exploitation. Abundance, fostered by the seemingly unlimited resources, was a basic determinant of Amerikan culture.[45] This unique combination of historical forces offered a situation in which the Western worldview could expand free from the restraint of Europe's traditions.[46]

Some American Myths

As time passes the frontier's unlimited abundance has been shown to be a myth. But the power of myth should not be underestimated; one need not delve too deeply to see the importance of the frontier to Amerikan culture, even though actual physical frontiers are hard to find in the modern world. If television is seen as a medium for preserving modern myths, the longevity of the 1960s television program *Star Trek*, recently revived with a new cast of stereotypes, qualifies it as an Amerikan myth cycle. Any "trekkie" can quote from memory the introduction that precedes each episode:

> Space—the final frontier. These are the voyages of the starship Enterprise, whose five-year mission is to explore new worlds, to seek out new civilizations, to boldly go where no man has ever gone before![47]

It is hard to imagine a better credo for the frontier/abundance myth. When the frontier ceased to be earthly wilderness, it became space, a place of an infinite number of wildernesses. One need only leaf through a sample of modern elementary and secondary school textbooks to see that the image of pushing back frontiers frequently appears as window dressing for chemistry, math, or biology lessons. The frontier/abundance myth is a typically Amerikan version of the exploitative Western worldview. It says, "as long as there is a perpetual frontier, there will be perpetual abundance to exploit."

Another worldview expression that devalues stability and favors constant change is the "fountain of youth" myth. The value placed on youth and the belief that aging can or should be slowed, is not entirely based on a fear of death. It is related to the growth economy, to changes in goods, jobs, and situations. The individual must be willing to accept superficial newness as a requirement for becoming an Amerikan worker/consumer. Old people are assumed to be inflexible, impediments to change. Thus, the emphasis on youth provides a rationale for early retirement and for the physical separation of generations.[48]

More directly, youth sells. The consumption/growth economy relies on the fountain of youth myth to support constant buying. The judicious manipulation of the Amerikan fear of aging and death by the advertising industry, made easy by the concept of humans-distinct-from-nature and the physical isolation of the individual from the environment, makes Amerikans vulnerable to appeals from the consumer industry. Women are especially vulnerable to this manipulation because their status in society depends so heavily on their ability to catch and hold a husband, which, given the Amerikan youth aesthetic, depends to a large extent on their ability to appear youthful.

The Amerikan "melting pot" myth represents yet another change-oriented value. It reflects the influence that immigration diversity has had on the culture. A persistent theme in Amerikan folklore, embodied in the nineteenth-century works of Horatio Alger, is the immigrant boy who becomes rich through hard work and enterprise. This immigrant hero embodies the Amerikan ideal of achieved status over the European ideal of acquired status. He demonstrates that no matter what one's racial or cultural origins are, there is no one who cannot be melted down and recast as a successful Amerikan in the great Amerikan melting pot.

That the melting pot myth can also be found in a phrase like "all men are created equal," or in the more contemporary slogan "equal opportunity employer," suggests that equal opportunity is something to be made explicit rather than something to be assumed. Yet school children are still taught explicitly and implicitly that individual self-interest starts, and group loyalties end, at the door of the employment office. They are encouraged to believe that the ticket to higher education, the route to the top, is a competitive score on their

Scholastic Aptitude Tests. Millions of minority-group members, members of the working class, women, and many unemployed Ph.D.'s know that there is more to it than that.

The Western emphasis on the individual is also made explicit in Amerika by the myth of the "rugged individualist," an incipient hero found in newspaper accounts of Harry Truman, who chose to ignore warnings from geologists and died in his cabin on the slopes of Mt. St. Helens when the volcano erupted in 1980.[49] His tragic death was a human interest story for weeks after the event, always reported in tones of amazement, awe, and back-door admiration. Millions of people considered him a fool for bucking the experts, yet admired his courage in sticking to his convictions. He was an exception, proving a rule, that Amerikans place more faith in science and experts than they do in their own judgement. He was so readily accepted as a hero because there was already a mythical category in which to place him, that of the rugged individualist.

It is paradoxical that while "the rugged individualist" is a folk hero in Amerika, one of the most striking characteristics of Amerikan society is conformity. Margaret Mead explains this conformity as a function of the newness and lack of tradition in America. Because there are no long-accepted rules for behavior, people are forced to look to each other for guidelines.[50] Much can be explained about Amerikans in terms of self-reliance, which is an extreme version of the Western idea of individualism.[51] This emphasis on self-reliance prevents interdependence, giving rise to insecurity, which takes the form of racism, conformity, and violence. The self-reliant individual provides a sanction for competition and economic relationships within a capitalist economy.[52]

The apparent conflict between individualism and conformity is one of those paradoxes that undergird the tensions within a culture.[53] The individualism/conformity continuum is important to both Amerikan and Mateelian cultures. The differing contexts in which it appears explains how individualism can be a positive environmental value in Mateel and a negative environmental value in Amerika.

Faith in science and technology is codified in the Amerikan myth of "Yankee ingenuity." We like to think that the "Yanks" are more ingenious than anyone else. But the notion has been called into serious question by economic activity in the Far East and Europe. Marvin Harris amply demonstrates the mythical quality of Yankee ingenuity in his book on the quality of American goods and services.[54] The Green Revolution may fail in the long run because "Yankee ingenuity" does not extend to making new technologies appropriate to non-industrial social and economic settings. Gene Marine's compendium of failed U.S. Army Corps of Engineer projects suggests that "Yanks" may have destroyed large segments of the American natural environment through the application of their "engineering mentality."[55] Yet, there are those who look to Yankee ingenuity to give us a technological edge against our potential enemies, the Russians. The "Star Wars" program, and calls on educators to de-emphasize the humanities in favor of math and science, are moves apparently calculated to give "Yankee ingenuity" its best chance. The significance of the myth lies both in its ability to fuel the economy by creating a demand for technological gadgetry and its potential to divert attention from social, philosophical, and cultural solutions to environmental problems. In Amerika, faith in ingenuity forms the basis for making short-range technological choices over holistic long-range solutions.[56]

Amerika, then, possesses all of the characteristics found in industrial civilizations and epitomizes the Western dualistic worldview, individualism, belief in unlimited growth, and faith in science and technology. It demonstrates these beliefs by perpetuating series of interlocking cultural myths related to the special historical circumstances of the United States.[57]

Friends dance around the groom at a wedding reception.

Chapter Five

The Primitive Model

Once there was a way to get back homeward....

—*the Beatles*

John Bodley has called primitive societies the "only proven cultural systems man has ever known."[1] He is not advocating an unequivocal return to that system, nor are any of those who study primitive societies for clues as to how to reestablish ecological balance. In fact, a simple return to the primitive form might only serve to start the whole process of environmental degradation all over again.[2] However, understanding what it is that made them so stable might suggest some directions to take in changing our industrialized culture. The interest of Ecotopian writers and Mateelian individuals in tribal societies is based on this possibility.

A crucial question currently being asked in anthropological circles is to what degree primitive societies are, or were, balanced parts of their respective ecosystems. John Bennett claims that stable primitive cultures represent mere "pauses in the overall historical tendency toward exponential increases in environmental use and impact." His position is that the only difference between industrial civilization and primitive culture is in the level of technology. In other words, if primitive people had the know-how to overuse their environments, they would. In his view, it is an "ethnological fallacy" to look to primitive people for solutions to environmental problems associated with industrial civilization. The very word "primitive" has fallen into disfavor with some anthropologists because of the attitude exemplified by Bennett, that there is no essential difference between it and industrial culture. This change has occurred because the word has taken on negative connotations within some developing countries composed primarily of formerly tribal peoples. Elsewhere, however, Bennett is forced to admit that there have been pauses in cultural evolution during which small, isolated communities have exhibited "relatively stable, sustained yield systems of resource utilization."[3] How long this stability has been maintained varies, but there are cases in which the "pauses" to which Bennett refers may have in fact lasted for millennia.[4]

John Bodley takes a position on this question that is almost exactly opposite to the one Bennett proposes. Bodley, who argues that primitive cultures "are totally different from our own" and that they "represent an almost total contrast in adaptive strategy to our own unproven cultural experiment."[5] He would retain the word and concept of primitive because of this extreme difference, which renders the two cultural forms so incompatible that the primitive one could not survive contact with the civilized one. Bodley believes there is:

> ... little doubt that most primitive peoples could easily produce a "surplus" of food above their own immediate subsistence needs ... [but] there is a cultural lack of incentive to raise production. . . .[6]

It is not technology or resources that limit the environmental impact of primitive cultures, but built-in cultural restraints, among these "defining maximum good at easily sustainable levels."[7] If Bodley can specify one way in which the cultural system itself restrains overuse of the natural environment, there is no reason to think that there are not more. Some of these might well be adaptable to the modern situation. When Bennett dismisses primitive cultures as possible sources of information for cultural change in industrial societies, he does so without knowing what the explanation is for their apparent viability. Given that these groups have maintained rough environmental equilibrium for periods of time much longer than industrial civilization has been in existence, and given the fact that it is unknown just how they did it, how can we reach the conclusion that they have nothing to teach us about ecological balance?

The position taken here is that: 1) primitive cultures are qualitatively different from industrial civilizations; 2) they do exhibit tendencies toward ecological balance and stability, and; 3) it may well be that aspects of their cultures which kept them in states of equilibrium are adaptable to the modern situation. Bennett correlates the increasing environmental impact of civilizations with the amassing of wealth, differential evaluation of products, saving and investing, and competition of individuals for material and social prestige.[8] To the degree that these traits are not characteristic of a culture, it is considered primitive. Pre-civilized, small scale, food-producing groups are included with the proviso that the primitive traits listed are most characteristic of hunting and gathering groups. Since Bodley has presented the essential differences between industrial civilizations and primitive groups so well, there is no need to go beyond a quote:

> ... primitive societies are quite small in scale, with ... maximum total population sizes of seldom over a thousand people divided into basically self-sufficient, kinship-based bands or villages of from 25 to a few hundred people. ... Status is normally a matter of sex, age and personal qualities; and there is generally free access for all individuals to natural resources, food and shelter. ... Primitive economies are locally self-sufficient, subsistence based systems characterized by reciprocal exchanges and built-in limits to growth.[9]

In addition, the impact primitive cultures have on the environment is more gradual than that of industrial civilizations and more analogous to natural processes.[10] Primitive characteristics to which Mateel is particularly comparable derive from the smallness of scale, continuity of membership in the group, and the direct experience of the natural environment that is implied by smallness and self-sufficiency. The smallness of primitive societies, in combination with the fact that people tend to stay in the same band or village over time, has several implications. The first has to do with the relationship between the individual and the collectivity. Individuals are prevented from pursuing their own interests at the expense of the group by 1) the absence of the concept of the individual as separate from the tribe and 2) the effectiveness of controls on behavior internal to the individual, or what we call the individual conscience. This internal kind of behavioral control stands in contrast to the authority based, external control typical of most civilizations. The internally controlled group may employ sanctions against maladaptive individual behavior.

Second, internal control implies homogeneity of values and expectations. In other words, smallness and continuity limit the opportunity for the individual to get access to ideas that are incompatible with those of the tribe, and raise the degree to which people have similar ideas.

Third, the modern conception of individuality as the highest value is something alien to tribal people.[11] That is why sanctions internal to groups, such as ridicule, gossip, ostracizing, and exile, work for tribal people. Another effect of smallness and continuity is that relationships are personal and multi-functional. Social and economic roles are embodied in the same persons, with economic implications attendant to such roles as friend, brother, mother-in-law, or head of the extended family. Therefore individual economic behavior is the legitimate concern of one's friends and kin. There is little conception of "minding one's own business" because one's own business concerns the business of the group. In addition, no one can become *only* a leader. Leaders cannot concentrate power without the constraints placed on them by their kinship and tribal membership roles.

Many Ecotopian writers have recognized the value of the small-scale tribal model in addressing environmental problems. Goldsmith and his coauthors point out that when a society is too big, the bonds holding it together are of "an ever more precarious nature" and "in a small, stable society, all citizens will have the good of society at heart." They observe that the mobility and large scale of industrial societies reduces the power of public opinion and thereby the society's capacity for self-regulation.[12] Slater describes small-scale communities as situations in which "nothing can go too far in any direction without corrective forces coming into play."[13] All of this means that even if one is not restrained from furthering self-interest at the expense of the group by internal controls, one will be restrained by other members of the group through sanctions internal to the group. Smallness of scale and multi-functional roles also improve communication, enhancing the ability of the group to act collectively with regard to the environment. Information does not have to travel such a large "social distance" from those who deal directly with the environment to those who make decisions regarding it. They may well be the same persons, or if not, the decision makers are obligated by kinship, reciprocity, and tribal membership to make decisions that are for the long-term good of the group, not the short-term good of a small part of it.

Another aspect of primitive societies especially comparable to Mateel is the fact that they experience the natural environment more directly than industrial civilizations. All of the individuals in the group are equally subject to weather, resources shortages, endemic hazards such as predators, and direct perception of the ecosystem of which they are a part. This implies several things. For example, there are simply more eyes and ears gathering environmental information that, because of the smallness and equality of the group, can be pooled effectively. Also, what Bennett calls "humility in the face of Nature—in other words, more restraints on human behavior" is enhanced.[14]

The arrogant, exploitative attitude toward Nature exemplified in modern, industrial society can be partly explained by the fact that only a small percentage of modern individuals ever really experience Nature. They are so insulated by technology that the consequences of bad environmental decisions are seldom experienced directly or immediately. Primitive people are in much better positions to experience directly the consequences of their own environmental decisions.

There is much ethnographic evidence to show relationships between aspects of religious behavior and worldview on the one hand and regulation of economic behavior on the other.[15] For instance, primitive rituals can operate directly to limit population growth, dispersal in space, and resource use. Mythology can also serve to codify crucial information about the environment and to educate the young about key ecological variables—animal behavior, location of resources, hazards, etc. Primitive people lack the modern technology that insulates them from direct experience of the environment. Thus, they incorporate their experiences into religious behavior because it is the most profound reality they comprehend. In doing so they express the interdependence and identity of the tribe with the natural world. Their religion helps them to maintain this relationship in a balanced way. Primitive religions and worldviews include ideas that express the interdependence and identity of these people with the natural world.

Primitive societies, then, are small, self-sufficient, kinship based, internally controlled, more or less in balance with resources, self-regulating, and have religious rituals and worldviews that express interdependence with and membership in their ecosystems.

Waiting for the morning circle at a three-day encampment ceremony. The rotting stumps remain from earlier logging in the area.

Chapter Six

Worldview

Here comes the sun. . . .

—*the Beatles*

It is in the area of values and worldview that references are frequently made to "the hippie movement," which spawned the culture of Mateel.[1] This is usually, but not always, accompanied by some kind of a disclaimer limiting the usefulness of the counter-cultural model. It is also in this area of discussion that Ecotopian planners who give highest priority to economic motivation dismiss the counterculture as superficial, inept, naive, etc.[2] The present research contradicts this assessment, at least in the case of Mateel. The changes in worldview that began with the discontinuity experience deepened, broadened, and were reinforced by the experience of living in Mateel and interacting principally with others whose individual worldviews were undergoing similar changes. That segment of the counter-culture which ended up in Mateel proved politically sophisticated, pragmatic, and competent enough to have implemented the changes in ways I believe will prove long-lasting—through their institutions, their children, and their real influence on mainstream activities.

The crucial historical factor that led to the creation of the Mateel community was the widespread experience of "dropping out." Mateelians individually came to some experience or series of experiences in their lives which dramatically threw them off the track they expected and were expected to follow. For the vast majority, mind-altering drugs—psychedelics and marijuana—were a major part of this "discontinuity" experience. Although marijuana and the psychedelics are chemically different, the subjective experience associated with each is similar enough that researchers are uncertain how to describe the differences.[3] In any case, they were functionally similar in their historical impact. They revealed to those users who became Mateelians the importance of subjective experience and placed it at the top of the list of Mateelian values.

The use of these substances is both an individual and a collective event. It is individual in that some parts of the experience cannot be shared. Actual hallucinations, images, and streams of consciousness, as far as is known scientifically, are specific to one mind. Yet the experience can be collective in that the feeling of increased perception of the environment accompanying the use of these substances includes the feeling of increased perception of other people.[4] The experience of increased subjective activity is a shared experience even though the specific hallucinations, images, and perceptions are not.[5] The discontinuity experience, likewise, had both individual and collective aspects for Mateelians. One was not only thrown off one's own path, which experience may have been intensely individual, but having been thrown off, those who came to Mateel discovered hundreds of other people who had a similar experience. Having learned a new way of perceiving the human and non-human environment and with their knowledge of the possibilities inherent in exploration of subjectivity increasing, they began creating new lives, individual and collective lives. The primary change had been in the mind. In anthropological terms, a new worldview had begun to take shape.[6]

The concept of worldview has had, relative to other anthropological concepts, little theoretical polishing. The main effort in this direction was made by Robert Redfield. Redfield distinguishes several categories which he sees as universal to all world views. Though the degree to which a particular culture may be separate—these categories and the relations between them vary—Redfield maintains that they may be discerned in all cultures. The first distinction is between the "Self" and the "Not-Self." Within the category Not-Self a distinction is made between "other humans" and two categories Westerners would call "God" and "Nature." The Self incorporates a part which addresses the outside world and a part which observes the addressing part.[7] These two parts of the Self correspond to what G. H. Mead called the "me" and the "I," respectively.[8] The ethnographer infers all of these categories from such aspects of culture as ceremonies, language syntax, explicit religious statements or "cosmologies" and other aspects of behavior. Redfield's conception of worldview includes the categories themselves, their content, and relations between them. Also included in Redfield's scheme are conceptions of time and space. Closely allied to worldview are the moral orientation and values of a culture.[9] This chapter will focus on these categories, and their relationships, time and space conceptions, and the moral orientation of the Mateelian worldview.

In a recent work, Michael Kearney has updated the concept of worldview by applying a systemic and materialist viewpoint to the traditional idealist conception established by Redfield. Kearney sees worldviews as being in a feedback relationship with the environment, a relationship in which each affects the other over time:

> ... humans, working with the conditions given to them by history—technology, environment, social structure, worldview and their social relations with other peoples—create their own society. ... A people live and work within such constraints. ... A worldview is linked to reality in two ways: first by regarding it, by forming more or less accurate images of it, images that mirror the world; and second, by testing these images through using them to guide action. ... in the process of acting, the actors modify the world they perceive.[10]

This quote describes exactly how the changed worldview of Mateelians has been translated into the physical, everyday culture of Mateel. Kearney sees the different categories of worldviews interacting with each other in a manner analogous to biological evolution, so the ideas tend to be compatible with each other as well as the rest of the cultural system.[11] In the case of Mateel, the interaction between worldview and environment has taken place for only fifteen to twenty years. There is not at this point enough data to rigorously determine the positive and negative effect Mateelians may have had on the environment. I suspect that, within the six core watersheds, the overall effects have been more beneficial than not, but there are Mateelian environmentalists who disagree with me. Fifteen years has, at any rate, been sufficient for the different categories of the Mateelian worldview to have become compatible with one another. The embryonic Mateelian worldview is sufficiently cohesive that it may be compared to the Amerikan worldview with regard to potential impact on the environment.

Mateel, as has been mentioned, is in some ways similar to a revitalization movement. It is in the aspect of what is called "mazeway re-synthesis" that this similarity to revitalization movements is most obvious. Mazeway re-synthesis is an extensive cognitive reorganization which occurs to certain individuals in societies that are undergoing a period of cultural distortion. In what appears to be a "last ditch collective attempt to survive," these individuals become the sources of a new worldview which is, hopefully, more consistent with the new reality than the old.[12] The discontinuity experience of Mateelians can be compared to "mazeway re-synthesis" but, rather than this process happening to one or a few individuals who then became prophets, it occurred to almost everyone in the culture. The worldview that is developing as a result of it, is the collective response of a large number of individuals who have, to differing degrees, experienced this deep-seated reorganization of perception, behavior, and values.

Diversity and Tolerance

The first difficulty presented by an analysis of Mateelian worldview is the incredible diversity of Mateelian individual philosophies. In a society of long standing the ethnographer would look for evidence of worldview in specifically religious behavior, but there is no one consistent pan-Mateelian religious system. There are, however, some regularities which emerge from observation of what organized religious structures there are. Atheism—the belief that neither God nor anything supernatural exists—is rare to non-existent. I have met only one Mateelian atheist. Soon after he proclaimed to me that there was no Supreme Being, no life after death, and no spirits he left Mateel to return to his former profession as a foreign correspondent in Asia, thereby ceasing to be within the scope of this study.

I have never met a Mateelian who actively practiced the religion originally enculturated. People either counter directly the religious training they experienced as children, or incorporate a diluted form of it into a personal system which includes remnants from many religious traditions and elements generated from individual experience. People who were raised in families actively involved in a highly structured religion may retain an openness towards the supernatural, but reject organized collective efforts to communicate with it. They tend to be eclectic and fickle in their attachments to particular religious systems. This category includes many former Mormons, Baptists, Catholics, and Jews.

An example of this eclecticism was a marriage between a semi-practicing Jew and a person of unspecified religious background. The ceremonial part of the occasion lasted altogether two hours, took place outdoors in an oak grove, and was attended by more than one hundred people. It consisted of a series of unrelated ceremonies borrowed from other cultures and invented by the couple, their family and friends. These included a fire ceremony conducted by a resident Hindu Brahman, group singing after the manner of the Yoruba conducted by a drummer in the local Santeria[13] group, readings from the Bible, Christian prayer, and the manipulation of ritual paraphernalia from Celtic and Native American traditions. Guests were asked to contribute further rituals "just to be sure we didn't leave anything out." The request was more serious than not.

Another large category includes those Mateelians who became involved with a highly structured group. These people were either not trained in a religion or peripherally involved with a religion that required less single-minded devotion than those listed above. Members of fundamentalist groups might have described them as "Christmas and Easter Christians." Included in this group are Mateelians who became fundamentalist Christians, giving local mainstream fundamentalist churches an unexpected shot in the arm. (When Mateelians become Christians, they almost always become fundamentalists.) Also in this group are people who became involved with modern cults such as the followers of Bagwan Sri Rajneesh or Swami Trungpa. The more active such an involvement with an outside leader is, however, the more likely it is that the individual will leave Mateel, thereby ceasing to be within the scope of this study.

By far the largest group are those who, no matter what their previous religious training, evidence a great interest in the supernatural, but reject rigid religious structure and dogma. Only a handful of Mateelians encountered in this study went from highly structured religious training as children to the same highly structured religious practice as an adult. In spite of the enormous increase in population in the six core watersheds, none has ever produced a functioning traditional church. In the entire geographical area of Mateel, where the population has more than doubled in a decade, no new church has been established, although some already established fundamentalist churches have grown and added facilities. One exception is the Living Waters Commune in Whitethorn, a heavily evangelistic fundamentalist Christian organization which was active for several years before it moved from the area. The basic Mateelian distrust of leaders, structures, and labels and the corresponding emphasis on individuality, self-reliance, and personal responsibility prevents either the fundamentalist Christian organizations or the modern cults from taking much advantage of the Mateelian openness to the supernatural. With the exceptions mentioned, most Mateelians approach theological ground with a potential for awe and a sharp eye for dogmatism.

Obviously, consistency in religious behavior is not especially valued. The dominant value is spiritual seeking itself, with a concomitant value on tolerance for the spiritual seeking of others. Orthodoxy and evangelism do occasionally appear, however. The response of the community to evangelic groups has so far been highly predictable along the lines suggested by the following two cases.

In 1976, representatives of a group called "Shivalila Commune," based in the mountains outside Bakersfield, California, appeared in Mateel. The leader of the group was a man who called himself Ogbra Lut, claiming to have been given the name by a Himalayan guru during one of Lut's many pilgrimages to the East. This same man, it so happens, is the person on whom Yablonsky based his early work about hippies, Lut's given name being Gridley Wright.[14] Lut's representative, Akbar Sat, spent some time in the Mateel community, calling unexpectedly on single women in an attempt to recruit them to the Bakersfield commune. One of these women described his *modus operandi*. First, he would flatter them by telling them he had heard of their spiritual prowess and was only looking for those advanced in consciousness, then he would attempt to establish sexual relations, after which tactics borrowed from the encounter group movement in combination with LSD would be used to break down their resistance to joining the commune.

Sat's only successful recruit returned from a two-week trial stay in the commune to get her children and take them there. In the words of a closely related informant:

> I happened to be caring for the children while she was gone because their father was my old man. Lut, the mother, Sat, and perhaps two or three other members of the commune, literally invaded my house and proceeded to denounce everything about it. She showed up with her head shaved, wearing a Tibetan pagoda-type cap. It took me a while to recognize her. They don't approve of nuclear families, so my one double bed was attacked because it showed I normally sleep with my old man. They ridiculed my TV set, they don't approve of those either. My two-year-old still wore diapers to bed and because of them I hadn't gotten around to taking off his diaper. They yelled at me that that was why he had a runny nose. Diapers are bad, right? My old man decided this was a good time to make himself scarce, so he took off on an errand, leaving me to handle the whole scene alone.
>
> Then they started in on me, screaming that I was a bitch who could not possibly be allowed to continue caring for the two children, who now belonged to the commune. I had at one time pursued a career, and no professional woman could be fit to mother a child. When one of the children began to cry that she didn't want to go because they would shave her head like her mother's and prevent her from learning to read, Lut, who was six feet tall and probably scary as hell to a kid, stalked over to her and said "R., you have no choice." At that point I flipped and screamed at all of them to get the hell out before I called the police. This was, of course, an empty threat, since the nearest phone was two miles away. Because the mother promised they would be in the area for several days, I allowed the children to go with them, making sure they knew that neither I nor their father would ever allow them to be forced to go.

The whole group returned to the mother's house, where Lut essentially held court for several days while dozens of people who had heard the story, including myself, came to check him out. The mother having appeared to be, up to that point, a pillar of the community, curiosity ran high as to what could have induced her to leave so precipitously. During their stay in the Briceland area, the Shivalila group invaded another house where they had heard that a highly regarded Zen Buddhist from San Francisco was on retreat. The story circulated that they had "trounced" him spiritually and left him in tears. They bragged of this to me.

Lut skillfully changed his approach for everyone who came to see him, being charming to some and obnoxious and combative to others. The philosophy of the group was based on the idea that one must be destroyed in order to be reborn. They saw their function as providing the destruction. The reaction of Mateelians to this extreme assumption of spiritual superiority is highly instructive. Those who were not directly attacked were amused, receiving with glee such of Lut's statements as "I can whip Jesus Christ in dharmic combat." No one, other than the one recruit mentioned, was inspired to join him. No one accepted him as any form of spiritual leader. Those who were secure in their own religious outlook, including several Zen Buddhists, enjoyed the diversion. Those who had been directly attacked regarded the group as dangerous, bigoted "mind-Nazis."

Everyone was concerned for the safety and well-being of the mother but no one felt empowered to prevent her from leaving with them, even her closest friends and family. Short of her forcibly removing the children, it was felt that she had an inalienable right to follow any "spiritual" path she chose, even to the point of endangering her life, a situation which many suspected might actually be the case. (When she returned after a month with the commune, she confirmed that excessive use of LSD and encounter group tactics, as well as the interception of her welfare check at the post office by the commune had caused her to fear for her safety. She had had to essentially escape from the commune, leaving her belongings there and hitchhiking home.)

A second such case occurred several years before the Shivalila episode, when a recent arrival became caretaker for land newly purchased by a community group intending to build a school on it. This man claimed to be an architect, which made him seem an appealing choice on land where a non-profit school would soon be built. Somehow he suddenly began drawing followers around him as a spiritual leader. Again, women formed the bulk of the followers, and again, sexual activity loomed large in the attraction. This time, however, the "harem" consisted of some married women who left their husbands to live with the new guru.

Again, the community tolerated the situation up to the point where a legitimate community interest came into it. The relevant question was, "How many people can we allow to live on community land for free when we are going to use it for a school?" Since the land is located in the middle of one of the small towns, where there had been a history of violent confrontation between "hill people" and "locals," there was also the question of relations with the local mainstream community. When asked to leave, the caretaker resisted until pressure became strong enough to force him to leave. At no time were his religious pretensions questioned collectively. Individually, Mateelians were inclined to joke about him. Only a handful can be said to ever have followed him. Those directly concerned, the aggrieved husbands, again, saw him as a mind-Nazi.

The tension between tolerance and orthodoxy arises frequently. Generally speaking, it is not until some group takes the position that they have the only path to the Supernatural, that tolerance becomes strained. Christians who refrain from evangelizing are completely accepted. The sanction against orthodoxy starts with ridicule and culminates with expulsion where possible and/or ostracizing. I have never heard of legal moves being made, even when there could be physical danger to the individual, except when the well-being of children was an issue.

Against this background of extreme diversity and tolerance, with community interests placing the only lid on cultism through ridicule and ostracizing, a beginning analysis of worldview may be attempted. The experience of discontinuity, in addition to creating the population of Mateel, formed the basis for the development of the worldview categories which are implied by Mateelian culture. The following discussion may be viewed as covering the lowest ideological common denominators among the many philosophical and religious outlooks to be found in Mateel

The Mateelian Universe

The first statement to be made about the Mateelian worldview, then, is that the Mateelian universe includes an enormous range of phenomena routinely excluded from the Amerikan, but not the primitive, universe. The experience of discontinuity opened individuals previously indifferent or antagonistic to the supernatural to an acceptance of the possibility that rational laws do not explain everything in their universe. Individuals who may never have been introspective suddenly became aware of a welter of subjective phenomena for which their lives as Amerikans had not prepared them. Extremely rational people became fascinated with such things as Jungian "synchronicity,"[15] omens, precognition and systems of divination such as The Tarot, astrology or the I Ching.

Since these phenomena are not considered to be accessible to rational explanation, they will be referred to as "non-rational inputs." This does not mean that rationality is abandoned, as is often claimed by critics of the counterculture, but that the laws of science are seen as being of limited use in describing the complete universe.

Mateelians will argue that this inclusion of non-rational inputs is more truly scientific than science as practiced by Amerikans, because possibilities have not been excluded from consideration without proof of their non-existence. (Anthropologist Edward T. Hall, incidentally, makes a similar argument.)[16] In the absence of proof to the contrary, Mateelians assume non-rational inputs. Individual experience, which may or may not be susceptible to scientific proof, is not only accepted as a valid source of data but as the most valued source of data.[17] A more important point is, however, that "data" for many people is superfluous. They simply have faith. Telepathy goes without saying. Omens are part of everyday life. Healing begins in the soul. It is an uneasy transition for those who had been most committed to the procedures of Amerikan science. Ambivalence, humor and inconsistency surround this culturally sanctioned openness to non-rational inputs, indicating some degree of conflict or paradox associated with it. Yet, relative to the accepted Amerikan view, Mateelians are remarkably open to non-rationality.

In the Pure Shmint play *Vibram Soul*, Spring tries to make gardening decisions:

> Well, I've thought about it for a long time and I've meditated on it, too. I threw the I Ching and I did the Tarot, and I looked into Ruby's crystal ball. I finally came to a decision. I'm going to cut down a tree. . . . I need the sun on my garden and the tree is blocking the sun. . . .

Spring presents the extreme of non-rational decision making. She is presented in the play as something of a caricature, indicating the tension between non-rational and rational input. Her "ex-old man," Jack, exemplifies a more typical attempt to relate objective to subjective, rational to non-rational. The following soliloquy brought down the house in Mateel:

> Six years. I spent six years with Spring and then it's Hello Swami and Good-by Jack. I mean I could see it if it was another lover, but what possible chance do I have against some prayer beads and a picture? And to top it all off he is the ugliest swami I've ever seen in my life. I mean I even tried hiding his picture once. I hid it under a stack of magazines in the outhouse. I thought she'd never find it. She comes home one day and says "Where's swami?" "I don't know." "Well, I'll have to meditate until swami calls me to him." So she meditated for seven hours and after seven hours, nature called her to the outhouse before the swami did. And she found him. The next morning at dawn she was making the shitter into a shrine. So every time I took a crap I had to look at his face. It made me very regular, though, I have to say that. I don't know, I tried to get into her trip. I really gave it an honest try. I even listened to his tapes. The swami has these tapes. He'd say things like "Death is not necessarily life and life is not necessarily death. And neither one is necessarily necessary." Now what in hell does he mean by that? What the hell does he know about death? What does anybody know about death? What do I know about it? I mean I read about it in the papers. I see the dead deer along the freeway. . . . I don't know, I don't know, I don't know anything. I know he doesn't know anything, that's for sure. You know, but I do wonder, I wonder where the spirits of those little creatures go when they die.

Basically skeptical about gurus, Jack is nevertheless open to the idea that something outside of objective reality affects him. "It made me very regular," "I tried to get into her trip," "I wonder where the spirits of those little creatures go when they die."

The practical problem facing individuals in the counterculture when the world of subjective reality opened up to them, was how to arrange their lives so that exploration of it did not interfere too greatly with physical survival. Over time they have come to incorporate non-rational input fairly smoothly into the practical side of life. Scientific, rational, logical approaches may prevail in fixing one's car, building a house, curing allergies, or laying out a water system, up to the point where rationality fails. For instance, if a car won't start there are certain logical actions one may take to start it. One checks the gas, cleans the battery terminals, wiggles wires, makes sure an automatic transmission is in "Park." In Mateel, if all of these actions fail, and the car does not have an automatic transmission, an attempt will be made to roll-start it. (Volkswagens are popular in Mateel just because they roll-start so easily.)

Chances are good that by the time all of these approaches have been tried and have failed, a small crowd of sympathetic people will have accumulated. Someone is bound to say "O.K., try the starter again and everybody concentrate." This suggestion may well be accompanied by smiles and laughs and facial expressions indicating play. Yet, chances are that everyone will make a serious attempt to concentrate, at least once. No one will become embarrassed or walk away in disgust. The attempt will be made.[18] The point is that whether or not everyone believes that the concentration of a non-rational source of power may start an otherwise disabled car, everyone will act as if they believe it. No one will seriously argue that such a procedure is a foolish waste of time. Self-consciousness in engaging in such an activity will vary widely from individual to individual, but even the most skeptical Mateelian will "play along," indicating that the possibility of success is more valued than the maintenance of apparent rationality.[19]

The Power of Consciousness[20]

There is power to be gained from the manipulation of non-rational inputs. This power is made accessible through what Mateelians call "expanding consciousness." One expands consciousness by exploring and learning about subjectivity. This process, which may start as a going inward, leads ultimately outward, to oneness with the Universe. If one accepts the idea of the power of consciousness as an ideal, one acts with reference to it. The more one accepts it, says the Mateelian, the more it works.

A moral corollary to this belief is that it is not only possible to become more conscious, but that one is obligated to become more conscious. The Pure Shmint play "Growing Pains" postulates a future in which a large earthquake has turned the mountains of Mateel into islands. Mateel has made an unsuccessful attempt to secede from the union and establish the "Federated Co-op of Sensimillan[21] Islands." Part of the constitution of the quashed revolutionary government expresses the obligation to expand consciousness:

> We, the people of the Federated Co-op of the Sensimillan Islands, declare our loyalty to the harvest, the Earth and the Earth's mother. We strive for our growth as conscious beings, in pursuit of achieving perfection within ourselves and for the realization of the divinity of humankind.[22]

The obligation to expand consciousness derives from the concept of manifesting reality. The omnipresent adage, "you make your own reality" is a moral assumption underlying much Mateelian behavior. One, but not the only source of this idea, is the writings of Jane Roberts, a medium whose guiding spirit, "Seth," is said to speak through her body. Roberts's books describe a whole philosophical system in which "simultaneous time" and "manifesting reality" are outlined.[23] They are widely read in Mateel. One manifests reality inadvertently through one's attitudes and actions in life. This idea is also referred to as "karma," although its resemblance to the traditional Hindu conception is open to question. The more conscious one is, the greater becomes one's power to change karma and choose the reality one manifests. Thus the expansion of consciousness is a way of making your own reality.

In *Vibram Soul*, Jack dies without having used well his chance to expand his consciousness through love. In his post-death world, he finds himself tossing a baseball around. He hears the cheering crowd; he becomes Mickey Mantle in the bottom of the eighth. He stops, suddenly, light bulbs flashing in his brain, so to speak, and announces, "Hey, I can play any game I want. It's whatever you want it to be." The band plays the theme from the old television quiz show "You Bet Your Life," a bird descends on a string from the ceiling with a placard around its neck reading "whatever you want it to be" and Groucho Marx comes out with his cigar, saying "You said da secret woid. You win." Jack says, "Why didn't I remember that when I was alive?"

In the dance sequence that follows, he accepts and embraces the figure of Death, who has haunted him throughout the play, and begins to sing what becomes the Grand Finale. The refrain goes:

> Round and round and round the wheel of reality. . . .
> What do you want it to be? Hey!
> Now he's come around to see
> There ain't no such thing as reality.
> Reality turns out to be whatever you want it to be.

Again, when he is told that he failed to grow and expand spiritually in life, he responds:

> I blew it, she's right. But we all blow it. I'm trying, I'm learning. Uh, I feel warm all over. . . . I feel my roots expanding deep into the earth and into the sky. . . . Outward, outward towards the Source and the Source is my heart. I don't fear the truth. I am the truth.

This soliloquy sums up the Mateelian view of the relationship between Universe, Self and Not-Self. The crux of the Mateelian worldview is here, as well as the kind of imagery often used to describe it. Realizing fully the limitations of two dimensional visual aids, I have attempted to approximate this view with a mandala in Figure 4. Self and the human segment of Not-Self each contain the "me" which acts and perceives and the "I," which observes the "me." Both of these are conceived of as having only a nebulous separation between each other and the universe. (Many Mateelians of a Zen or Vedantic orientation would say that both the "I" and the "Me" aspects of Self are illusions of separation from the consciousness which is the universe.)

The expansion of consciousness goes first inward (Jack's expanding roots) through individual subjectivity— the "I"— until it

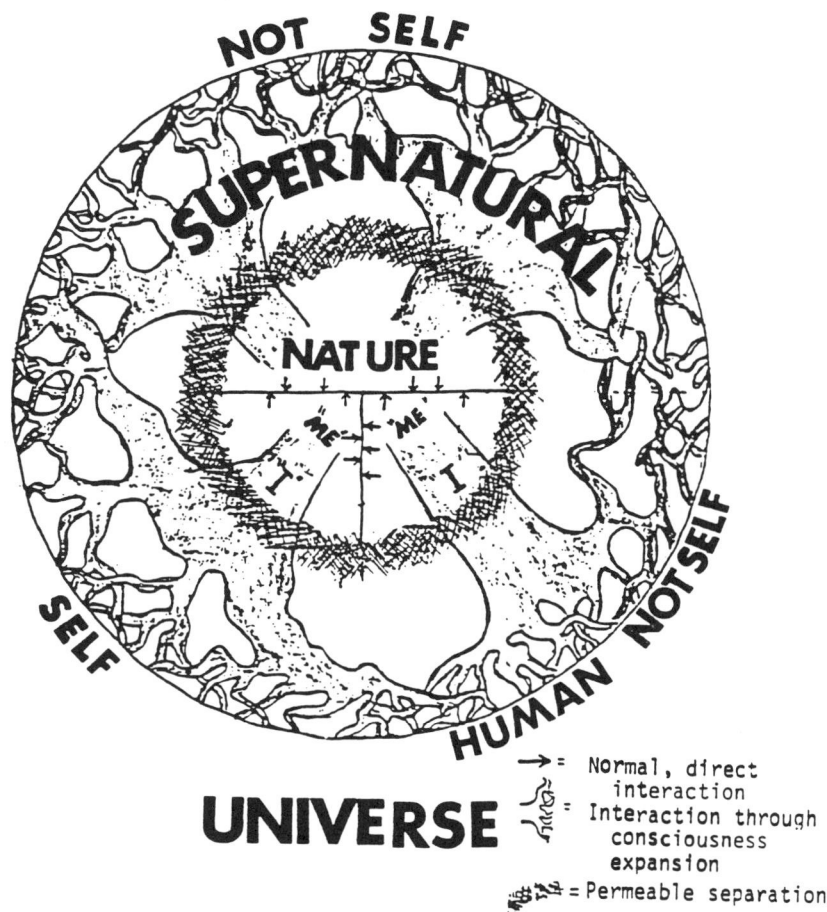

Figure 4. Mateelian Worldview Categories

connects with the universe. Jack's roots expand through the "I," into the Earth (nature) to the Source (the Universe/Supernatural). The Source is his own heart because he is continuous with the universe. He is the truth because the ultimate truth is the unity of the Self and the universe. There is no separation between Nature and the Supernatural, since what Westerners consider supernatural may well be a natural process which cannot yet be explained by science. Not-Self may be perceived either through the senses or through co nsciousness. The latter is free of the biases imposed by culture. Perceiving Not-Self through expansion of consciousness inward leads outward to the universe by a route which does not involve the illusory Self.

The Physical Not-Self

One might ask why this moral imperative to create a new reality. The answer is that the present one includes a world that is dying. Mateelians are survivors. They came to Mateel to preserve what they see as their integrity, their souls, their bodies, their freedom, their sanity, their children. I have never talked to anyone who came to Mateel before 1976 who did not come there in response to some negative experience with Amerika. Although many will respond to the question "why did you come here" with the statement that they wanted to build a house and be self-sufficient, further questioning on the order of "why would you want to do that?" elicits the negative experience. Common reasons stated include:

> I wanted to forget the war (veterans and radical pacifists).
>
> I wanted to get away from my spouse (battered, abused and neglected wives and psychologically abused husbands).
>
> Someone was after me (political refugees, military deserters, former revolutionaries).
>
> I could no longer stand the city. Specifics of this one are: traffic, violence, pollution, overcrowding, lack of low-cost housing, police harassment, involvement with hard drugs.
>
> At least three people had some health problem they believed was terminal and came to Mateel to die. (None of them have.)

Many came from a combination of these reasons. The most common reason is the expectation of the death or serious decline of the world in general and the cities in particular, as the result of nuclear war, environmental disaster, economic disaster, earthquakes (which are more dangerous in the city) or racial violence. It is believed that short of a total nuclear war, one increases one's chances for survival of these catastrophes by establishing a life in the country, by setting up one's own systems rather than remaining dependent on systems which are likely to collapse in any of these events. Whether their quest for survival is seen in terms of personal choices exclusively or as part of a social movement, the demise of the Earth and/or the human species has infinitely more reality for a Mateelian than it does for the average Amerikan. From this, the following general statement is inferred. The physical world has a limit of tolerance. The image of "spaceship Earth" is not a political cliche in Mateel. It is a motivating fundamental concept. Mateel is seen as a hope for survival either individually, or collectively, or both. For some it is seen as the last hope.

To survive, Mateelians must not continue the kind of life which has placed the world in such danger. They must make it over from scratch. This attitude of starting from scratch and making everything over will be referred to as the concept of "funky." Funky is a word in the hippie vernacular which has taken on a particular connotation in Mateel. It was originally used among Blacks in the 1960s to mean "smelly" or "dirty." It is from this meaning that the noun "funk" probably derived, expressing a psychological condition in which one is too depressed to move (or wash, or clean up one's environs, or "take care of business"). Somewhere in its etymology the word "funky" began to take on the sense of "smelly and dirty but somehow appealing nevertheless," as in the 1960s Motown hit record "Funky, Funky Broadway." The implication of the song is "it's smelly, dirty and the source of 'bummers', but somehow it works anyway."

When disenchanted Amerikans gave up their expectation of clean, operating, efficient Amerikan material culture (cars, houses, plumbing) and moved onto completely unimproved land to live in school busses, tepees, tents, sheds, and under large pieces of plastic, with no money for vehicle repair or home improvement, the concept of funky came to be applied to whatever they developed to meet practical needs. A person might improvise a part for Volkswagen repair out of what was available in a neighbor's junk pile, see that it works and announce, with a broad grin, "Well, I fixed the bug. It's funky, but. . . ." Or a plumbing job which cleverly combines ten of the wrong size connections to take the place of one unaffordable or unavailable one will be complimented by a smiling "Pretty funky!" When applied to a practical project, then, the word funky implies that the problem presented by lack of money, which is the result of having dropped out, has been solved by patience, determination and a tenacious willingness to put up with whatever hassle goes along with having a funky solution. Although it probably has nothing to do with etymology, one might say that funky is short for "functional, but just barely," analogous to classified advertisements for used cars which read "$500. It runs."

I am here taking the liberty of applying the concept to abstractions like institutions and personal relationships because the attitude which produces a funky shelter is the same attitude which is taken toward social and spiritual experimentation. As a component of worldview, the concept of "funky" is a rejection of the Amerikan enchantment with experts, specialization, written law, and dictated morality. It is, again, consistent with the value placed on personal responsibility and self-reliance. In a sense, it expresses a return to "Yankee ingenuity" as a reality based on ecological limitations rather than a myth in the context of abundance. Mateelians assume that they will solve problems as they come up, with whatever is handy in the way of concepts, changed assumptions and perceptions, new information, appropriate technology, empirical observation, "vibes," and whatever is in the junk pile, and they have cheerfully tackled the problem of creating a new social and physical reality with this attitude.

The following incident illustrates how "funky" applies to social behavior. During a summertime recreation program sponsored by one of the alternative schools, a group of older and younger children, babies in arms, mothers and other adults, walked several miles up the north fork of the Eel River. The campsite chosen featured a beautiful sandy beach in a small cove. A latrine area was specified in a sandy area inland and downstream from the camp proper, and furnished with toilet paper and shovels. The walk from the camp area to the latrine was through an area one might call "snake heaven," complete with rocks, holes, and crevices.

On the second day, an enormous rattlesnake was spotted sunning on a rock between the camp and the latrine. Confusion ensued as mostly urban-raised people with only a few years experience in the country tried to decide what to do. The children were advised to stay away from the snake, but whether the group should leave it alone or not was unclear. Before a decision was reached, two teenage boys, counselors for the recreation program, began stoning the snake, by dropping large rocks on it from the cliff above. (There were no guns or other weapons available.) Finally the head of the program, who had been against killing the snake, was forced by compassion to help finish the job rather than leave it half dead. The snake was skinned, with one of the boys claiming the skin and rattles, and the carcass was roasted over an open fire. A group of naked children ate the meat while the mothers carried on a heated discussion.

One mother felt vehemently that the snake was an unpredictable danger to her toddler. We were justified in protecting our young, getting the snake before it got us. Since we did not waste the meat and the skin, we had done no wrong. Another mother felt it would have been sufficient to scare it back under the rocks, move the latrine, and warn the children away from the area. A third mother felt that short of killing the snake, the only solution was to move the camp—an enormous hassle—since no amount of warning the children away from the area would insure that the children would not forget, or that the snake would not be drawn into camp by the heat of the camp fires. A long ignorant discussion on snake behavior followed this statement. It was pointed out that where there was one snake, there were extremely likely to be more, therefore moving camp could only result in placing us in some other snake's territory. In addition, we knew there were rattlesnakes around when we moved here. Life is full of danger and death, only some of which can be avoided.

About the time that a consensus was being reached that what was done, was done, and further discussion was a waste of time, one of the mothers who had been silent throughout burst in with a dramatic statement. The snake was old, as its size testified. It had lived there in peace for who knows how many years, just being a snake. Then one day we burst in on its scene, establish our territory, label its world according to our needs, and kill it for simply sunning on its own rock. If we had to kill it, it was good that we ate it, but did we need to flaunt its death by allowing an adolescent to turn its skin into a hat band? And what right did we have to kill it? What makes us think we are more important than the snake? She asked, "What kind of karma is that?" This speech was followed by absolute silence as the speaker looked with dead seriousness at each one of us in turn. Then she broke into a self-deprecating smile, shrugged and said, "I just thought I'd put in a word for the snake." The whole speech had been delivered, incongruously it seemed to me, in a New York accent, but it was so compelling that not another word was said about the snake the remainder of the trip.

The fact that such a discussion took place at all illustrates the "funky" Mateelian need to establish non-Amerikan guidelines for conduct. Where there are none, they must be created together and any incident may provide the occasion for such creation. Some further aspects of the concept of funky are also illustrated. There are no experts, or rather, experts need not be deferred to without further discussion. The assumption was made that everyone present had an equal right to contribute to the discussion. A Mateelian might say, "No one has the truth; it comes from all of us. We start from scratch." No one assumed that some potential course of action was more "right" per se than any other or that there was any person in a position to declare what was right and have it accepted. The teenaged boys were chastised mildly but not authoritatively, not for killing the snake, but for acting without authorization from the group.

The anecdote illustrates another aspect of the Mateelian relationship to the natural environment. There were no weapons available to kill the snake because one begins interaction with the natural environment with the assumption that humans have no special claim to it. Even though it includes unsavory creatures like snakes, it is not something hostile from which one automatically needs to defend oneself by carrying guns.[24] The mothers, from the one who felt killing the snake was mandatory, to the one who felt we had wronged it, all accepted that the snake had some rights, that there must be a reason for taking its life, and that it would be wrong to "waste" it after having killed it. All would have been opposed to killing a harmless snake such as a gopher snake. No one said "I hate snakes" as a justification for killing it.

Lengthy observation of Amerikan tourists in Mateel, suggests that most Amerikan campers would more than likely have had a gun, shot the snake, taken the rattles as a souvenir, left the carcass for the vultures and never given the matter a second thought. Alternatively, they would have panicked, packed everything up and left. Primitive people, unless they observed special taboos relating to rattlesnakes, would probably have done the same thing the Mateelians did but more efficiently and without second thoughts. The point is that even though confused and relatively ignorant about the natural environment, Mateelians, unlike Amerikans, related to it with respect.

Mateelians respect Nature in the hope that, if the respect is sufficient, the potential for environmental destruction can be forestalled. This idea forms the basis for the conception of "The Land," a phrase one hears constantly in Mateel. In general, the use of the article "the" is preferred over the use of the first person singular possessive "my" with the word "land," unless possession needs to be stipulated. (The question of ownership and possession of land is more thoroughly covered in chapter eight.) The phrase "The Land" may mean "my land," as that part of The Land which is in my keeping, or it may mean the Earth in its potentially undestroyed state. The concept of The Land has a connotation of "place," that is the location or area, but no connotation of either individual or collective ownership or political designation. It is quite distinct from the concept of "my land," town, county, state, or nation. The concept of The Land implies personification. The Land is seen as a living, breathing entity with whom one has a personal, interactional relationship and which more or less corresponds with the Supernatural. This personal relationship to the physical world called The Land is also reflected in naming practices.

The function of names as "symbolic orders of person definition" has been established by Clifford Geertz in his discussion of naming practices in Bali.[25] Whereas the Balinese system de-emphasizes individual experience by making the personal name a combination of nonsense syllables and seldom using it, Mateelian personal names are always highly meaningful and emphasize personal values and experience. The common practice of changing one's name is most often in order to symbolically express the results of the discontinuity experience. Secondary reasons are to hinder being located by someone, or as a statement for individuality and against the experience of having a common name like "John," or because of some negative meaning attached to one's original name. Children's names and CB "handles" also conform somewhat to the principles of the following discussion.

Table 1 is a classification of Mateelian chosen names drawn from attendance lists at three alternative schools and from general observation. The school attendance lists are complete, in order to show the proportion of ordinary mainstream names to relatively unusual ones. The general observation list represents names which would be unusual in mainstream America only. The table is divided into seven categories, according to the meaning of the name. These are:

1) Names referring to a spiritual value, either related directly to The Land or not, more frequently with an Eastern or Native American origin than a Western origin.

2) Names referring directly to some aspect of The Land, including names of mythical creatures associated with aspects of The Land.

3) Biblical, ethnic, and old-fashioned names.

4) Political names.

5) Ordinary American names.

6) Unusual names on which I have no information.

The spiritual/mythical names are a reflection of values and an interest in the cosmologies of other cultures. The third category is connected to identification with The Land in that it consists of names typical of American pioneers, peasant and tribal peoples, all of whom live on The Land. Biblical names are included in this category because, as namers explained to me, they are typical of American pioneers, not necessarily because of the Biblical meaning of the name or associations with the Biblical character.[26]

Table one shows that only a handful of chosen names do not refer directly or indirectly to The Land, and the majority of those which do, place the referent squarely into the natural environment, reflecting the sense of belonging to The Land or being a part of it. Those remaining reflect identification with other people who traditionally live on The Land, or with personifications of aspects of The Land. It will be remembered that the collective name, Mateel, refers

	Children		General	
Spiritual Values, not The Land	Rama Yang Om Pilar Tao	Sita Freya Shantidavi Damara Dia	Bindu Abracadabra	Spirit
Spiritual Values, Land	Kupiri	Cybelle	Kali	
Place names, aspects of The Land	Rainbo South Gimli Sunshine Acacia Sunny Day River Osha (ocean) Mateo Joaquin Khola Dawnflower Trilium (C.B.)	Sky (2) Sun Cedar Joshua (tree) Heather Panama Rain Thane Utahblue Solar Rio Watershed (C.B.) Tall Trees (C.B.)	Sierra Sun Man Douglas Fir Iris (2) Yerba Buena Wind Hummingbird Autumn Wind Rainbow Raven Guthrie Flower Hog Drops (C.B.)	Tree Man-who-walks- in-the-Woods Star Columbine Weasal Songbird Owl Sunsong Mattole Sky Deerhawk Otter (C.B.)
People who live on The Land, pioneer, old-fashioned names, ethnic, peasant, tribal, Biblical	Sarina Brenden Jesse (2) Sara (2) Daniel Benjamin Nicole Uvea Lee Ann Roxanne Mara Jessica Jomra Anders Lauriel	Reidar Jason (3) Caitlin Honna Eva Olin Marco Sebastian Jubal (2) Obadiah (2) Nile Laeben Ezra Emma Laura Jo	Ruby Omar Moses Jentri (Gentry) Jonn Melody Aaron (2) Jacob Gabrielle Tito Jonathan Vivian Johanna Lauren	Aia Yan Sally Bell Dotsolali Sasha Melissa Indigo Frances Lela Sara Seth Alexis Lacey
Ordinary Names (children)	Rosie Andy Candy Michael	Danny (2) Tony Jill Brent	Gary Diana Eric Jenni	Todd Bob Lisa William
Unusual, meaning unknown	Koree Ali Casey	Reb Pandora Sailas	Kyra Bo Mika	Allysa Kalina Alison
Political	Devlin (child's name, after Bernadette Devlin)		Woman (last name, feminist statement)	

Table 1. Mateelian Names
Meanings may be found in Appendix Three.

directly to the two main rivers, Mattole and Eel. This name has been regarded ambivalently by the "hill people" since its inception. Excluding those persons who object to it on aesthetic grounds, disliking the association with such an unpleasant creature as an eel, I have the impression that there is a geographical gradient describing the differential acceptance of the name. It runs from Garberville to the sea. Residents who reside furthest from Garberville defend the name, some vehemently. Those who either reside or work in town are more likely to reject it or be indifferent to it. This pattern of acceptance/rejection, if valid, would support the notion of naming patterns being a reflection of the concept, The Land, in that those whose residence indicates a willingness to be most involved with The Land physically are most likely to value a community name referring to it.

Categories of People

Discussing the categories Mateelians use in ordering that part of the Not-Self which is comprised of other people conflicts directly with the Mateelian repugnance for labels. In accordance with the dictates of the funky mentality, every interaction and every relationship is to be as much as possible, generated from scratch, without prior assumptions, prejudice, or stereotypes. On the other hand Mateelians, like everyone else, cannot avoid using categories because they are fundamental to thinking. The psychedelic and marijuana experience provided an image of pure feeling, pure truth, pure knowledge free from categories. This experience is crucial to the understanding of the culture in that it is an ideal which informs Mateelian behavior. Yet the undeniable truth of that experience is that no matter how often one has it or what means is used to produce it, it ends. Where it ends, thinking begins, and thinking requires categories, even stereotypes.

A great effort is made to base definitions of relationship on individual attributes and Mateelians are probably among the most tolerant of people regarding personal eccentricity. Practically, however, relevant categories of people are, as they are in every culture, unavoidable. In Mateel these categories are kept implicit as long as possible, understood to reflect continuums, and are relative. They are also provisional in that individuals can move rapidly from one to another without experiencing a great deal of social pressure to be consistent. The overriding value is always personal freedom and the ideal is always "we are all one."

With that caution thoroughly established, it is possible to describe implied Mateelian categories of people. The most basic one exists in all cultures, the division between "us" and "them." The degree of ambivalence surrounding this category in Mateel is enormous and many Mateelians are placed into a paradoxical situation with regard to it. On the one hand, the discontinuity experience tells them that they are different in some basic way from the other members of the culture in which they grew up. This information comes from the highest valued source, personal experience. On the other hand, they know that wars are predicated on perceived differences between people, they believe that the way to end wars is to end warlike behavior in themselves, and many feel a moral obligation to do so. One of the highest cultural ideals is peace. Many informants were antagonistic to this study on the grounds that it "draws lines between people." Others agreed with my defense that the lines are there already, created with no inordinate help from me, and that, as an anthropologist, I am merely "doing my thing" in describing them.

The local poet, Deerhawk, speaks for the experience of "us" and "them":

> decide, which side am i on, lord, which side are you on:
> Down in Selma, Alabama, which side are you on?
> or in Desperate Nicaragua, which side are you on?
> up in filthy Chi-town, which side are you on?
> Town in the smog of Watts town, which side are you on?
> and here in the grace of Mateel land which side are you on, tell the truth, which side are you on?
> never forget, brothers and sisters, fathers, mothers, friends, foes,
> the sacred tribe here growing, evolving now, celebrating today on the banks of Sinkyone Eel River
> dwelling here in the grace of Mateel was forming in the madness a dozen years ago
> today was coalescing in the sun bright white light
> that dissolved the doubt of being that renewed the opening of hearts hungry for Love's dominion,
> starved for Aquarius![27]

The local politician, Alan Katz, speaks for no distinctions between "us" and "them" in a letter to the editor of the local newspaper, *Star Root*:

> If I'm a cowboy, I deny the Indian. If I'm a hippy, I deny the redneck. The price we pay for our cultural institutions (the Moose, the Hippies) is that we must deny a part of ourselves; for the truth is that we are all cowboy and Indian, hippy and redneck, Christian and pagan. That's why we need the secret handshakes, the costumes, and the mumbo-jumbo: to reinforce the lie. . . . [28]

The contrast between these two positions derives from a confusion of two levels of thought, the ideal and the real. The ideal level is what Katz refers to elsewhere in the same letter as "the one-ness of being." It is a concept derived from the experience of expanded consciousness in which thinking is replaced by something else. "One-ness of being transcends the two sources from which knowledge is derived in ordinary consciousness, experience, and logic. One who values experience over logic must accept the distinction between "us" and "them." One who values logic over experience is free to rationalize the distinction away in an attempt to realize the ideal. The logical paradox comes from trying to equate the higher category of "one-ness of being" to something which it includes, the experience of the categories, "us" and "them."

To resolve the conflict between ideal and real, a conflict which Mateelians find especially bothersome since they are so idealistic, Katz attempts to rationalize back to the ideal. He makes a false assumption that the mere existence of even relational and provisional categories necessarily implies prejudice, and he denies the necessity of real-world humans to use categories for thinking, whether they are thinking about humans or vegetables. In this rationalization process, he contradicts the findings of experiential truth, which suggest that categories are real because they have been experienced. The poet recognizes the truth of experience, categories, and people, and understands the limitations of ordinary consciousness. He knows that the one-ness of being includes all three sources of knowledge—experience, logic, and the "something else" of expanded consciousness. The poet does not attempt to reconcile the conflict between ideal and real in any way other than by seeking higher consciousness.

Katz is in the end forced to admit the value of identification with a group while inadvertently describing how most Mateelians in fact resolve this paradox, or at least live with it:

> And then there are those rare human beings who get beyond the "us" and "them," who no longer need to wrap themselves in cloaks of patriotism or drugs, costumes or religion, who simply are what they are, who try to stay open, alive, growing . . . they share in the oneness of being; they are hill folk and town folk, but they don't need to live behind their masks or their locks. Though they may find strength in a set of beliefs, a sense of identity, or a tradition shared with others, they take the responsibility of breaking out of the protective and ultimately smothering shell of communal identity and begin the painful, joyous game (or dance) (or task) of being human.[29]

A perusal of other letters to the editors of local newspapers throughout the 1970s shows that while both "locals" and "hill people" perceive differences, enlightened persons who would identify themselves as members of one or the other group are always trying to resolve the conflict between the need for human beings to use categories for thinking and the ideal of no prejudice-generating divisions between people. The following example is from a rather long exchange. The exchange was started by a local "straight" real estate man who asserted that the "newcomers" did not pay taxes and therefore should not receive federal CETA funding for their community projects. A letter defending the newcomers mentioned that they did pay taxes when they earned enough money to owe them, but that many were so poor they didn't even have hot running water. This prompted an anonymous reply that that must be the reason why they brought the parasite, scabies, to the public schools. The following letter from Rettie Schille answers that "clean" or "dirty" are not good criteria for assignment to categories because these characteristics are true of individuals in both camps. The writer does, however, acknowledge a philosophical difference:

> . . . the eyes of prejudice see what they want to see, never recognizing that worn clothing, faded clothing, and mended clothing can also be clean clothing. Such clothing is a deliberately chosen visual statement of the "refugee" philosophy— waste not, want not; let us leave some for our children's children. And indeed, why not wear one's philosophy? The 'locals' do it, too. It reads: see how prosperous I am. My clothes are new and crisp.[30]

Beyond that, she reaches for an explanation of the dirty stereotype in differences in material culture:

> My observation is this: those who are very new are building and working and living under quite primitive conditions, and find it next to impossible to maintain the standards of cleanliness their mothers taught them. Ever been camping? Imagine camping for two years straight. . . .

Characteristically Mateelian, she includes a plea for the idea of transcendence of categories:

> Do we really need to have this war? I firmly believe there should be enough psychological space in this country for all forms of belief and philosophy. . . . Let's try to find more . . . common bases from which to regard the world positively.

The distinctions of sex and age are relevant to both of the categories "us" and "them." They are not, however, relevant to the same degree or in the same way that they are in most cultures. In keeping with the concept of funky, sex becomes relevant as it becomes a factor in the relationship. Given the high degree of tolerance for ambiguity, the revolution taking place in sexual relations, and the large obvious homosexual segment of the community (see chapter ten), it is not too ridiculous in the context of Mateel to say that even the categories, "male" and "female," are reflections of what is more accurately thought of as a continuum. There are some activities from which persons may be excluded on the basis of sex, but these exclusions are always open to question. For instance, both men and women attend births, but the advisability of having male midwives has been a controversial question. The fact that there is a contingent of midwives who also oppose the idea of female midwives who are not mothers, suggests that the objection to male midwives is not that they are men per se, but that they belong to a wider category of those-who-have-not-given-birth.

There is some sexual division of labor, perhaps even more than in contemporary mainstream Amerika because of the physical nature of work in the absence of labor-saving devices, but again, this is situational in nature. There are no taboos preventing members of either sex from engaging in any activity of which they are capable. The ultimate line is physiological—men cannot nurse babies or give birth. There is no corresponding ultimate line for female behavior, and female activities are limited by the strength of the individual woman rather than by taboos or negative sanctions. This is not to say that Mateel is free from sexism, only that it is likely to take on a much more implicit, interactional form.

Age as a category is, again, not nearly as relevant as it is in other cultures and the Mateelian urge to deliberately break down or deny categories applies especially to age. The tiniest babies are spoken to in tones implying honest interest and basic equality. Children are considered persons certainly from the moment of birth and for some time before. They are usually interacted with on an individual basis rather than as members of an age group and are admitted into decision-making on the basis of individual maturity rather than by arbitrary age lines. Older people are probably the least tolerated age group *de facto*. Even here, however, the explanations given for any intolerance are not based on age explicitly, but on personal attributes which may or may not be a factor of age. The rapid rise of people over sixty in recent years has resulted in many attempts to include them in community activities. The ideal is certainly a population as diverse in age structure as it is in personalities.

Residence distinctions enter into the classification of people, who are classified first as "townies" or "hill folk," then with reference to the particular town or watershed or ridge-top. A certain amount of stereotyping goes on, inevitably, and there is some basis for it. For instance, persons in Watershed A are seen as artistic, creative, cliquish, colorful, tribal and, with a few outstanding exceptions and until recently, apolitical. They drive Valiants. Watershed B persons are seen as consisting of two types. They are either gay, which category has its own attributes, or they are seen as especially funky, likely to dress in jeans and flannel shirts rather than picturesque ethnic clothing, drive heavy-duty beat-up vehicles, and strenuously reject labels, leaders and organizations. They are thought to be pragmatic rather than abstract or "arty," a fact expressed physically by the presence of a junk yard at the entrance to their road, and not to be inclined especially to spiritual pursuits. They, too, are seen as apolitical.

Ridge-top A and Watershed C people are seen as bourgeois, intellectual, spiritually arrogant, elitist, and most likely to have or have had a profession. They are seen as especially political and inclined to organization. Watershed D people are thought to be most like Amerikans economically. When marijuana became a profitable cash crop, it is widely believed that they were the first to grow big. They are seen as least communal, most oriented to the traditional style nuclear family with traditional male-female roles. Town A is seen as the skid row of Southern Humboldt county. Residents are thought to consist of hard drug addicts and drunks, to be dirty, sexually promiscuous, spiritually deprived, anti-intellectual, non-productive, inarticulate, prone to violence and a source of hepatitis and parasites. Residents of the various towns and watersheds mentioned often joke about the stereotypes, even about themselves as displaying the stereotype, in a way which indicates that they acknowledge and accept that there is some degree of truth to them. These stereotypes and others appear prominently in Pure Shmint plays.

Other minor distinctions are "gay" versus "straight," which is of interest not for purposes of discrimination, but because of its relevance to courting practices. Another distinction is between "old-timers" and "newcomers," again not for purposes of discrimination, but in order to evaluate the degree to which experience informs statements about the local environment or community.

Time

The Mateelian concept of time is stated in the often repeated phrase *Be Here Now*, which is the title of a book by Baba Ram Dass, formerly the Harvard psychologist, Richard Alpert.[31] It is difficult to say how much the concept in Mateel is related to the book, since I am sure the phrase has been spoken to me by people who never read the book. Nevertheless this particular book is one frequently found on bookshelves in Mateelian houses and copies are always in stock at the local book store. To give a sense of the way the phrase is used in Mateel, an example from an informant:

> My family once went to visit another family by a route which included a bridge which had supposedly been fixed. It had been

washed out for years. When we got there we found that it hadn't been. Horses, motorcycles, and pedestrians could cross it, but we were faced with either a quarter mile walk up a thistle choked, rocky, not-quite-dry creek bed to our friend's place, or a one-and-a-half hour drive going the other route. Since I wasn't prepared, I was in favor of the drive, but was unable to convince my son's father. So, carrying a large bowl of potato salad in my hands (leaving no hands free to catch myself should I slip on the non-path and begin to fall through the thistles into the creek bed), wearing Birkenstocks on my feet and packing a six-month-old baby on my back, I followed my son's father and three small children up the creek. On the way, we had to fight off heat stroke and yellow jackets, the kids and I fell into waist-deep pockets of water (almost head deep for the children). We got there soaking wet, worn out and frazzled. I immediately began expressing my anger to my hostess. I was angry at the person who supplied the original misinformation, at the person who told us that there was a path next to the creek, and at my son's father for insisting that we walk rather than drive. When I said it reminded me of another time, another situation, in which I had been mad at another person for similar reasons, my hostess cut me off with a finger to her lips and said, "Well, let's just be here now."

In this example it appears that the "now" one is to "be here" in is in contrast to the past. The informant was allowed to be angry for present reasons, but not past reasons or at someone not present, here, now. If one is forbidden to compare the present to the past, it would appear that learning from past experience is considered to be of no value. "Be here now" would then seem to imply that one may only determine appropriate action in a situation on the basis of the situation itself.

Seeking to verify this idea, I consulted a woman who had spent six years in India and is regarded by some as a spiritual interpreter. I asked whether living only in the present did not tend to counter good psychological practice by preventing one from "working through" feelings of anger or grief deriving from the past. I also asked if it did not imply that there were no lessons to be learned from the past which could be applied to the future. Her reply:

Oh no. That isn't at all what it means. You're supposed to be here now in the present *with* your past and your future. Everything that you were in the past is here with you now and everything that you can be in the future is here with you now. It is not that only the present exists. It is that the past, the present and the future are one in this moment.

This statement suggests the concentration of past, present and future into one point rather than the separation of these from each other. It is more consistent with my observations than the first example in expressing what most Mateelians appear to mean by the phrase "be here now."

Edward T. Hall has written extensively on the subject of time. He distinguishes altogether eight different kinds of time depicted in a mandala,[32] reproduced below in Figures 5 and 6. A subdivision has been added to the category "micro time" that Hall makes elsewhere. The new categories are "monochronic" and "polychronic" microtime. Those areas most relevant to the Mateelian and Amerikan cultural systems have been rendered in lighter or darker shades corresponding to Hall's interpretation of their importance in Amerika and my interpretation of their importance in Mateel. Without going into too many details, the definitions of the different kinds of time may be listed as follows:

> *Physical*: time as related to measurements of physical phenomena. Includes Newtonian time, geological time, astronomical time.
>
> *Profane*: explicit cultural time, as measured by clocks and calendars.
>
> *Sacred:* mythical time, experienced as no-time, such as in ceremonies. It differs from metaphysical time in that it is chosen, rather than experienced spontaneously.
>
> *Micro*: implicit, subconscious, cultural time. It is monochronic, that is, consisting of a single line moving deliberately ahead, in which one can only do one thing at a time, or polychronic, i.e. assumed to contain several lines at once.
>
> *Biological*: related to biorhythms.
>
> *Personal*: time as experienced by individuals as a result of their inner state.
>
> *Metaphysical*: spontaneous "no-time" experiences such as *deja vu* and precognition.
>
> *Sync*: time related to interaction with others.
>
> *Meta*: time as discussed by philosophers.

The Mateelian approach to time is probably related to the use of marijuana and hallucinogens, which are known to cause a distortion in the perception of time.[33] Using Hall's schema for analysis, it may

Worldview 101

A MAP OF TIME

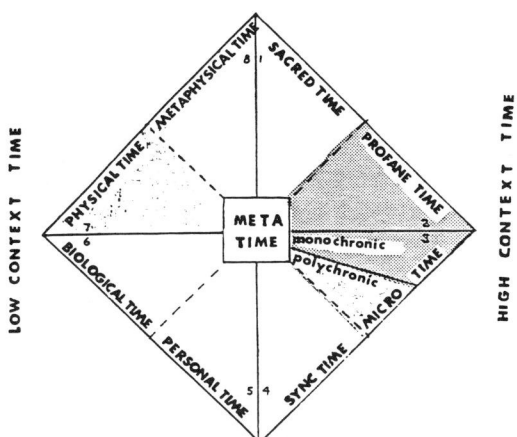

Figure 5. Amerikan Use of Time.

A MAP OF TIME

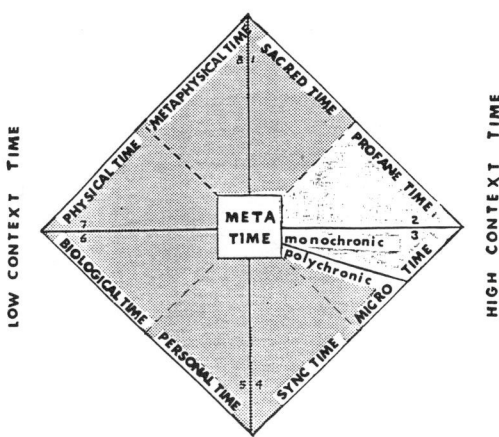

Figure 6. Mateelian Use of Time.

be said that these substances revealed to the users all the dimensions of time which Amerikan culture does not normally include. Ideally, Mateelians would prefer to be constantly in the highest possible state of consciousness. Experientially, this is a situation in which time does not appear to exist. Hall's Sacred time sounds similar to descriptions of the timelessness described by informants as characteristic of highest consciousness and to the kind of timeless experience towards which Mateelian ceremonies aim. Sacred time does not move forward or backward, one is simply in it.

A slightly different state of consciousness allows one to remain experientially in Sacred time while "taking care of business." This concept may be seen as belonging to the Mateelian "little tradition" of Zen. Only a few Mateelians claim to be practicing Zen Buddhists, but the conception of being one with the task at hand, of everyday activity as meditation, is widespread. The ideal way to work is to "be here now" in the activity. As Hall points out about Zen:

> In the East, time springs from the self and is not imposed. The purpose of Zen is to attune one's self to nature and to "eat when hungry and sleep when tired."[34]

Hall does not relate this Zen conception of time to his mandala, but it seems to me that it includes aspects of sacred, biological, and personal time. At any rate, the "be here now" of the ordinary Mateelian resembles Hall's description of Zen time more than anything else.

When Mateelians are not in Sacred or Zen time, the most relevant time is physical time. Physical time is so real to Mateelians because they live so close to the natural environment. Seasons, with accompanying drastic changes in weather, are of paramount importance to Mateelians both because they are farmers and because so many people live on roads and in dwellings which are severely impacted by the rain. Many follow the moon cycles because of the astrological belief that they affect planting and also because the moon is outdoor lighting in a place where street lights are unknown.

Mateelians acknowledge personal time because of its connection to subjective states. Occupations which require specific hours are perceived as impingements on personal freedom because they preclude adjusting activities to subjective states. This is such a factor for some that it explains why they are in Mateel—they could not work at a "straight" job because the imposition of clock-regulated, profane time on personal time is seen as an intolerable limitation on personal freedom. "Nine-to-fivers" are strenuously avoided for this reason, which does nothing to raise the employability of Mateelians in Amerika. Great tolerance is allowed for personal time in social relations also, so that arriving and leaving a social gathering, or even a conversation, may operate in a way which Amerikans perceive as erratic, as people respond to individual perceptions of time. The high value placed on personal experience and subjective reality means that no one is expected to "mark time" in a social situation which is dragging for them, with the exception of community meetings. In that case it is considered a necessary sacrifice to ignore personal time in order to remain at a meeting to "take care" of collective business.

Mateelians give lowest priority to profane time, and regard it as a great but sometimes necessary evil. When forced into profane time by cross-cultural contact, primarily getting children to school or keeping appointments with Amerikans, they surround the situation with humor, cynicism, and other behavioral indications of ambivalence. Inability to operate on profane and monochronic micro time hampers environmental and peace groups and has often effectively sabotaged potential group creations. Rectifying that disability too well opens one up to suspicion of losing respect for sacred time. "Be here now" is probably such a prevalent phrase because it serves to remind one of the ideal of sacred or Zen time when a danger is perceived of it becoming relegated to second place. The tension created by different individual orientations to Amerikan profane and micro time is probably one of the most prevalent obstacles one encounters in Mateelian cooperative efforts.

An example is provided by the effort to build a special building for the teaching of the martial art, Tai Kwan Do (TKD), to school children. The TKD teacher is a study in Mateelian time, operating polychronically when in micro time at all, but most often in every time other than micro or profane. When he tried to donate his labor, organizational skill and charisma to build a TKD building on the community-owned land, he received enthusiastic support from his students and the students' parents. Donations of money and material began to emerge. Benefits were held. The students, mostly boys between the ages of eight and eighteen, energetically began to level the building site and place pier blocks for the foundation. Physical time, now Summer, was passing, with the imminent threat of Autumn rain, which would effectively end construction projects until spring. However, there were rules, which came from the necessity of the non-profit community organization to abide by laws made by profane monochronic people. The building code must be satisfied. Architects' and engineers' plans must be submitted—and before, not during, construction.

    An enormous split developed on the board of directors. There were those who felt that it was mandatory to take advantage of the energy of the children and not let it dissipate, simply because of Amerikan rules; to seize the chance to let them create their own building. But there were those who did not want to jeopardize the already precarious standing of the organization with the building inspector by building even further without authorization. The wrangle was not resolved, the pier blocks stood bare over the winter, the energy of the children dissipated and the building has advanced only slowly from the pier block stage.[34] The children, whose main contact with profane time was through the alternative school, which minimizes its importance, found it difficult to understand.

    Some directors said, "Good, they must learn to deal with the outside world when they have to." Others said, "We have allowed the outside rules to let us miss a chance to teach the children self-reliance, cooperation and carpentry at the best time, when they were into it." In addition to illustrating Mateelian conceptions of time, this story is a perfect illustration of the way in which Mateelian cultural development is constrained by its Amerikan context. It also illustrates a tension in the educational sector on the question of how much to train the children to deal with Amerika and how much to act to them as if Amerikan culture is not important.

    If Mateelians are bad at operating in profane time, they are worse at monochronic micro time. The dominant micro time in Mateel is polychronic. Profane and monochronic micro time are only necessary at all in town. People organize "town trips" so as to accomplish everything as polychronically as possible. If a monochronic appointment is made, it disrupts entirely the flow of polychronic activities, which fact is the source of much Mateelian "hassle." There is no more fruitful place to observe Mateelian polychronic behavior than in the laundromat. Because of the shortage of electricity, washing clothes at home is one of the most difficult technical problems Mateelians have had to solve. Gas-powered washing machines do exist as well as, more recently, generator-operated electric washing machines. Dryers are much rarer, especially since they are needed only during the rainy winter season. The laundromat for many people is therefore inescapable. Large numbers of Mateelians made a "funky" social adaptation to this problem by coming to interpret the laundromat as a place for social as well as practical activity in much the same way that peasant peoples the world over wash clothes together on rocks by the river.

One entire scene in the play *Vibram Soul* reflects both the social importance of the laundromat and the way activities are conducted polychronically. Loretta, a female "biker," and Spring, the female, celibate, spiritual seeker, are washing clothes:

Loretta: Yeah, laundromats and laundry day. It's a real bummer, huh.

Spring: Oh, I kinda like it. Do you ever really listen to the washing machines? They kinda go "Ommmmm." And the dryers. If you really get into the dryers and watch those colorful clothes go around and around. It's just like a mandala.

Loretta: Yeah, well, whatever gets you off. (Enter Jill, the liberated country woman, crying.)

Spring: Jill, Jill, what is it? Hey.

Jill: Oh, it's nothing Spring.

Spring: Of course it's nothing, but nothing is everything.

Loretta: Well, it must be something.

Jill: It's nothing. I guess it's something. Oh, it's everything. It's just that this morning my car wouldn't start, and I had to get to town on time for a welfare appointment, and I had to do my laundry because my kid has lice, so I ended up running four miles down a dirt road in the rain and the mud. Then when I finally got a ride on the county road, the guy had a flat tire. Then I got to the welfare office and found out that my check's gonna be a week late and I'm already flat broke and I still gotta get up the road and . . . oh, it's nothing.

Loretta: Hey, Jill, don't worry about it. I'll give you a ride up the hill.

As it turns out, after a long intimate discussion between the three women, which includes the weather, the lack of men, and the fallacy of looking to the opposite sex for the solution of one's personal problems, Loretta forgets her offer, which has by now expanded to include stopping off at the local bar, and Jill, altogether. Spring, after giving Jill permission to "go after" her ex-old man Jack, discreetly leaves when Jack enters with his laundry. Jill has "spaced out" putting hers in the machines while talking to the other women. Jack and Jill engage in a silent comedy routine, bumping into each other, dropping laundry, picking it up, mixing it up. Finally Jack starts a conversation, offers to take Jill out for a pizza, then home. The romantic plot of the play emerges from this laundromat scene.

The expression "go with the flow" is a sort of dynamic "be here now" in that activities will be organized with reference to "whatever's happening" around the actor. In the above scene Jill has come to town for a monochronic appointment, but is "going with the flow" from there. Loretta can drop everything and offer her a ride home, which in Mateel might mean a two hour drive. Loretta and Spring drop everything to deal with Jill's psychological crisis. Jack and Jill go quickly from doing laundry to starting an affair. Jill leaves the laundromat with Jack for an unplanned three day visit. There are manifestly no schedules apparent in any of these lives, except for the restraint imposed on Jill by the fact that she has a child. In this case, she was able to go off indefinitely with Jack because she knew her child was safe with his father, who appears later in the play, incensed because Jill has left the child with him without notice. His complaint is one of the actions that establishes him as the villain of the piece. He should be able to "go with the flow" which brought the child to him for an unplanned three day stay.

Anything can happen in the laundromat because, aside from the monochronic limitations imposed by the automated, timed machines, everyone is on polychronic time. I have conducted parent-teacher conferences while sorting dirty socks and observed others working out deep marital conflicts publicly while folding sheets. Cars are repaired and knitting lessons take place during the washing and drying cycles. Polychronic time leaves room for spontaneous courting and impromptu therapy, but Jill's whole day was required to get her to her monochronic welfare appointment. Among Mateelians it is understood that when monochronic appointments are made, polychronic time is intended. Anything from the weather to a forest fire to a breakdown in cars made prone to it by bad roads may interfere with strict monochronic time. The absence of telephones precludes last minute changes or advisories. Only the fact that polychronic time is understood in common by all members of the culture enables them to operate collectively at all.

"Sync" time is time in relation to unconscious rhythmic messages between people. Hall cites the work of William Condon in explaining the importance of the rhythmic messages exchanged between people at the unconscious, primary level of culture.[35] Using video tapes of interacting people and analyzing them frame-by-frame with the aid of computers, Condon found that when people talk their body language is perfectly timed with speech rhythms. There is, in addition, a synchrony of the body language of each with the other. Using electroencephalograms in combination with the videotapes, Condon also found that brain wave patterns "lock" in conversations. In Hall's words, "When we talk to each other our central nervous systems mesh like two gears in a transmission." Condon found that schizophrenics, dyslexics and autistic children experience aberrations in this synchronized pattern, and that parents of battered children had never learned to "sync" with their babies.[37]

Hall's work in this field shows that people everywhere "sync" when listening to music, that there is a relationship between love and whether people are in close synchrony, and that in any performance, the more perfect the rhythm, the easier it was for the audience to see the details of it. He found that people in American and European cultures favor one side of the body over the other in synchronizing body language with speech, in contrast to Black and Native Americans whose body language is better balanced and synchronized. Hall states that "the power of the rhythmic message within the group is as strong as anything I know."[38]

Hall sees "sync" time as especially important to polychronic cultures, maintaining that polychronic cultures avoid dissonances because people stay in sync better than they do in monochronic cultures. He cites Japanese culture in which people who must live and work closely together in space manage this by staying coordinated in their rhythms. The quick-reading of social cues among polychronic people is related to their high ability to stay in sync.[39]

The polychronic culture of Mateel shows signs of being like other polychronic cultures in the importance of sync time. One indication of this is the high incidence of those activities which Hall states raise the probability that people will "sync" well. These activities are anything which raises awareness of the body or rhythm sense. He also states that music releases rhythms present in the individual.[40] Mateelians are probably much more in sync with each other than their Amerikan counterparts, because of the high value placed on consciousness of the body and the enormous interest in such activities as dancing, music, particularly drumming, drama, mime, and martial arts, all of which involve careful timing, and other forms of body consciousness training such as Hatha Yoga and Tai Chi. It is uncanny how so many Mateelians can pack into such a small space for a boogie, and dance vigorously without bumping into one another. A careful study using Condon and Hall's methods might well validate that this is possible because Mateelians are good at "sync" time.

Space

The last of Redfield's categories of worldview is space. The concept of The Land is an aspect of spatial conceptions as well as of relationship to the physical world. Areas of space which are still visibly The Land are distinguished from areas of space in which The Land can no longer be readily perceived. The Land away from Mateel is important and Mateelian environmentalists will travel hundreds of miles in efforts to protect it, too, but Mateel is seen as a special place for Mateelians. It is seen by the majority of Mateelians as the place they intend to stay for the rest of their lives. Deerhawk's poem, *A Song of Twelve*, expresses the sense of place and the feeling of continuity many Mateelians feel with the Sinkyone and Mattole Indians who lived there first. This feeling is expressed by the folklore that Mateelians are reincarnated Native Americans, gathered there to bring in the Age of Aquarius; or that Mateel is a place where astrological lines of power converge to generate especially high energy; or that it is a "power spot" in the terminology of Casteneda's *Don Juan*;[41] or that it is one of the nine places most likely to survive a nuclear war.

Space which is not The Land is viewed negatively and visited only when strictly necessary. Los Angeles is especially a location which is in space but is not The Land. On the Household Energy Budget Questionnaire, subjects were asked to say how often they visited what they considered to be "town," Eureka, San Francisco, or Los Angeles. Five informants who gave a number estimate for the other choices were not content to put a zero in the space for Los Angeles, but wrote in NEVER with multiple exclamation points.

Personal space is flexible, varying with the situation. In general, Mateelians are able to tolerate more indoor crowding than Amerikans, but only in order to live on The Land, where outdoor space is much more available to the average person than in Amerika. Especially in the early stages of residence in Mateel, people can manage to live in situations incredibly crowded by American standards. Some examples:

> A single mother with two teenage daughters in a twelve by sixteen foot, one-room cabin.
>
> A single mother with a live-in lover, a three-year-old and a newborn baby in a twelve by seven by six foot tool shed.
>
> Ten to twenty members of a commune in a school bus. The same commune in one old four-bedroom bunkhouse.
>
> A land partnership of two childless couples in a ten by sixteen foot converted chicken coop.
>
> A single father and a two-year-old daughter in a pup tent.

These are typical situations, each of which lasted through at least one long, rainy Humboldt County winter. One factor that makes these situations tolerable, if not pleasant, is that Mateelians are generally an affectionate group. Spontaneous physical contact between people of all ages and sexes publicly and privately is the norm. Mateelians, in fact, appear to delight in cramming themselves into impossibly small places, passing a "joint," (marijuana cigarette), and socializing for hours. Visiting Amerikans frequently become nervous and irritable in such situations, evidencing every sign of claustrophobia.

Another interpretation of this ability to tolerate crowding is that Mateelians value social interaction over a strict interpretation of personal space and have trained themselves to suspend preferences with regard to personal space when necessary, in favor of the interaction.

Variables in the degree of crowding tolerated include duration, social proximity ("how much we love each other"), motivation to live on The Land and/or be part of the community, how much the situation impinges on personal freedom and privacy, and the value placed on privacy. This last varies greatly from individual to individual, as it does in Amerikan culture. Also, the fact that all of these spatial situations take place in the context of The Land allows the participants a safety valve which is not available to urban dwellers. One may be stuffed into a tiny cabin with children, dogs and cats on top of one and no elbow room, but one can at any point step outside where one is instantly on The Land with, if it isn't raining, an infinite view of Space. There is, however, a limit. "Cabin fever" is a widely known and feared phenomenon associated with winter. Here it is the inability to get outside and the duration of the crowding which allows it to reach an explosion point.

Another important variable is that Mateelians include inner space as part of their conception of space. If one is in a situation where physical space is limited, one may simply sit still and travel in inner space by whatever means one employs for this, marijuana, psychedelics, or meditation. This is true also in a general way, in the belief that the more one has mastered inner space, the less confined one will be by limitations of physical space.

Another parameter in the conception of space may be seen in the use of space as a metaphor in social relations and to refer to psychological operations. The expression "give me some space" may refer to literal physical space, as in "back off, you're crowding me," to time "give me some time to work out my problems," and to freedom "don't hold me back from growing." When used by couples, it often is part of a transition to some other relationship and is part of a physical separation implying sexual freedom. It calls a sort of interactional "time-out" which may or may not precede physical separation. The expression "spaced-out" refers to a psychological state in which one has moved from physical space into inner space. The word "space" in this context is intended to call up the image of outer space as a metaphor for inner space. It is also a reference to the folklore that traveling in outer space is likely to cause one to become so entranced with one's perceptions that operations in the physical world will cease to be important.

Summary

Mateelian worldview sprang from the discontinuity experience. An important part of this experience was the widespread use of marijuana and psychedelics. Some of the particular clinical effects of these substances, such as increased awareness of subjective phenomena and distortion of the time sense, formed the basis for concepts which presently are central to the Mateelian worldview. As a result of the common experience of expanded subjectivity, the Mateelian universe includes non-rational inputs. The Mateelian universe is continuous with the Self, other selves and those categories the Western worldview calls God and Nature.

The Not-Self part of the universe is composed of the physical environment, which is divided into The Land and not-The Land, other people, and non-rational inputs. Both The Land and other people are living, feeling, thinking entities with whom one is expected to interact with respect. One is also expected to act toward both humans and nature without prior assumptions, constructing relationship through interaction, using whatever is available. This expectation is the concept of funky. Humans may have an impact on the physical and social Not-Self, they may manifest reality, to the extent that they gain power by expanding consciousness through exploration and manipulation of subjective reality. They gain the power to manifest reality this way because once they have traveled inward past the illusion of Self, they realize that they are the universe. Humans are obligated to gain this power in order to manifest a better reality because the physical Not-Self, their environment, is in danger of termination. Central to this moral obligation is the belief that the natural environment can only be rescued through the expansion of human consciousness.

When in the highest state of consciousness, both time and space are non-existent. When in everyday consciousness, time comes from within and personal space is flexible. The ordinary Mateelian strives to stay in the highest possible state of consciousness for the longest possible time. The inability of the individual to do so indefinitely creates various cultural tensions between the ideals predicated on experience of this state of consciousness and the inability to stay there.

A crucial difference between the Amerikan worldview and the Mateelian worldview is in the relationship between Self and Not-Self. In Amerikan culture, the Self is seen as separate from and acting on the Not-Self.[42] In Mateelian culture, the Self is an illusion. Whereas the Amerikan frontier/abundance myth sanctions exploitation of the environment, the Mateelian myth of The Land personifies the physical universe, includes humans in it, and sanctions respectful interaction with it. The Mateelian conception of a limited physical environment is the exact opposite of the Amerikan view of the world as capable of surviving infinite economic growth. Mateelians see the *inner* universe as capable of infinite growth, but the physical world as limited.

Since the comparison between Amerikan, Mateelian, and Primitive views of the Self involves concepts more appropriate to what will be discussed in chapter ten, it will not be explored here. The Amerikan faith in science and technology is not reversed exactly in Mateel, but placed in a more limited context. Mateelians do not deny that their lives depend on such items of modern technology as plastic and automobiles, but they see these as unavoidable and hopefully transitional. Modern technology is not seen as the primary or exclusive way of surviving. Paraprimitive technologies employing biodegradable and natural, rather than synthetic near-indestructible materials, and the substitution of cultural, rather than exclusively technological solutions are preferred. The Amerikan myth of "Yankee ingenuity," which originated in Amerikan technological know-how is modified into the concept of "funky" in Mateel, where it includes the ingenuity required for living in a limited physical environment.

A major factor which distinguishes the Amerikan conception of space from both Mateelian and Primitive is that most Amerikans do not experience the natural environment as directly as do Mateelians and Primitive peoples. Amerikans stay inside, reinforcing their conception of humans-as-separate-from-Nature.[43] The rise of modern technology is surely responsible for this because it so insulates people from the natural environment. Modern technology has another, more subtle, effect on the Amerikan perception of space. Because of modern science, it is possible to divide land into territories, using straight lines or streams as boundaries and paying no attention to ecological units like watersheds or vegetation zones, which are the spatial realities for people who live on The Land. The fact that land is seen as primarily a commodity to be bought and sold, giving it no status as a living entity, encourages this arbitrary chopping up of land. Planning, zoning, buying and selling of land all fail to take the actual character of the land into consideration, a procedure which would probably make a great difference in such matters as road-cut erosion, overuse of water resources, and distribution of housing sites.

In Amerika, space is a criterion for reality. Only that which measurably occupies space is considered real.[44] Anything related to inner space is not considered "real" by Amerikans, whereas these subjective phenomena may be "real" to Mateelians. Mateelians aspire to expand into inner space through the power of consciousness; Amerikans hope to expand into outer space through the power of technology. Amerikans and Mateelians are basically similar in their requirements for personal space and privacy, or at least no generality can be made about a difference as yet. However, Mateelians are much more flexible about this and able to suspend these requirements much more readily than Amerikans if the situation demands it.

Primitive cultures, notwithstanding the generalizations made in chapter four, are extremely diverse. It will therefore be more useful to compare the Mateelian worldview to a particular primitive culture or culture area than to the general model. For this purpose, Kearney's discussion of Northern California Native Americans is particularly useful, since their worldview was developed in interaction with the same general environment as Mateel.[45] There is much in the worldview of Mateel which is strongly reminiscent of the aboriginal northern Californians. How much of this similarity should be attributed to conscious emulation and how much to the fact that both groups occupy a similar environment is impossible to say.

In particular, the lack of clear distinction between Self and the social and physical other is similar. Also, the tribal northern Californian concept of power and how to gain it resembles the Mateelian manifested reality. In both, power is immanent and potential in all things.[46] It is a continuum of more powerful and less powerful. The native northern Californian gains access to personal use of power by visiting the mythic time when creation was taking place and obtaining it from the heroes like Coyote, who exemplify "the underlying unity" of things.[47] Similarly, Mateelians gain power by being in the highest state of consciousness, a timeless state. Both of these are examples of Sacred time. The indigenous people of California saw the soul as a "personalized manifestation of power."[48] Mateelians see personal consciousness as a source of power which may, like the California aboriginal soul, be increased and focussed for purposes of healing, astral projection, and obtaining extra-rational knowledge. One indication that the Mateelian Self is seen as being involved with the Other, as it is in California Native American culture, is the concept of the "contact high." Originally this countercultural idea referred to the widely reported experience that persons who had not taken any mind-altering substance could experience the effects of intoxication when in the presence of others who had.[49] In Mateel, this idea is an assumption which has broadened to eliminate the necessity for anyone to have taken mind-altering substances. A contact high can be obtained from those who are "high" from any intoxicating experience: meditation, drumming, dancing, singing, playing softball, massage, sex, love, giving birth, or being involved in a ceremony designed for that purpose. Whether or not the contact high experience could be "proved" with empirical measurements is irrelevant. The belief in the contact high indicates that there is a conception of direct involvement between Self and Other.

There are important differences between Amerikan and Mateelian conceptions of time. Hall has analyzed the American conception of time in detail. He describes it as linear, meaning it is conceived of as moving from a point of origin steadily ahead. It is monochronic—there is only one such line and people can do only "one thing at a time." It is compartmentalized, i.e., heavily and rigidly scheduled. It is driven to closure; tasks have a beginning and an end and Amerikans have a low tolerance for leaving things "unfinished." Time is objectified—time units are linguistically objects rather than verbs or adverbs as they are in the Hopi language. Status is related to time in that high status persons are allowed more freedom to disregard schedules. Even though one moves from past to future, the past is fragmented and thrown away and the future is the short term future. The distant future is unreal.[50]

Americans, according to Hall, are self-centered and alone in time. It is a conveyor belt filled with empty containers. The individual must fill these containers alone and will be evaluated by how well they are filled. Conflict between externally imposed time, the clock-on-the-wall, and personally experienced time is the cause of enormous tension and stress in modern society.[51] To this picture may be added the idea of progress. Kearney speaks of the developmental American view of time which actively seeks change as opposed to the California Native American view, which seeks stability.[52]

Kuhn's discussion of the connection between science and the idea of progress illuminates the importance of the progress-oriented Amerikan view of time, since science plays such a leading role in the Amerikan worldview. Kuhn asks, "Does a field make progress because it is a science, or is it a science because it makes progress?"[53] The education of scientists as described by Kuhn offers a good example of the way in which past and future are disregarded in Amerikan time. He points out that students of art, philosophy, history and social sciences must read the classics in their field and thus become aware of the eternal questions and the array of possible solutions, whereas the student of hard science gets a narrow and rigid education which relies on textbooks and secondary sources. This creates a drastic distortion in the scientists' perception of the scientific past: More than practitioners of other creative fields, he comes to see it as leading in a straight line to the discipline's present vantage. In short, he comes to see it as progress. No alternative is available to him. . . .[54]

Kuhn points out that Darwin's crime was that his scheme had no goal, it moved away from a primitive beginning but toward nothing specific. It threw out the idea of progress.[55]

In contrast to Amerikan time, primitive time places a high value on the past and tradition. The California aboriginal past is seen as a source of power, which has been running down since the time of creation. World renewal ceremonies are held to offset the inherent degradation of power, to reverse the effects of time, and to insure that the present continues intact.[56] The mythic time of creation is visited for the purpose of obtaining power. Endless repetition with little change is a desired condition. Elapsed time is unimportant, and the past can only be discussed in relation to known events.[57]

The Mateelian conception of time is much more like the primitive than it is like the Amerikan. In fact, rooting out the Amerikan attitude towards time as part of the deepest seated level of culture, is one of the most distinctive features of Mateelian culture. The concept of "be here now" coincides exactly with Hall's description of Quiche time in which the past, present and future are compressed into one point. He quotes Barbara Tedlock, "at no given time past, present or future, is it possible to isolate that time from the events that led up to it and which flow from it."[58] One only needs to listen to a few Mateelian life histories and the manner in which they are told, to realize that Mateelians, too, find it difficult to isolate an event from past and future.

Hall contrasts the Hopi tolerance for a proliferation of unfinished buildings to the American emphasis on bringing things to a conclusion.[59] In the course of fifteen years, I have visited hundreds of owner-built Mateelian homes, but I have never been in one which the owner was willing to declare finished. As much as Mateelians love ceremonies, there was never a formal ribbon-cutting, opening ceremony for the Beginnings community building, because there was never a clear point when it was finished. Mateelian houses, like Mateelian institutions and Mateelian personalities are never finished, but always in a state of becoming. Hall speaks of Hopis as living in an eternal present, preparing for the ceremonies which will place them in Sacred time. Ceremonial life is also important in Mateel, even though there are few traditions to follow in preparing for it.

Amerikan calendar ceremonies are celebrated but with much complaint and displays of behavior denoting ambivalence. As one informant put it about Christmas, "We do it, but it really isn't *our* kind of holiday, is it?" Ceremonies from older traditions, such as Equinoxes and Solstices, are widely celebrated with the attendant expectation and experience of Hall's Sacred Time.

From the above comparisons, it is clear that in the area of worldview, Mateelian culture is much more like the Primitive model than it is like the Amerikan model. It has not been compared to the Ecotopian model because only general statements have been made by Ecotopian writers about a hypothetical worldview and these mostly in terms of religion specifically.

The author standing in her garden holding her infant son.

Chapter Seven

Political Behavior

All you need is love. . . .

—*The Beatles*

If you ask the Mateelian-on-the-road to characterize the hill people politically, you will probably be told that they are anarchists. A dictionary definition of anarchy might include the following:

> The absence of government or governmental restraint; a state of society without government or law; political and social disorder due to absence of governmental control; in general, disorder due to want of a controlling and regulating agency.[1]

Anarchists are defined as "advocating the violent overthrow of government." Mateelian anarchy departs in some important ways from these definitions. Mateelians as a group do not advocate violence for any reason. Neither do Mateelians prefer disorder to order in general, no matter how disorderly they, their children, and their organizations may appear to outsiders.

Mateelians are frequently characterized by others as apolitical and they frequently characterize each other this way. Yet it only took a decade for Mateelians to claim half of the positions on the Board of Directors of the Southern Humboldt Unified School District. In 1984, Alan Katz, a former resident of one of the core watersheds, missed being elected as county supervisor from the Southern

Humboldt district by twenty-eight votes, amid accusations of irregularity in the election procedures.[2] The fact that he came so close in a district of which the geographical area of Mateel comprises only half, is an indication that if Mateelians ever were apolitical, they are rapidly becoming less so.

Why, then, do they see themselves as anarchists? Even though it is true that early in the history of Mateel, an atmosphere of distrust of the Amerikan political system prevailed and many people did not vote out of a sense of futility, some Mateelians must have elected the Mateelian school board members. The answer is that Mateelians do not conceive of their political power as residing exclusively or even mainly in their right of suffrage, but in the power of their local organizations as agents of change and in themselves as agents of change. In describing themselves as anarchists, they are referring to the rejection of remotely located governing agencies, not to regulation that they themselves generated.

In addition, there is the fact that Mateelians define areas appropriate for regulation (public matters) and areas considered inappropriate for regulation (personal matters) differently than do Amerikans. When Mateelians describe themselves as anarchists, they are referring partly to this distinction. Mateelian personal areas include victimless crimes, manipulation of personal consciousness by the use of any substance, method, or religious system whatever, the design of owner-built homes, right to suicide, right to die, personal health and medical care, funeral practices, and reproductive matters—childbirth methods, birth control, abortion, form of family and sexual practices. Public areas include: violent crimes, crimes with victims, fire prevention, environmental concerns, road maintenance, and child welfare and education up to a point.

Mateelians are not, then, really anarchists as the word is traditionally defined. They are extremely willing to accept local authority in matters they define as being of public concern and do subject themselves to agonizing efforts to produce egalitarian organizations that meet this description. It is unclear at this point whether the emphasis on local government pertains to all matters. Civil rights, for instance, are vigorously supported, yet they derive from federal, not local, law.

The emphasis on personal development is important to Mateelian political philosophy in its relation to the realization of group over personal self-interest. To the degree that one is self-realized, i.e., has transcended neurotic motivations, personal self-interest, material and psychological, can be laid aside. To the degree that self-interest is laid aside, the correct decisions are believed to emerge from group interaction rather than individual leadership, hierarchical structures, or formal procedures. The assumption is that the group is the repository of ultimate wisdom and that this wisdom is emergent in the interaction of self-realized individuals. It is seen as the task of responsible individuals to not only participate in the kind of interaction that will produce group wisdom but to become the kind of individual who is able to engage in the right kind of interaction. This interaction involves complete communication, complete honesty, and complete equality. It is the political implementation of the moral obligation to "raise consciousness" (see chapter six). This political philosophy can be called "magical anarchy."

Magical Anarchy

Magical anarchy usually appears utterly chaotic, even senseless, to the outsider. It is magical because no one can explain how it works. The assumption is that if everyone is "in the right head" and enough "group energy" is generated, it will "just happen." Like magic anywhere, it has an element of danger, and has been known to backfire, resulting in a decision that no one would have anticipated, or that turns out to be of questionable use. Nevertheless, Mateelians cling to the belief in magical anarchy both because of their bedrock repugnance for externally imposed, that is non-Mateelian, authority and because of their belief in the efficacy of higher individual consciousness. Their histories have convinced them that almost anything is better than the political organization of technocracies as they actually operate. These, it is often pointed out, have led to intolerable environmental and social conditions and to the constant threat of nuclear annihilation. This is seen to be true whether the political organizations are left or right, capitalist or communist, democratic or dictatorial. No matter how frustrating and confusing it may get, Mateelians assume that the decisions generated by the group will be best in the long-run and that the spiritual, social, and psychological rewards of magical anarchy are more than worth the "hassle."

Ad Hoc Group

A description of the political system of a society is a description of control. The threat of force or incarceration, the use of police, are controls external to the individual and, depending on whose police do the incarcerating, the control is external or internal to the group. City police, for instance, are internal to the municipality, but may be seen by an ethnic group within the municipality such as, say, Hispanics, as an external control. Public opinion, which uses the sanctions of ridicule, ostracizing, or gossip, enforces values commonly held by the group. It is a control internal to the group who holds the common values. The values themselves, followed because of individual conscience or guilt, both of which represent the internalization of group values, are controls internal to the individual. To the degree, then, that values are held in common by a close-knit group, control may be internal. To the degree that individuals with disparate values must be controlled, those controls will be external.

An examination of some examples of the forms magical anarchy can take may provide some clues as to what kind of control it exerts, who has the power, and why "it just happens." The first is the case of ad hoc groups assembled to make decisions about local crisis situations. In 1982, a parcel was purchased on one of the large subdivided ranches by a group from Los Angeles, the "Institute for Creative Studies." This parcel was in a central location, in Briceland, adjacent to the land owned by Beginnings, Inc., a community organization that includes two alternative schools and a volunteer fire department. It also adjoined and/or was visible from at least a half dozen parcels owned by Mateelians of long standing.

Soon after the purchase, an article appeared in the Garberville Redwood Record describing an elaborate plan filed with the Humboldt County Planning Commission by the Institute. This plan included an auditorium, several residences, a barn/studio, a swimming pool, tennis courts, a parking lot and several roads. The outcry in the Briceland area was instantaneous and vehement. A meeting was called at Beginnings to which the Institute of Creative Studies was invited to justify the plan to the community.

The meeting was a study in magical anarchy in a crisis, as well as a gauge of the political energy that can be mustered in Mateel when "outsiders" threaten the local environment. It is worthwhile to quote extensively from the transcript of the tape of this meeting since it reveals several points about the operation of magical anarchy. I arrived about a half hour late and was therefore unable to determine if any effort had been made to establish a format for it or if anyone had attempted to lead it. If such an effort had been made, it was apparent to me on arrival that it had failed. When I arrived, Keith, the "head" of the Institute for Creative Studies was seated in the center of an angry group of about fifty to a hundred people, including children, most of whom were talking to him or each other. A local "old timer" who had lived in Briceland for thirty to forty years was speaking. The following is a composite of the tape transcript, my field notes, and later interpretations. Remarks in brackets relate to later discussion, according to the following key:

G.D.: Statements which function to establish group definition.

Comm.: Statements relating to communication, which in Mateel includes non-verbal communication and verbal information usually left out of Amerikan communication.

Env.: Environmental concerns.

Fairness: Statements representing attempts to be tolerant and fair.

P.M.: Profit motive.

G.A.: Group authority.

Process: Relating to how the meeting is being conducted.

Excerpt from meeting to discuss the new arrivals:

Old-timer: We don't like your style, Mister, and we don't want you here. I'll run you out of town myself, if necessary.

(Cries from the group "you bet," "right on"). [G. D.]

H. A.: (to Keith) If you're gonna get bigger, tell us you're gonna get bigger, if you can. First you tell us you are, then you tell us you're not. That's double talk and I don't like it and I want you out of here, too. [Comm.]

G.M.: (German accent) I want to know if you gonna have, you know, your electricity and your telephones. You know, we're looking down at you, you're going to have stuff going on at night, now, I can't look up at the stars if you're gonna have lights and stuff going. I can look over there and see the lights of Garberville, and so you're going to have stuff happening, too, maybe some ground lights and stuff, I don't know, I don't want that. [Env.]

S.: Are you gonna have poles strung all across the beautiful Briceland Meadow? [Env.]

Keith: I don't know, at this point. [Comm.]

J.: (astonished) You wouldn't, you wouldn't consider that, would you? You wouldn't consider that for a minute, would you? [Env.]

Keith: (drowned out in the uproar. Children making a ruckus right next to tape recorder. Can make out phrases "plan," "consider," "county road.") [Process]

J.: You know, I really would, that question I just asked, I really would like an answer. That was a serious question. (She is trying to be heard, people beginning to quiet down.) I really would like to know if you would, if that would be something you would seriously consider. Would (complete silence now) you seriously consider, for one second, putting telephone poles up this meadow? Yes or no. [Comm., Env.]

Keith: I think I said, we have very little money. . . . [Comm.]

J.: Right [Comm.]

Keith: P, G & E (Pacific Gas and Electric Company) wants $5,000 dollars. . . . [Comm.]

J.: Yes, I know, but I'd like to have a yes or no on that one. That's a real simple one. [Comm.]

Keith: Yes, I'd consider it. [Env.]

J.: (amid shocked silence): You would consider it. Well, that's a piece of information I'm glad I have. [Comm.]

(A period of Pandemonium ensues, with conversations everywhere.) [Process]

(I have a conversation with J.E., who is a former resident of Los Angeles, in Mateel fleeing urban decay, and S.M. and P.R., some founders of Beginnings.)

S.M.: I think it's very important that we're talking to them. If they're going to be here, this is how they know where we're at. [Comm.]

P.R.: Yes, but they never came to us and said this is what we're going to do. [Comm.]

J.E.#1: They're not doing a very clear job of it at all. [Comm.]

S.M.: You know what happened? When we planned Beginnings, we sat in the trailer, me and P.R., and K.R., and K.P., and a lot of other people sat in the trailer and drew the plan up and my job was to go to the community with these plans. . . . [G.D.]

J.: And nobody could find the community, if I recollect. [G.D.]

(laughter) [G.D.]

S.M.: Oh yeah, it was at the swimming hole! (laughter) [G.D.]

J.E.#1: (angry, about Keith) He's not doing this out of the goodness of his heart. He's making money doing this. How can you be so naive? He's making dough! He's not doing this out of the goodness of his heart. He's come up here from L.A. to [pig?] everything out. [P.M., Env.]

P.R.: You don't have any real basis to say that. [Fairness]

J.E.#1: No basis! From all the information I've been able to gather, and he hasn't given us any this evening so far, so I have to draw my own conclusions. . . . [Comm.]

P.R.: All right. What is it that you'd be open to hearing from him? [Fairness]

J.E.#1: The straight scoop. It's been "creative" this and "artistic" that all evening. [Comm.]

S.M.: That's about their philosophy and their program. In terms of practical. . . . [Fairness]

(interruptions from several people at once) [Process]

P.R.: He's explaining that. He's explaining what the philosophy is. In terms of what they're trying to do right now he's now saying two buildings, right? [Fairness]

(protests, more people are joining our conversation, it is becoming the focus of the main group) [Process]

P.R.: Nooooo! He's saying they're abridging that plan and asking for a new conditional use permit for just the two buildings they're talking about. For any new buildings, they'd have to go to the Planning Commission. I agree with you. We need to be aware, we need to ask questions and find out, you know, like what their philoso. . . .

(interruptions) [Comm.]

P.R.: Maybe they're just neighbors moving in. . . . [Fairness]

J.E.#1: (breaking in on P.R.): If they were just neighbors moving in, they'd build a house, and a chicken coop next to the house, and they'd be just like the rest of us. [G.D.]

P.R.: All of that sounds like [prejudice? bullshit?]. Some people come in trailers, people come in tepees. . . . [Fairness]

J.: All of us are different. . . . [Fairness]

J.E.#1: Most people don't bring thirty-five people from L. A. with them. [G.D.]

P.R.: How is that any different from what lots of us are doing? [Fairness]

J.E.#1: (sarcastically) It's a lot different from what most of us are doing. [G.D.]

S.M.: Different from Hoka Hey? [a commune which became a group of land partners who define themselves as a family] [G.D.]

A.J.: (female member of Hoka Hey, generally a very unobtrusive person) How can you say anything about Hoka Hey? [Process]

(interruptions, the male voices are dominating, A.J.'s soft female voice persists, J.E.#1 roars "Go ahead, A.," people fall silent.) [Process]

A.J.: I have something to say about Hoka Hey. When we first came . . . O.K., ten people, eleven people . . . twelve people, and people were really afraid that we were gonna set fires, that we were gonna burn up the community . . . (it gets lost in the rising bedlam. Angry voices getting louder and louder, they are from the people located furthest away from A.J. in the group, probably can't hear her and don't know what's happening.) [Fairness, Process]

(Yells from the rear, "What about J.E.?," "Yeah, he put telephone poles right up in the woods.") [Fairness]

J.E.#1: . . . trying to make a living. . . .

(long period of inaudible ruckus.)

[Process] I take the opportunity to go and talk to B.B., who had stated at some point that these people were "totally different from us." I asked him how he could tell.)

B.B.: Oh, yes, it's different, it's totally different. [G.D.]

Me: Would you say it's a different way of perceiving their environment, because they are fresh from L.A.?

B.B.: Oh yes, there's that, and they have no respect for their neighbors, they act like they can do anything they want, you know, King of My Forty Acres. [G.A.]

(uproar now becomes so loud that it is impossible for me to hear B.B.'s words on the tape although the recorder was right in my hand, 18 inches from his mouth. J.E.#1 in particular can be heard, phrases "my personal," "No way." His voice becomes clearer and clearer, people are listening to him, finally focus is restored.) [Process]

J.E.#1: It's not a homestead, it's not a house, it's not a family, and that's what this whole meeting is about. This whole area, as far as you can see, is families on homesteads. [G.D.]

Keith: Don't you think that what we want to do is similar to what you want to do? [G.D.]

(cries of NO, NO, NO) [G.D.]

Keith: We're artists, we're trying to find our creative. . . .

J.E.#2: (She is both an artist and a dancer and is clearly offended by Keith's arrogant tone): We have a lot going on here, too, you know. Most of us are artists of various kinds already. Lots of creative things are happening already in this area. Maybe you should watch us, come here with your family, and participate in what we've got going already. [G.D.]

M.E.: I think what rankles a lot of people who don't want you living there is that our perception of Beginnings is that we live all around it in the hills and this is where we come together to. . . . [G.D.]

E.L: Beginnings is our own. . . . [G.D.]

[Implication is that since the Institute land is adjacent to Beginnings, the presence of another complex of buildings would ruin the symbolism of having the community buildings and schools right in the center of the valley].

Keith: That's our philosophy also. We don't plan to have 365 people living on this property.

M.E.: How many do you plan to have? [Env.]

Keith: I plan to live there.

M.E.: and who else? [Env.]

Keith: and there might be room for two or three others to live there, but as I say, that's the maximum. We've got 65 acres there. That would mean that we could have, three-and-a-half times four. . . .

(laughter) [G.D.] (I think the three and a half was people per acre or something and people are laughing at the image of a half a person, also at the serious manner of Keith, who obviously is naive enough to think that you can plan. It is a sort of cosmic laughter acknowledging the power of Fate to disrupt plans.)

Keith: (looking mystified at the laughter): Now shall we go on with the slides and talk about the rest of this after?

E.L.: Yes (everyone settles down for a slide show. Children are captured and seated, young ones climb into mother's laps and begin to nurse.) [Process]

Keith: (opening slide) : We do the work ourselves, that's part of our program.

M.E.: (open sarcasm): Oh, that's nice. [G.D.]

(Everyone laughs, but in a controlled way. Tone is now more subdued, resigned to politely listening to Keith's rap. There are isolated jokes and laughter in the crowd. My impression is that people are growing tired of being lectured by someone so far behind them in this kind of social experiment. Keith's last line, for example, landed strangely in a crowd where work is so obviously crucial to survival. The idea that you'd incorporate work into a creative studies program for some reason other than "if you don't work you don't eat," was incongruous.)

Discussion after the slide show:

H.A.: I heard that you had an auditorium in your plan and the Redwood Players came up to you and asked if they would be able to make use of your auditorium and you said "Well, no." [G.A.]

(Sudden interest, general pricking up of ears)

Keith: That's not true.

H.A.: (a radical and outspoken homosexual man): Weeellll, I hear all kinds of things. . . .

(Everyone laughs at his insinuating tone. The meeting now disintegrates for a full minute as giggles take over. A joke contest ensues as everyone speculates on what it might be that this particular outrageously "up front" gay man might have heard.)

(Some more discussion about possible sound pollution from performances or parties at the proposed auditorium. This part has gone beyond the bounds of rationality because the sound pollution from the practicing of the children's rock bands at Beginnings as well as dances there can be heard for miles. This is generally o.k., however, because it's "us" and "our kids," not "outsiders" making the noise.)

W.D.: You say that your main man is an electronics expert. I really object to electronics. Electronics are used to control nuclear weapons.

Science has brought us to the brink. . . .

J. (cutting in angrily): All right, now, that does it. As a bona fide real live scientist, I object to this bigotry. [Fairness]

(W. D. stops, startled, and looks around for the source of the comment, thereby losing the floor.)

K.R.: What about water? [Env.]

Keith: As I said before, we've got several different sources of water. And we've got persons who can deal with any kind of water crisis.

(Groans, probably expressing disgust at the attempt to snow the group with talk of experts.) [G.D.]

K.R.: Orchards, a greenhouse, a garden, a swimming pool. A lot of us here know just how difficult that is. We've been struggling with water for Beginnings for years. [Env.]

W.D.: (something about fires, W.D. is a volunteer fire fighter), he's talking about a well. I was up there yesterday. There is no well. So there is no water. [Env.]

(W.D. begins to run on and on, soon everyone is ignoring him and talking among themselves. People begin to yell at him to sit down and shut up. He responds with "I'm an individual. I can talk if I want to." Finally, Y.I., who is well over six feet and quite ferocious appearing when necessary, dives across the room and grabs him. J. yells "Y., you're non-violent!" He shakes W.D. and says "We've listened to you enough, you individual asshole," but does not harm him and releases him. W.D. sits down and shuts up.) [G.A., Process]

B.B.: What you've told us is that you have the same idea in coming up here that we have. And there have been a lot of people in the room who have told you, after hearing what you want to do, that we don't think at all that what you're doing is in any way similar to what we're doing. [G.D.]

S.: (artist with a reputation for dramatizing things): This community is a very special community. Now here you are, you're coming from some place else, and we don't know if you realize that this is a very special place, a very wonderful place. [G.D.] You might laugh and think that I'm getting hysterical or overreacting when I say I'm horrified at the thought of PG and E lines going across the Briceland Meadow. I'm sorry, but that does make me hysterical. You have to realize, now I'm a very emotional person, I'm a nervous wreck, fine, but this is what you must take into account. [Comm.] You're moving into a very tight community. This is a family, this is not a block in L.A. [G.D.] And you've got to understand something damn basic here. If you put PG and E nuclear bastards across our meadow, sir,

I'm sorry, I am not going to look down from my hill and see PG and E lines! (crying now) I refuse! [Env.] Not while PG and E is murdering my brothers and sisters (reference to nuclear investment and investments in S. Africa). You don't realize where you're moving to! I have given it part of my life, a great part of my life. (complete silence in the room, she is speaking "from the heart" for all of us). But we have to realize where we are. You cannot simply move into this community that has grown here in a certain way and totally ignore it. [G.A.] You cannot do it. You must look into your heart!

J.E.#1: Well, what happens to my water, when you tap into it? [Env.]

H.A.: It'll get sucked out.

S.: Not for one family. Not for two families, but God, it's five years later, look at all these people coming to your beautiful Institute, now there's a hundred people coming to these things, and maybe a little bit more.... What happens.... How did.... You must think about your environmental impact! You must think about the Earth. You must. [Env.] This is not L.A. This is simply not L.A. And if you can't integrate with people I love, your sisters and your brothers, I know, it's all idealistic, but it's all really true here. [G.D.] You have to think of where you're putting all those bodies. [Env.]

(This speech is followed by ten seconds of complete silence during which hands reach out to S., patting her on the shoulders, the people nearest her hug and kiss her. Although some eyes roll upward in an expression which says "Oh, there goes S. again, beating her breast with emotion," the group can be seen physically drawing closer together. It is clearly the climax of the meeting, to which very little may be added.) [G.D., Comm.]

The meeting ended about an hour after this point, four hours after it started, with families leaving one by one, as tired children required dinner and naps, and as individuals reached their limit of tolerance for meetings. When I left there were still a few people asking questions of Keith. Probably this smaller group continued to dwindle and there was never a formal adjournment. Formal decisions in such cases are rarely made beyond setting up another meeting. No group action in fact was ever taken, to my knowledge, beyond this meeting. Yet, the Institute of Creative Studies never implemented any part of its plan. The three members of the Institute residing in the area soon disappeared. When the Beginnings Volunteer Fire Department attempted two years later to locate a key for the locked gate on the access road to the property, for emergency access, no one was able to produce a valid address to write for one.

Several points emerge from an analysis of this tape transcript. One crucial political process taking place at this meeting is that, in spite of the "we-are-not-here syndrome" (see chapter one), the group is stating their conception of who they are in opposition to who the Institute is. This is indicated by the statements labeled G.D. for group definition. These statements show that if there is no name for the community that everyone can accept, there is nevertheless no lack of group identity. The most repeated complaint about the Institute for Creative Studies is that they are outsiders who show no evidence of a desire to become insiders. This is one of the rare situations in which the extreme tolerance of the community was finally exceeded and a clear message was sent that "you don't belong here."

The two factors that precipitated the message that "you don't belong here" were the threat of negative environmental impact [Env.] and lack of respect on the part of the Institute for the authority of the group [G.A.] to input on decisions that might affect it. By filing a formal plan with such obvious environmental impact in the form of increased traffic, strong outside lighting, excessive water use, possible erosion from grading steep terrain for building sites, parking lots and roads, and the ugliness of utility poles, the Institute made its intentions clear enough to force Mateelians to object. Any family or group arriving new in Mateel is a possible environmental threat, but there had never been a situation where it was so easy to prove it.

The message that the Institute would not accept the authority of the community to regulate environmental impact was sent by their failure to contact the community before filing the plan. It was then exacerbated by Keith's incommunicative interaction strategy, which could only be interpreted in a Mateelian context as "sneaky." What happened on an individual level when W.D. responded to group criticism with the statement that "I am an individual. I can talk if I please" happened on a group level when the Institute made it clear that they did not acknowledge the community's authority. Individualism is fine, even preferred in personal matters, but it is subject to severe negative sanction when it involves matters seen as legitimately the concern of the group. Environmental impact is one of the most accepted of legitimate community concerns.

Politically, then, the whole episode demonstrates that there is such a thing as a Mateel community and that individuals are expected to acknowledge its authority in matters that affect everyone in it. The constant references to "L.A.," to incidents in Mateelian history, the use of in-jokes, and the direct statements concerning differences are indications of the strength of group definition. That this group definition and solidarity stops short of bigotry is suggested by the spontaneous appearance of "devil's advocates," arguing the Institute's position in the interest of fairness [Fairness]. The possibility has been suggested to me by informants that the motives of the defenders of the Institute might have also included some kind of hidden "deal" with them by which Beginnings could profit from the Institute's presence. No substantiation of this has ever presented itself to me and I am inclined to think that if there were some motive for defending the Institute beyond an interest in fairness, it was probably just a typically Mateelian desire to be perverse for fun.

The apparent reluctance of Institute personnel to acknowledge the existence, history, talent, value and authority of the community greatly reduced the tolerance that normally greets any newcomer. Aside from a modicum of cautious suspicion, based on many bad experiences with "rip-offs" and freeloaders, the distrust of the group toward newcomers usually arises only after honest efforts to obtain information appear to have been thwarted. The definition of the group includes a certain pride in its achievements. This is demonstrated by their implied reprimand to Keith for his stance as bringer of higher culture to the rural hinterlands. The arrogance of the Institute's assumption that they were in the area to teach creativity rather than to learn it was infuriating to people who see the best achievement of the community in terms of its artistic expression.

This episode also illustrates how free flowing, apparently random and unstructured interaction brings desired events to pass without explicit action ever being taken [Process]. Even though there was no official procedure or chair at the meeting, there are some regularities to be seen in the pattern of interaction displayed there. It was emotional, but it never really became violent. One situation, it is true, threatened to disintegrate into a fight, but it was met with instant group pressure for non-violence, to which both parties responded without complaint. Efforts were made to insure that even the quietiest voice was heard, efforts that were not completely successful, it is true, but efforts nonetheless. The rhythm of group interaction moved from periods of complete group focus to periods of small group focus to periods of complete disintegration that always moved back through small group focus to complete group focus again. The periods of complete disintegration were ended by group humor,[3] by one or several strong speakers slowly gaining the attention of small groups that then coalesced, or by group agreement. In one extreme instance, group focus was restored by a physical display that did not move beyond display to real action.[4]

The expectation of complete honesty from members of the community on community and personal matters is clearly demonstrated in the many statements regarding Keith's apparent dishonesty [Comm.] and in S.'s inclusion of statements about her personality as part of the relevant information in her speech. J.E.#1's main complaint was that the Institute was apparently withholding information. What he suspected them of concealing was a goal to make money [P.M. for Profit Motive]. Making money is, of course, an acceptable activity in Mateel, which has not succeeded in seceding from the Amerikan cash economy. However, making money at the expense of the environment or one's neighbors, making too much money, or masking the profit motive with high-flown statements is not acceptable. (This is not to say that it has not been done, especially at the height of the marijuana boom.) J.E.#1 suspected the Institute of all three crimes. He was especially suspicious, it may be assumed, not only because the Institute land constituted most of the view from his land, rendering him one of the most potentially impacted parties, but because he had arrived in the community from L.A. more recently than many of the other participants and his memories of it and reactions to it were fresher. For him, as well as for most of the others, the worst mistake Keith made was to appear dishonest.

The Institute, whose representatives were interviewed before and after the meeting, claims that they had only submitted such an elaborate plan to the county because they had been instructed to submit "the most inclusive program they would ever consider" on that property. They had already, in the Mateelian view, made a mistake in identifying themselves as an "Institute" rather than a commune. This move had put them into a category with the Planning Commission that required more stated plans than would have been required of a commune. Since they were completely new to the area, they hadn't the slightest idea of the strength and solidarity of the local community. It therefore never occurred to them to make inquiries. They were accustomed to dealing with Amerikan bureaucracies. They therefore assumed that the more developed, organized, and technically competent they appeared, the more likely it was that their plan would be approved.

It is my impression, based on subsequent interviews with participants, that the Institute could have saved at least part of their plan, had they only told their story with candor, demonstrated their willingness to be a part of the community, and appealed for sympathy on the basis of urban ignorance. Their story lent itself perfectly to a plea that "the Planning Department made us do it." This plea would have aroused the instant sympathy of the community, which has a long history of wrangling with the planning department and the building inspector. Their choice to conceal these facts from the community, a perfectly acceptable Amerikan strategy, proved disastrous in Mateel.

The community felt that it had won, as indeed it had. Magical anarchy had won some years previously against an attempted oil well in Briceland. In this case, a local rancher invited an oil company to place an exploratory drill on his land, in the hope, obviously, of getting rich quick. The hill people were immediately offended by the ugliness, strong lights at night and the noise, but the major complaint was the potential impact if oil should be found, since most of the deeds for the sub-divisions owned by Mateelians exclude mineral rights. If oil had been found, individual land owners could have been forced to allow such rigs on their own land. It is to this that Deerhawk's poem (see Appendix) refers when it says "worry about that [mineral rights], when you see oil rigs in Briceland, har, har."

Ad hoc meetings were held at Beginnings to combat the oil exploration. A class action suit was filed. A group of meditators met across the road from the oil rig in an attempt to "change the group karma." Suddenly, one day shortly thereafter, the rig was gone. A rumor circulated that a key piece of equipment had broken before there had been any sign of oil, rendering the whole venture financially questionable. Whether the law suit had scared them away, the venture had been successfully hexed, it was an early case of "ecotage" (sabotage for environmental reasons), or it was pure coincidence that the oil seekers left just when the meditators met and the suit was filed, there was a great sense of relief, joy, and solidarity. The apparent victory contributed greatly, it may be assumed, to faith in the community's ability to stand together when threatened. Certainly, the failure of the oil venture at exactly the time that the community was taking rational and irrational action against it did nothing to discredit the philosophy of magical anarchy.

Service Organizations

Another vehicle for magical anarchy is the long-term service organization that, rather than effecting one large goal, must maintain its services over time. Here a certain degree of order is imposed by the legal requirements of the mainstream society. It is the task of the organization to balance these "straight" legal requirements against local Mateelian expectations. It is quite a balancing act. To legally own property as a community group, status as a non-profit organization is required. This entails, among other things, the production of by-laws, officers, account books and minutes of meetings, a Board of Directors and a defined membership. In addition, health, sanitation and building codes must be followed where applicable. Funds must be raised and accounted for. Insurance may be required.

All of these requirements conflict directly with the basic assumption of Mateelian culture that control should be local and adjusted to local conditions. Insurance is especially galling since so many potential experiments are precluded by insurance rules based on statistics deriving from Amerikan culture. Philosophically, the whole idea of insurance is in direct conflict with the idea of manifested reality. Boards of Directors and officers conflict with the Mateelian repugnance for hierarchy.

There are several possible approaches. One is the famous "paper lie." The group generates everything required by the law and all of the necessary paperwork, then submits it properly with the understanding "among ourselves" that it is "only for them," that "we don't have to necessarily abide by the by-laws." The problem with this approach is that it is often difficult to get much consensus as to where the rules applicable to the group, the "us," stop and the rules applicable to the paper, the "them," starts. It assumes dishonesty. Magical anarchy is thus obstructed by this approach, which is why it is usually rejected in favor of one that does not require any kind of dishonesty.

Another approach is to accept the necessity for a Board of Directors, etc., and try to incorporate enough flexibility into the by-laws to keep power decentralized, while staying within the letter of the Amerikan law. Here the concept of funky reigns supreme. One organization, for instance, leaves the number of members of the Board open, "to be decided at the discretion of the membership at each election." At elections, a call is made for volunteers, the membership approves them and declares that the Board of Directors this year is whatever number is equal to the number of volunteers.

Other organizations follow the spirit of the law but in so doing lose the support of their Mateelian membership, who are likely to fight "Amerikanization" of the organization individually, dropping out in disgust when they fail, rather than organizing a caucus to preserve the Mateelian ideals. Two members of a local service organization, including one of the founding members, were not re-elected to the Board during a time when compliance with mainstream regulations was an issue. Both individuals were outspoken defenders of Mateelian ideals and felt that their "purist" stance was the reason why they were dropped from the Board. The logical result of this approach is that the organization is soon indistinguishable from local Amerikan organizations and vulnerable to accusations that it has "copped out." Representatives of the Community Credit Union, formerly the Mateel Community Credit Union, have informed me that the organization no longer even pretends to be any different from Amerikan credit unions and many of its decisions support this assertion.[5]

Among those organizations that manage to keep their Mateelian support while remaining within the bounds of the law, magical anarchy emerges in process rather than structure. Decisions tend to be made on-the-spot by whoever is present, meaning that power comes to be invested in those who are most frequently on-the-spot. There is an explicit principle for this in Mateel, which is that "if you care about it, you will make yourself present. If you don't, you have no right to make the decision." The idea here is that those who work hardest and contribute most should be the ones who make the decisions. Absentee landowners, for instance, to whom land is only an investment, are generally considered to have no right to comment on road maintenance decisions, whereas their tenants do. The right decision, then, is assumed to emerge from the interaction of people most directly concerned with the situation. Other assumptions are that the members of the organization are in close enough contact that the grapevine will work, that everyone will know everyone else's opinion on major issues, and that no one would presume to take an action known to be disapproved of by large numbers of people.

It will be recognized that the concept of funky operates here also. Problems will be solved as they arise with whatever is on hand and whoever is on hand and nothing much is assumed. The concept of "be here now" also operates in that whatever decisions may have been previously established by a larger group of people who are "not here now" may turn out to be of lower priority than the decisions of the on-the-spot group. The obvious disadvantage of this is that those who may have invested time or money into a project based on expectations deriving from a decision-making group in which they were included, feel betrayed when their efforts turn out to have been donated to something else. The planned greenhouse turns into a school building, the elementary school building is transformed by the carpenters on the spot to a primary school by the simple expedient of lowering the windows so that they are better situated for smaller children. The disgruntled then drop out of the organization, increasing the power of the on-the-spot group.

A major component of this form of magical anarchy is trust. It only works as long as the organization is small, individuals are in frequent contact, common goals and assumptions are shared, and people trust that everyone is placing the good of the group above individual self-interest. In the past, all of these assumptions were completely reasonable ones. However, as federal and state funding and marijuana-based donations raised the number of persons who could be employed and served by the organizations, and the general population continued to increase, creating a less committed and enculturated general membership, the decision-making, on-the-spot group has tended to be increasingly smaller and composed of the same people over time, many of whom are also employed by the organization. The more members of an organization who consider that they have met their social obligation by donating money rather than attending meetings, the more concentrated the power becomes.

The constant pressure of meeting requirements generated from mainstream culture increases the frustration of this small overworked core of people so that they tend to solicit general input less and arrive at decisions more often from interaction with each other. One of the great deficiencies of this form of magical anarchy is that it cannot maintain itself as anarchy and begins to be transformed into benevolent oligarchy, not unlike the early stages of political hierarchy in tribal societies. Interestingly enough, one large local organization exhibits strong patriarchal tendencies, while another exhibits strong matriarchal tendencies, increasing the similarity to tribal kin-based hierarchies, in which power tends to reside with a group of people of the same sex.

Ongoing service organizations, then, operate on magical anarchy in inverse correlation to size of the constituency and the degree to which they must meet mainstream regulations. The smaller and more isolated they are from the mainstream, the more they operate on magical anarchy. At any point in the history of any Mateelian non-profit organization, it is attempting to cope with the contradictions between the Amerikan political philosophy of representational democracy, which is hierarchically structured and ideally impersonal, and the philosophy of magical anarchy, which assumes complete equality and is, ideally, highly personal.

Pure Shmint

An example of a group that is able to operate completely on magical anarchy without resorting to a formalized procedure is the improvisational drama group, Pure Shmint. A description of their process is a paradigm of magical anarchy. Pure Shmint has no official director, scriptwriters, or Board of Directors. They improvise all of their plays as a group, working from plot lines contributed by any inspired player. They have no membership list. One becomes a "member" by coming to rehearsals and contributing work. Decisions on practical matters are made by the group, using a conversational format, or particular persons simply become, *de facto*, responsible for certain kinds of decisions because they have some special skill in that area. Since the group is composed of actors and people interested in drama, the decision-making efforts of the group often become "scenes" and points of view may be acted out as well as presented verbally. It is sometimes difficult to determine the exact point where a conversation becomes a scene. This is a completely acceptable way of operating and everyone is quite accustomed to it.

Decisions on play-related matters, lines, timing, etc. are made by those present, with priority being given to the actors directly involved in any particular scene. The function of "director" is filled by different people at different times for different lengths of time depending on the situation, sometimes more than one at once. Often the "directing" is done by other cast members who are not in the scene currently being considered. Any given play may have several directors from the beginning of rehearsals to the last performance. Persons who try to interact with Pure Shmint as director, producer, choreographer, or "star," in the traditional way, expecting the authority that normally comes with their title, are quickly frustrated by the egalitarian, apparently unstructured way Pure Shmint operates.

Yet Pure Shmint is a highly successful creative (and sometimes financial) venture. Incredible order emerges, along with coherent plots, continuity, meaningful and funny scripts and performances that are comparable to any traditionally structured drama group. One is hard-pressed to explain how this happens and it certainly appears magical, but there are some observable contributing factors. Pure Shmint operates on what E.T. Hall would call "high context" messages.[6] Much is inferred from prior knowledge, from the immediate context, from time and space usage, and from body language rather than from the spoken words alone. Because the social actors are also dramatic actors, they are especially sensitive to high context messages and adept at sending and receiving them. These invisible, implicit, perhaps only partially conscious messages result in individual adjustments in points of view and behavior that are undetectable to the average observer but change the outcome.

The history of the group explains some of the ease with which these individual adjustments become group decisions. While it is true that there is no definition of membership and anyone can become involved, it is also true that there is in fact a consistent core of people who are the moving force in Pure Shmint. Many of these are also fewer members of Hoka Hey Commune, now land partners. They have therefore established implicit understandings and assumptions simply by virtue of their long relationship to each other. They are used to working together in making decisions about their land and they have engaged in purely economic ventures such as a communally owned cafe. New members quickly pick up on the high context message exchange or become so uncomfortable that they leave. This unspoken selection process tends to result in a group of people who work together well because they read each other well.

Another factor perhaps related to reading each other well has to do with Hall's "sync" time (discussed in chapter six).[7] Pure Shmint players are all performers, singers, actors, dancers, and comedians and they have by definition an acute sense of timing. Were a videotape made of a Pure Shmint performance and replayed frame-by-frame, as Hall and his students have done with various interactional situations, I suspect that the establishment of the "group dance" would be obvious among the players and probably also the audience.

Consensus Procedure

In recent years, magical anarchy has become codified and formalized into a procedure known as "consensus decision making." The most enthusiastic advocates of this method are environmental activists who learned it from anti-nuclear groups. It is thus an import from a non-local movement of people who are generally sympathetic with Mateelians, but who are accustomed to dealing with mass movements and urban participants. The formal consensus procedure is accepted as compatible with Mateelian life, but is only accepted as *the* proper decision making method to varying degrees.

Consensus procedure consists of rules, roles and special terminology. It may be said to be an attempt to maintain the ideal of magical anarchy while reducing the chaos and the amount of time it requires. "Consensus" does not mean that everyone necessarily approves the decision, but that it is within everyone's limit of tolerance. They can "live with it." Reaching a decision, however, is of lower priority than maintaining group solidarity. The procedure, it is hoped, insures that everyone has a chance to express an opinion, regardless of individual levels of articulateness, shyness, or expertise. It is seen as a way to ascertain the group will without creating a minority of disgruntled losers.

Some fairly intricate rules are specified, mainly to control time wasted in repetition, reminiscences, anecdotes, irrelevancies, and trying to handle more than one issue at a time. "Dialoguing," in which two people become engaged in statements and responses to the exclusion of the group, is forbidden. There are no leaders. At every meeting, participants select a "facilitator" to see that consensus procedure is followed and to assess how close the group is to consensus. The facilitator is assisted in this by a "timekeeper," a "vibesreader," and by the group itself.

At every meeting, participants must be seated in a circle.[8] An agenda is formed by passing around a paper on which participants enter items. The group prioritizes items and allots fixed periods of time for discussion of each. The group can, of course, rearrange these priorities and times at will. The timekeeper monitors the allotted times for agenda items. The "vibesreader" gauges the emotional tone of the group and how close it is to consensus. The facilitator calls on the contributor of each agenda item to speak. Others who wish to speak to the item raise hands and the facilitator designates a few at a time to speak in the order in which they were chosen. If someone changes the subject, speaks out of turn, or if a dialogue goes beyond one or two exchanges, any participant may call out "Process," "Procedure," or "Focus," thereby requiring action from the facilitator.

Once a proposal has been made, all speakers must address it. The "question" is never "called," to use the terminology of parliamentary procedure. Alternative proposals may not be submitted until it has been determined that the current one will not produce consensus. The facilitator at some point will ask "Have we reached consensus? Are there any strong objections?" The participants may then state objections, what amendments will make the proposal acceptable to them and their reasons, or may state that they oppose it and are willing to "block" it.

Any person may block a decision, provided that a reason can be stated. "I have a hunch it's wrong" qualifies as a reason, but puts the blocker in a less defensible position than a more specific reason would. A defensible position is important, because the blocker will then be submitted to intense group pressure, including a discussion of personal motivations. If the blocker survives this with the opinion intact, the group may not proceed with the proposal. The majority does not, in other words, rule.

The provision for blockers would seem logically to be one that could render consensus procedure unusable, but decisions are in fact rarely blocked by a single person because of the commitment of the group to reach consensus.[9] In addition to this factor, blocking is limited by the concept of "affinity groups." As one consensus teacher explained it, if one person is always blocking the group, that person should look for another, more compatible group to work with.

This is what in fact happens with magical anarchy in general. Individuals move freely from one group to another until they find one compatible with their personalities. The selection process described above in relation to Pure Shmint renders it essentially an affinity group in consensus lingo. Unlike representative democracy, which is appropriate for a culture that encourages conformity and routinely treats people as if their only inputs were statistical, magical anarchy assumes a diversity of individuals. Room for great individual differences in motivation, modes of operation, personal idiosyncrasies, are incorporated into consensus procedure in the idea of affinity groups and into magical anarchy by the tolerance displayed for individualism. There is no loss of face and usually no bad feelings when an individual leaves one group and joins another. The dictum that one should "do what you feel" supports a flexible approach to membership, so that the formalization of this in consensus procedure as finding your "affinity group" prevents the overuse of blocking and results in groups that are composed of people more or less compatible with each other.

There are some supplementary techniques to that described above, the purpose of which is to maximize input. A "go-round" may be called for in which every person present must either make a comment on an issue or stipulate that they pass. "Brainstorming" may be used in smaller groups, in which "process" is suspended and participants are encouraged to freely contribute ideas and to dialogue more or less on the subject. "Role-playing" may be used to practice responses in model situations on which the group may be trying to make a decision. Pure Shmint players are valuable additions to these situations. In large meetings, it is common to break into smaller groups for discussion, then reconvene with what is called the "spoke" presenting the small-group decisions. The larger group then uses these as input for higher-level decisions by the whole group.

Consensus decision-making is taught at formal workshops by volunteers with experience in the method. Because these persons are committed to the method itself, above and beyond any particular organization, workshops provide a link between similar organizations within Mateel and create a network of people committed to consensus. The staff of Briceland Community High School was thus instructed in consensus procedure by a member of the Environmental Protection and Information Center (EPIC) and a member of the Peace Action Group.

This particular workshop serves to illustrate several points about the varying degrees to which consensus procedure is accepted in Mateel. After describing the procedure, a trial run was conducted in which a real issue was discussed using consensus procedure. A group critique of the effectiveness of the method elicited the comment from one of the male teachers that the same question could have been decided in half the time by the method used so far by the staff—unstructured, leaderless "conversation." The men in the group agreed with this statement. The women, including the person who had requested the workshop, disagreed. This incident supports the assertion by consensus advocates that the procedure favors those who are not powerful leaders or do not have strong voices and whose input is usually lost in structureless meetings or meetings based on Robert's Rules of Order. Those women who sometimes felt overpowered by the men felt that their views were more incorporated into consensus procedure decisions, whereas the men, who did not feel the need for such protection, saw it as an encumbrance.

Additional reasons for resistance to the method have been expressed. One person, who had been in a managerial position in a local service organization observed that, "Everyone was into consensus, but no one was into conceding." Another suggested that, "We never reached consensus about whether we were going to follow consensus procedure." She was referring to a situation in which a group of highly verbal people who felt constrained by the rule against "dialoguing" began to meet one hour before the regular meeting of the organization, ostensibly to discuss public relations, but in fact to get their dialoguing over with before the rest of the members arrived to use consensus. In general, resistance to consensus procedure is partly because of its relative formality and partly because the enthusiasm of its advocates simply backfires in Mateel, given the Mateelian sensitivity to any sign of dogmatism.

A comparison of consensus procedure and the Institute for Creative Studies meeting indicates that many of the goals and methods of consensus are visible in the latter, but poorly implemented. The consensus technique for handling large meetings by shifting the focus from large groups to small groups and back to large groups again, occurred naturally in the *ad hoc* meeting described, except for the periods of no focus, which consensus procedure aims to eliminate. Efforts are made to equalize input, to amplify soft voices and damp down overly loud or long-winded ones. These were less effective in the *ad hoc* meeting, more effective with consensus. Thus magical anarchy has to some degree pre-programed Mateelians to accept consensus procedure.

Consensus procedure has proved extremely effective in political situations that require interaction with Amerika. Decisions have been reached and implemented in highly emotionally charged situations involving large numbers of people who have Mateelian assumptions and experience in common, but who are from widely scattered watersheds and are otherwise strangers. The Citizens Observation Group, formed in 1984 in response to the paramilitary activities of the CAMP (Campaign Against Marijuana Planting) program, operates entirely on consensus procedure. The large meeting that spawned it was *ad hoc*, called anonymously, and conducted by consensus procedure. Being too large to "circle up" or to handle all input, it broke down into "work groups." COG was the product of one of the work groups, its purpose to non-violently, but efficiently, observe CAMP teams in the field to document violations of civil rights, property damage, or dangerous activities.

COG later also observed the activities of the California Department of Food and Agriculture in spraying the pesticide Imidan on apple and Hawthorne trees in an attempt to eradicate the apple maggot. CDFA often sprayed illegally and without following safety guidelines. The success of COG in obtaining a federal injunction against CAMP and in monitoring CDFA, which was eventually forced to drop the apple maggot eradication program, is a monument to the effectiveness of consensus procedure when it is properly followed. Whether consensus procedure will replace the other forms of magical anarchy described remains to be seen. My impression is that Mateelians find it quite an exercise to confine their enthusiasm to such a formal structure, but that the structure lends itself to enough flexibility that it obviates the tendencies toward benevolent oligarchy, "copping out," time-consuming chaos, general confusion and the loss of disgruntled individuals who quietly drop out of organizations rather than revealing their gripe. It might be the bridge from small group magical anarchy to large scale magical anarchy.

Hierarchy and Magical Anarchy

There is one last form of magical anarchy to be discussed. This is what happens when magical anarchy is applied to a situation that mandates hierarchy. The Beginnings Volunteer Fire Department is incorporated as a non-profit organization, raises funds, has insurance and owns fire-fighting equipment. It has no paid positions. It was organized by one of the least anarchical individuals in Mateel. For a decade, this person was also, by default, the Fire Chief. Default means that no one else would do it. Maintaining equipment, keeping up with the latest fire-fighting information, raising funds, coordinating with other fire-fighting agencies, etc., requires that information be centralized. Some one or two persons must always know the status of the organization's ability to respond to emergency situations and be able to co-ordinate response from widely scattered volunteers connected only by CB's and plectrons (dispatch radios). Such a huge responsibility is more than most Mateelians are willing or able to handle, so that the only person willing became the Fire Chief.

Experience, as well as willingness to take personal responsibility for the safety of the crew are basic to fire-fighting. This factor, in combination with the emergency nature of the goal of the organization and the need for centralized information dictates that there be a clear chain of command based on knowledge, experience and respect. Yet even in the VFD, the philosophy of magical anarchy operates where it can, given the need for hierarchy. Non-emergency decision making, such as selecting fund-raising activities, whether to build a firehouse and where to put it, whether to sell a wildfire truck to get a structure fire truck, and how to approach fire prevention education are decided even more anarchically than is the case in other service organizations. When the first chief expressed a desire to "retire" after ten years of service, the fire department had to decide who would be the next chief. There was never a formal discussion. Over a period of six months or so, the fire-fighters simply discussed it with each other, ran through the logical choices, based on experience and availability and looked expectantly at each other. Willingness was not a criterion because it was assumed that whoever was best qualified could be drafted. The new chief ended up being the best qualified volunteer. No one objected. Magical anarchy had chosen the chief.

Meetings of the VFD are conversational. No process is established, yet interruptions are rare. Topics flow into each other freely, with completely irrelevant subjects coming up and being followed. The assumption is that sooner or later the original topic will be returned to; that if it is important, it will be dealt with. An accepted part of the meeting is fire-story telling, reviewing fires fought since the last meeting, fires fought by other departments, and fire-fighting situations that occurred in the past. The format is dialogue, questions and answers. No one complains that time is being wasted in reminiscing because everyone understands the educational function of this fire-fighting folklore. The questions and answers, which would qualify as "dialoguing" in consensus procedure, are a good format for passing on folklore. VFD meetings are the least formally structured and simultaneously the least chaotic meetings one is likely to encounter in Mateel. The affinity group concept discussed above explains this. Like Pure Shmint, the VFD attracts a certain kind of personality so that members are similar in important ways and able to read each other's high context messages.

Unlike Pure Shmint, which attracts colorful, dramatic, expressive, highly individualistic anarchists, the VFD attracts less flamboyantly expressive people who value organization and the authority of experience, and can tolerate the chain of command structure, which is mandatory at a fire. There are other similarities between VFD members which would tend to make anarchical decision-making easy. Among these similarities are the fact that the hard-core, long-term fire-fighters tend to be engaged in businesses that require organization and planning and/or to have an occupational history of being employed in such positions. One couple, for instance, has a successful business manufacturing and installing ferrous cement water tanks. One of these individuals was formerly a psychiatric social worker, the other a state geologist. Other such occupations represented are surveying, construction, heavy equipment operation, holistic forestry and teaching. The first fire chief was an Air Force officer at one time.

Because of this professional experience, even though fire fighters are as much drop-outs as other Mateelians and as capable as anyone else of "being here now" when the situation does not demand action, they are more open to the tenets of professionalism, such as trusting expertise, assigning areas of responsibility to individuals, and then trusting them to fulfill them. They have a low tolerance for the kind of chaos displayed at the meeting to discuss The Institute for Creative Studies. Their businesses and professions, which serve both Mateelians and non-Mateelians, require them to operate more often in monochronic time than most Mateelians. They are, in short, efficient. Since efficiency is in all other situations in Mateel of lower priority than other values, VFD members tend to keep this preference low-key. However, a person who is unable to grasp the value of efficiency or hierarchy in fighting a fire will not last long in the fire department.

The "affinity group" principle is, again, aided by the fact that the hard-core members of the fire department have long-term acquaintance and have worked closely on many projects. Given the open kind of interaction characteristic of Mateel, this means that personal idiosyncrasies, preferences, opinions, and motives are well-known and a certain balance of power has long ago been worked out. It is another high context situation where decisions are constantly being made at an implicit level in response to non-verbal messages between people who know each other well. In such situations, much can be expected to simply "fall into place" without an inordinate amount of explicit planning.

Problems of Magical Anarchy

Even in a small scale situation, there are problems with magical anarchy that have yet to be solved. The history of Mateelians has created in them an almost fanatical distrust of leadership and expertise. There is a great confusion between power and responsibility that discourages would-be organizers. The expectation that all decisions are to be made by the group becomes unnecessarily unwieldy in ongoing situations, yet any move to restrict any class of decisions to a group smaller than those to be affected by the decisions is met with vociferous objection. Representation of any kind is viewed with great distrust. Many are the individuals with valuable professional training who have attempted to work in a situation created by magical anarchy and ended up turning away in disgust. They had discovered that there was no clear-cut area of responsibility in which they were free to make the most minute professional decisions, or that their valuable time was wasted through lack of planning.

The problem would appear to be in Alvin Toffler's words, an inability to "make the decisions at the appropriate site in the organizational hierarchy."[10] (For Mateel, one should substitute the word "structure" for the word "hierarchy.") There is also, in spite of the closeness of the community, a lack of trust, lingering over from the Amerikan experience. There is a streak of skepticism in the Mateelian character that strongly resists assigning definite areas of responsibility and trusting individuals to fill them. In this way, Mateel is different from the tribal societies they so greatly admire. In the tribal situation, the conception of the individual as separate from the tribe does not exist. Individuals occupy a highly specified place in a well-known kin-based social organization and, where organization is required, have well-known traditionally assigned responsibilities. Suspicion of individual aggrandizement beyond known cultural limits is correspondingly low. Where authority is needed, there are definite procedures for assigning it and once assigned, it is respected. Plains Indian secret societies that took turns acting as order-keepers at large tribal ceremonies are one example of this.

The problems with magical anarchy are easily related to the transitional nature of the cultural system. Insofar as the suspicion is a lingering artifact of Amerikan culture, one might expect it to diminish over time, if Mateelian culture can be maintained long enough. Hopefully, the conflict between skepticism and trust can reach a stage where any move toward efficient delegation of authority will not be interpreted as an attempt to grab power and it will be recognized that as long as areas of responsibility are distributed equitably, individuals are prevented from centralizing too much power.

Explanation—Part of Why It Works

Magical anarchy works best in ad hoc situations, in creative group endeavors that have no obligation to meet Amerikan regulations and in what may be called "affinity groups," borrowing a term from consensus procedure. It is hampered severely in long-term service organizations that must be legally incorporated, insured and ultimately regulated by Amerikans. These tend to become co-opted, to tread on legal thin ice, and/or to become benevolent oligarchies comprised of well-meaning persons who define themselves as family and believe that they are operating on consensus.

Some variables that enable magical anarchy to work are:

1. The degree which, as Mateelians would put it, participants are "centered" or, as Ecotopian writers might say, "self-realized."[11] From a political standpoint, one might say that this is the degree to which individuals are able to lay aside self-interest, economic and psychological, in favor of expediting group process.
2. The level of high context communication, or the degree to which participants are able to read each other without explicit statements being required.[12] This is in turn based on how honest individuals are with each other and themselves, a function of point number one, how well they know each other and how much they share common goals, expectations and assumptions. All of these interrelationships depend on the community being small and its members remaining a part of it for a long time.
3. Level of tolerance for apparent chaos, which is related to point number four.
4. The belief in the superiority of magical anarchy over representative democracy. This belief counteracts terminal frustration, abandonment of the scene, violence, and other behavior that might hinder the operation of magical anarchy.
5. The degree to which action must be translated into mainstream Amerikan terms and made to fit Amerikan expectations.

The key to magical anarchy is it assumes and depends on a high level of quality interaction. A starting point for understanding what kind of interaction makes magical anarchy work is provided by C. Wright Mills's definition of Fate. To Mills, what people call Fate is the "summary and unintended result of innumerable decisions of innumerable men."[13] Such decisions "are not in themselves consequential enough for the results to have been foreseen" and "the results of each decision are minute," yet all these decisions, "coinciding, colliding, coalescing—add up to the blind result...."[14]

Mills maintains that most historical events are beyond explicit human decision, because of the "mechanics of Fate."[15] The Mateelian position is the exact opposite, that "you [or we] make your [or our] own reality." On the face of it, these two positions are irreconcilable. Yet it only takes the addition of a little communication theory to make them compatible.

The innumerable decisions of which Mills speaks are inconsequential only if one regards them individually, and sees the decision maker in isolation. But humans are in constant communication with one another, exchanging conscious and unconscious, verbal and non-verbal messages and making decisions based on these exchanges. Bateson likens this ongoing interaction within a system of communication to thinking, or "mental process."[16]

Bateson also points out that not everything one perceives is selected for projection onto the screen of consciousness, but only a small part of it. What the mind selects to be conscious of is also a decision. This decision is made on the basis of values, or purposes, or presuppositions.[17] If one can then become conscious of one's values, purposes, and presuppositions and change them, then it follows that what information is made conscious will also be changed.

In fact, changing one's values, presuppositions, purposes, paradigms, habits of thought, or in short, one's worldview will influence every decision one makes at every level of consciousness, and all of these decisions will become messages in the greater societal communication system. Taken together, these individual and minute conscious and unconscious decisions, (microdecisions) represent the mental process of the mind that is culture. To the degree that individuals can control their microdecisions by changing their worldview, and to the degree that members of a society can read each other's microdecisions as messages, to that degree Mills's statement that historical "events are beyond explicit human decision" is untrue and the Mateelian view that "you make your own reality" is valid.[18] To the degree that magical anarchy works, it works because the worldview of Mateelian culture, as well as its small scale and relative stability, encourages maximal, high-quality, frequent interaction.

Ecotopia

Philip Slater lists four processes that will facilitate the creation of a more ecologically sound political system. They are:

1. decentralization of power, establishing lateral, rather than vertical channels of communication
2. deceleration, eliminating the high mobility of Americans
3. depolarization, the elimination of confrontation as a way of making decisions
4. reconnection.[19] Words like "reconnection," "attunement," and "commitment," tend to recur in Ecotopian writing.[20]

It is clear that, whatever they may call it, the Ecotopian writers are attempting to describe the opposite of alienation. This would be a situation in which individuals are maximally perceptive of each other's verbal and non-verbal messages, and of their own and other's motivations. Such a situation is made more likely in a culture such as Mateel, which gives high priority to psychological sophistication and subjectivity. The high value placed on activities that would tend to train one in perception of non-verbal messages and in synchronizing communication rhythms probably also plays a role in achieving maximal social interaction. Perhaps Hall's conception of informal culture approaches what the words "reconnection" and "attunement" are attempting to describe. In the communication system that is culture, the informal level is that level at which there are no senders, no receivers, no readily identifiable messages. Everything is in the process itself, which releases appropriate responses in others. Hall says of informal culture:

> In [technological] cultures like ours, it is at the informal level that the unspoken group wisdom resides. The informal level is the seat of the collective unconscious and, as a consequence, the ultimate threat to the demagogue.[21]

Magical anarchy takes place largely at the level of informal culture.

If this maximal social perception is accepted as an interim definition of what is being described by such words as "reconnection," "attunement," and "commitment" and it is accepted that the culture of Mateel values such perception and trains its members in it (see chapter ten), then it can be said that Slater's four criteria are increasingly implemented in Mateel— decentralization by conscious choice, deceleration by the commitment to stay in Mateel, depolarization through magical anarchy and reconnection through maximal social interaction.

Taylor's criterion for anarchy, that "the general will of the group shall be discovered" to which consensus members of the group will surrender their independence is also met.[22] Magical anarchy is a sincere attempt to discover the general will of the group, an attempt made more likely to succeed by the relatively low degree of alienation and other characteristics raising the probability of reconnection. Taylor's "true democracy" image of anarchy rests on the assumption of maximum and equal input from conscientious, educated and self-realized individuals.[23] Mateelian magical anarchy would seem to be a step in this direction, with consensus procedure as a step towards formalization of it.

Amerika

Magical anarchy and representative democracy are similar in that the ideal is the equal distribution of power among participants. Their respective formal methods, consensus decision-making and parliamentary procedure, are similar in that they attempt to insure that all points of view are presented. These are unlike, however, in the degree to which the ideal is implemented and in the degree of flexibility displayed by each. Magical anarchy mandates interaction among honest people. A post-Watergate description of representative democracy may well be that it is an exercise in shades of dishonesty. Magical anarchy attempts to arrive at a solution that can include everyone. The maintenance of group solidarity is given higher priority than taking action. Representative democracy gives priority to action over group solidarity, sets up a series of either/or situations, offers participants only the choice of "yes" or "no" and assumes that there will always be a more or less disgruntled minority even in the best compromise.

In Amerika, communication is impeded at every level. Representative democracy is the kind of communication system that is easily knocked off-balance by rapid changes that overemphasize one variable.[24] This occurs because Amerika is based too much on complexity and not enough on diversity.[25] The Amerikan dictum "mind your own business," as well as the Amerikan urge to conformity bespeak interaction that ignores non-verbal communication and constrains verbal communication to ritualized low-context messages.[26] Individuals are not encouraged to be perceptive of each other or conscious of their microdecisions. Communication between decision makers and those who are affected by decisions is also limited. It is a system in which people are making decisions based on their incomplete interaction with each other through media, such as telephones, computers, televisions, and written material that transmit only highly coded verbal messages. It is therefore a system operating on minimal rather than maximal input. Relative to Amerika, Mateelian decision making takes place face to face, in a circle for that reason, between as many individuals as possible. It thus incorporates more of the totality of their messages.

The small scale of the Ecotopian, primitive and Mateelian models of society versus the mass scale of the Amerikan model is probably the best single explanation for the difference in political structure and philosophy. Even rural Amerikan situations, small towns where long-term acquaintanceship, commonalty of experience, etc., are applicable, the model of representatives arranged in a hierarchical manner, reflecting an audience/podium spatial arrangement, and utilizing parliamentary procedure, is based on the assumption that majority rule precludes the development of a more flexible political philosophy adapted to small scale communities. Wisdom still ultimately resides with experts in ruling rather than in the discovery and implementation of the group will.

An example of the difference between magical anarchy and representative democracy is provided by the public and private road maintenance situation in Mateel. Five out of six of the core watersheds are served by the same county-maintained road. Once one leaves this road, one is on a privately maintained access road. If the county road washes out, how and when it will be fixed is a decision made by a person located eighty miles away in Eureka or perhaps even further in Sacramento, and based on cost-benefit analysis. Since fewer taxes are received by the county from the Southern portion, because of the lower population and the fact that the main income is illegal and therefore untaxable, this county road is less likely to be fixed than one located near Eureka and/or used by the powerful logging interests.[27]

If a washout occurs on one of the private roads, the decision as to how and when to fix it will be a function of how much the washout inconveniences the users of the road. A "best case scenario" is as follows: The washout is prevented by the immediate response of users, who stop on the spot to dig out a blocked drainage ditch and head off the damage. They are joined by other users who pass by, thus creating a spontaneous work crew which makes an instant preventative decision with never a relevant word being spoken. The work crew is verbally encouraged by users who cannot stop right at the moment. They are also splashed by the passing of vehicles driven by users well-known for slacking off on road maintenance. These shirkers may find themselves the recipients of curses, taunts, and crude gestures as they pass or perhaps an emotional confrontation sometime later. Some persons who pass are subconsciously excused by the work crew because it is anticipated that they will help next time. All of these actions and thoughts are microdecisions, messages and responses to messages that result in major collective decisions about fixing the road.

The point is that whatever the present condition of the road, everyone knows that the general condition of the road is the outcome of the responsible or irresponsible actions of individuals. The road maintenance decision is made by more than one person, in response to immediate information from the physical environment, in interaction with others who are personally affected by the decision. The decision is immediate, it is flexible, it is based on wide input, and on need rather than profit. Even in the more likely situation where one person or a small group makes the decision, everyone knows that those affected by it are going to respond and are located nearby, so that the decision is constrained by anticipated feedback from the locally affected group.

Without specifying the degree to which representative democracy is characteristic of Amerika and magical anarchy is characteristic of Mateel, it is possible to offer some valid contrasts between the two systems, which may help in understanding the depth of their difference. Representative democracy is compatible with monochronic, linear time. Magical anarchy is compatible with Sacred, personal, sync, and polychronic time. Magical anarchy is high context; representative democracy, low context. To use an analogy from general systems theory, magical anarchy is analogic; representative democracy, digital. Magical anarchy is qualitative; representative democracy, quantitative. Whether these contrasts are mere metaphors or empirical truths is yet to be established.

Primitive

Mateelian political structure is like the primitive in its high-context interactional basis and its equality, both of which are functions of scale and stability. Mateel is like a primitive small scale society in which individuals are members over a long period of time and thus come to know each other, facilitating total communication. In primitive societies, and to a smaller degree in Mateel, this knowing of each other is increased by the importance of kinship. Mateelian magical anarchy is greatly facilitated by the group definition of "us" as family (see chapter nine). This is, of course, fictive kinship, and may thus be of less importance politically than is the non-fictive kinship of primitive societies. On the other hand, even in primitive societies clans are composed of people who consider themselves related but cannot always specify the common ancestor or the exact relationships.

At the level of communes, close neighbors, and formal organizations, individuals feel an even greater sense of familial obligation toward each other. To the degree that individuals see their relationship to each other as familial, this relationship provides a basis for sanctions against pure self-interest. In primitive societies, the kinship lines are well-known and explicit, with power based on position in the extended family or clan and restrained by traditional expectations. Even in more hierarchical cases, the "big man" or the chief is conceived of as the head of the family. Mateelian "big men" or "big women" who redistribute economic goods and become foci of political power will be faulted if they simultaneously cease to behave like family. Persons who become powerful in some area or another of Mateelian social life are expected to act as if they were heads of extended families and the image of family is frequently appealed to as a reason for cooperation. In Mateel, in contrast to Amerika and Ecotopia, kinship, fictive and otherwise, is relevant to politics in that the feeling and conception of family is the basis for the trust and close communication essential to magical anarchy. Kinship is, in this case, a motivating image as much as a fact of life.

Magical anarchy is analogous to a healthy eco-system in which maximal information is exchanged, feedback is immediate, adjustments are easily made, response is flexible. The factors that make it work—to the degree that it does work—are those which increase interaction, maintain equality of input, and favor diversity, all elements present in healthy, ecological communities. To the degree that healthy human communities are like healthy biological communities as communication systems, Mateel is working on a political strategy with great promise for health. In this area, it is well on its way to implementing the Ecotopian model.

Residents of a core watershed confer on various aspects of bridge repair.

Chapter Eight

Economic Behavior

When you got nothing, you got nothing to lose.

—*Bob Dylan*

The discontinuity experienced by Mateelian individuals in their enculturation as Amerikans was first philosophical, then economic. Yet the economic break—the material side of "dropping out"—had the most profound long-term implications. The economic step—dropping out of graduate school or professional training, going AWOL from the military, quitting a job or a career, refusing an inheritance—was the step away from Amerikan culture that was the most obvious because in Amerika, one's place in society was based on one's position in the economic structure. Because this economic step was so incomprehensible to those who were left behind, the employers, parents, professors, a bias exists in favor of making evaluations of the counterculture on the basis of economics alone. It is therefore necessary to stipulate that the following discussion is not intended to define success or failure, but simply to describe regularities observed in Mateelian economic behavior. Economic experiments continue in Mateel and the data are not yet in. There is plentiful evidence to suggest that community economic assumptions and expectations differ significantly from those of Amerikans, even when Mateelians have not "succeeded" in becoming independent of the technocracy. Any social critic who sets up the "goal" as "complete self-sufficiency," and then gleefully declares that a countercultural entity has "failed" to meet it, does not recognize that the nearest thing the counterculture ever had to an economic goal was the general desire to withdraw from the technocracy as much as possible.

The hope, not the goal, of self-sufficiency was one of the main reasons for dropping out. For the more explicitly political of the dropouts, economic independence from "The System" was a moral issue, related to the concept of personal responsibility for war and inequality. The position that "everybody—and hence nobody—is responsible for war"[1] was partially accepted by Mateelian dropouts. They accepted the "everybody," but not the "nobody." One of the most fundamental questions to be answered in "offing the pig in yourself" was economic. The question was "how much do I personally contribute to the Vietnam War by participating in an economic system that requires wars to maintain itself?" The only way to be sure that one's talents and work efforts were not part of that unequal war-generating system was to withdraw them as much as possible from access by the system.

Less politically oriented reasons for attempting economic self-reliance included aesthetics. Many Mateelians are artists who may or may not have had a promising future in Amerika. For them the concept of handcrafting a holistic life as a context for their art included economic self-reliance. Personal freedom was another motivation toward economic self-reliance. The use of mind-altering drugs made the pursuit of personal consciousness the highest value. The need became great to follow individual activity patterns, to do meaningful work, and to eliminate the power of the "boss" to control intensely personal aspects of one's life. These needs are what many Mateelians are referring to when they cite "freedom" as a motivation in dropping out. Such freedom is incompatible with the demands of ordinary Amerikan jobs, with their hierarchical structure, insistence on the use of monochronic time, and the way they compel people to be overly concerned with conformity in highly personal matters. The vast majority of Mateelians were thus rendered not only unemployed, but unemployable when they chose freedom over security. This fact is crucial to the understanding of their economic behavior.

Mateelians attempted to reduce their economic dependence on the ordinary Amerikan job by means of four major strategies:

1. consuming less by redefining needs
2. scavenging that took advantage of the enormous waste generated by the Amerikan economy
3. evolving more adaptive social institutions
4. becoming producers. Each of these strategies will be discussed separately.

Consuming Less

One of the main ways in which Mateelians managed to consume less was by redefining needs at a level closer to the level of available resources. This re-definition of needs was accomplished through the common experience of going "back to scratch" economically. "Back to scratch" constituted different things for different people and was an intensely individual learning experience even for dedicated communards. One eliminated whatever was unnecessary, stayed at that level of consumption for whatever length of time was individually necessary to be sure that Amerikan assumptions about needs had been thoroughly questioned, then began to carefully and selectively reintroduce items, examining the extent and context of their necessity item-by-item. The specifics varied. Some went through a period of asceticism that was incomprehensible to their Amerikan associates. Minimal shelter, a diet of grains, honey and dried fruit, and whatever personal items one could get into a backpack might represent the "back to scratch" phase for a childless, young and healthy purist. It is this extreme that was most visible to social scientists and the media, and which inspired many self-satisfied "I told you so's" when these individuals began their economic reentry.

One person describes the conflict between his ideal of self-sufficiency and the growing awareness of the difficulty of achieving it:

> I'm talking about the years from about 1970 to about 1975, when I lived in that cabin, the most important thing was becoming grounded. Establishing myself on the land, I explored the land, I knew it, I mapped it, I gardened, I raised chickens, rabbits, built a house, that

was the guiding principle. It was an illusion that it was in any way independent, objectively. Economically it was so depressing. Every week I had to make out the lists and the lists were so long. They had so many things—toilet paper, peanut butter, on them that I could not grow and felt I needed.

For many dropout middle class wives, simply exchanging a claim to their husband's income for Aid For Dependent Children or the ephemeral hope of child support was a sufficient exercise in returning to economic basics. A common female story is giving up an ordinary suburban home, with all of the electrical labor-saving devices, for a cabin in the woods with kerosene lamps, no or sporadically running water, and wood heat. One informant speaks of periods of melting snow to wash diapers while the pipes were frozen and she had no vehicle to get to the laundromat. It is amazing how many women chose this exchange knowing full well that they faced it alone and, perhaps, without even a vehicle. Personal freedom for them was breaking away from economic dependence on a subordinate relationship to their husbands.

However one approached it, the exercise was to see just how much one could do without, then to add to that, evaluating carefully as items were reinstituted and often redefining the function of the item before reinstating it. Irons, for instance, were universally abandoned as ironed clothes were seen as unnecessary for anything but a statement of conformity to Amerikan dress standards. Seamstresses later reinstated them as it became clear that irons are tools essential to garment making, a legitimate craft. The need for some reinstated items only became clear as new problems arose.

Telephones, for instance, are on the increase in the Mateel community as the second generation reaches adolescence. This is because a need is recognized to balance the adult reaction to them as part of the paraphernalia of technocracy against the parental anxiety that accompanies the increased mobility and social awareness of teenagers. Mateelian children are given a childhood education that stresses independence, self-reliance, and personal responsibility. When the children become adolescents, most parents recognize the urgent need to be with peers as a natural stage of social development. Becoming socially mature is a paramount value in Mateelian child-rearing. Because they have been trained to self-reliance, Mateelian adolescents expect much more freedom than mainstream adolescents are usually allowed. In the physical context of Mateel, with distances so great between friends, school, and home, being with friends involves being away from home much more than in the mainstream situation.

Parents face a choice between giving their teenagers complete control over their movements, as many do, or restricting their social development by insisting that they be isolated on remote homesteads, an option generally considered unwise in the long run. For those who can afford them and are close enough to existing lines that it is technically feasible, telephones can be a compromise solution. Telephones have also become reinstated as appropriate technology because of their obvious value in medical and fire-fighting emergencies and because the increasing political awareness of Mateelians has redefined them as tools for political organizing.

Some people could only engage in the redefinition exercise by placing themselves into situations that automatically eliminate "things." The choice to live without electricity, alone, necessitates a redefinition of what one really needs. Electricity has now been re-introduced to many homes because of constantly improving alternative technology and the increase in income from marijuana cultivation. Yet, since twelve-volt systems cannot generate as much electricity per home as public utilities provide per home, judgements must still be made as to whether the utility of an item justifies the amount of electricity it consumes. The experience of living for some time completely without electricity helps individuals to make this judgement. Table 2, based on the Household Energy Budget Questionnaire, indicates what items most people re-introduced when electricity became available and compares the prevalence of these items to that of mainstream Amerikan homes.

Television is a good example of the need-assessing process. Even though only one household responding to the HEBQ reported having no electricity at all, and twelve-volt television sets are easily obtainable, only four out of twenty-six households reported owning one. My interpretation of this, based on conversations with informants in general, is that many Mateelians have eliminated from their

Electrical Items	HEBQ (1985)	U.S. (1980)
Clothes Washer	19.2%	71.4%
Clothes Dryer	11.5	59.8
Dishwasher	7.0	36.1
Freezer	11.5	37.0
Microwave Oven	3.8	20.7
Electric Range	0.0	53.3
Television	19.2	98.0 (1985)
Air Conditioner	0.0	58.0

Electrical Items other than above, no comparable figures, HEBQ only.

Radio/Cassette	20	Typewriter	3
Lights	19	Computer	3
Blender	12	Hair Dryer	2
Power Tools	10	Refrigerator	2 (both PG&E)
Iron	5	Water Pump	2
Guitar & Amplifier	3	Space Heater	2
Toaster	3	Film Projector	1

Non-Electrical Items	HEBQ (1985)	U.S. (1980)	Shasta (1980)
Vehicles: one	23.0%	36.5%	25.0%
two +	42.0	49.6	70.0
Gas range	100.0	46.6	

Housing Consumption	HEBQ	Garberville (1980)	Ferndale (1980)
Median Value of Home		See Below	$56,100
Owner-Built	88%		
Owner-occupied, incomplete plumbing	100%	34% (614)	5% (44)
No telephone	77%		7% (U.S.=3%)

Energy Use		U.S. (1980)	Shasta (1980)
Wood as primary heating fuel	100%	.9% (West) 5.0% (Entire)	31%
Public Utilities	11.5		
Solar Panels	80.0		
Water Wheel Gen.	30.0		
Gas or Propane Gen.	53.0		
Wind Gen.	11.0		

HEBQ=Household Energy Budget Questionnaire (see Methodology)
PG&E=Pacific Gas & Electric, Public Utilities in Humboldt County, CA
Shasta=Shasta County, CA, exclusive of Redding City
Ferndale=Ferndale Census District
Garberville=Garberville Census District
Humboldt County Tax Assessor estimates mean value of So. Humboldt County home, including negative value, as $4800.

Table 2. Consumption Patterns

lives the need for television, replacing it with more active forms of entertainment and deciding not to reinstate it even when they are financially and technically able to do so. Many Mateelians report that their experience of not having a television set has convinced them that it is not only unnecessary but actually harmful, especially for children.

There are no absolute requirements for the experience of redefining needs. There is a certain degree of social pressure in that the less one is able to "simplify" one's life, the more vulnerable one is to accusations of being "bourgeois." This is a weak kind of social pressure, however, generally over-balanced by the tolerance for individual idiosyncrasy, repugnance for dogmatism, and respect for the right of the individual to pursue consciousness in whatever way works best for them. "Whatever gets you high" or "off" is a common saying that states this respect for individual psychic needs. It is fair to say that if Mateelians had more possessions in 1980 than they had in 1970, these possessions were more carefully chosen, obviously useful, energy-efficient, long-lasting and of higher quality, than the possessions they disposed of when they dropped out, or than one might find in an ordinary Amerikan home. My observation is that Amerikan consumer items that are largely sold by advertising and social pressure and/or are produced in a wasteful, polluting manner are less likely to be found in Mateelian homes than Amerikan homes, although quantitative data on this has not been obtained.

Scavenging

Taking advantage of Amerikan waste was relatively easy early in the history of the counterculture because the Amerikan economy was in a period of boom. Middle and upper income dropouts could raid their relatives' attics, basements and garages. Other sources of discarded but useful items were thrift stores, junk yards, garbage dumps, flea markets, household garbage cans set out for pickup, and supermarket dumpsters. To use an ecological analogy, early countercultural individuals became excellent scavengers. They were able to do this by the simple cultural expedient of inverting the mainstream status connotations of using discarded items.

High status accrued to those who could make the best use of junk. Low status went to those who had to resort to buying from Amerika. This status reversal, in combination with the great creativity of Mateelians, opened whole new vistas of resources and instituted the concept of funky (discussed in chapter six). People became connoisseurs of junk and tips on the best sources of junk were passed eagerly from one person to the next. Later in the seventies, the reversal of status symbols necessary to scavenging was rendered less necessary by the spread of environmentalism, which established "recycling" as a perfectly respectable activity, at least in some areas of Amerika.

Mateelians were and are recyclers par excellence. In the HEBQ, the most consistent response, twenty-five out of twenty-six, was that households composted their organic waste. At one point in the history of Mateel there was at least one family who earned a few extra dollars by making "garbage runs" to Eureka, scavenging all the produce and dairy products supermarkets are required to discard, bringing it back to Mateel and selling it at a minimal price to persons unable to scavenge for themselves. One class of local Amerikans who became sympathetic to Mateelians early were the junk dealers, whose businesses suddenly began returning higher profits, and whose status was high in the counterculture. Because Mateelians redefined what was usable and what was not, they became expert at tearing down condemned buildings and recycling windows, doors, siding, hardware, and beams, all of which would have been simply dumped, and the use of which often violated the building code.

So eager are Mateelians to recycle and scavenge, that one must be careful to designate what is up for grabs and what isn't. Scavenging does have a tendency to fade over into stealing where the ownership of items can be interpreted as being in question and there are always a certain number of anti-social hangers-on who are willing to interpret items as unclaimed that are clearly claimed. The "rip-off" problem has always gone hand in hand with the positive attitude toward scavenging. Mateelians take the attitude, however, that the rip-off problem is not sufficient to condemn scavenging and recycling, even though means of combatting it are limited to negative sanctions such as gossip. One person got a reputation for siphoning gas out of parked cars because "it was an emergency." His formerly windowless house sprouted familiar looking windows at about the time that his neighbor missed some windows stacked up and intended for his own house. Record albums donated to a communal collection appeared magically on his turntable. This person soon found himself accused of every theft in the area and discovered that people were reluctant to do any kind of business with him or to permit him on their property. He eventually moved back to Texas.

Adaptive Institutions

More adaptive economic institutions created and rediscovered by Mateelians include communes, free boxes, farmer's markets, crafts fairs, rummage sales, bartering, co-operatives, work exchanges, and land partnerships. All of these are much more in evidence in Mateel than in ordinary Amerikan small towns. The commune, especially, was a route to self-sufficiency tried by many countercultural dropouts. Communes have had their greatest effect on Mateelian economic behavior as learning experiences for the participants. I know of no large operating communes in Mateel, but I know of numerous land ownership situations that would probably be avoided by most Amerikans. Their chances of success depend on the ability of the participants to co-operate, an ability greatly enhanced by the communal experience.

Mateelian economics has, over a period of fifteen years, taken a direction away from communal and socialistic ideals and toward small-scale capitalism. This general statement, however, fails to convey the great diversity that has always characterized the Mateelian economic scene. From the start, the economic unit has included large and small communes, nuclear and extended families of actual and fictive kin, and individuals acting alone. There have always been small businesses, freelance service providers, and temporary and part-time wage-earners. The shift in emphasis toward small-scale capitalism can be seen in the slow breakdown of communes into smaller economic units, and by the rise in the number of small businesses, self-employment, and services.

The most common arrangement for land ownership is the land partnership. This is because the zoning regulations for most rural areas of southern Humboldt county prevent subdivision below forty acres, but allow two homesteads on each forty-acre parcel. The number of buildings on one parcel is severely limited by the steepness of the terrain, so that parcels vary widely as to the number of possible residences. On the other hand, since Mateelians are capable of living in much smaller dwellings than Amerikans, they can make use of smaller areas of level ground.

The land partnership is basically a financial arrangement whereby partners buy "undivided" parcels—that is, the parcel cannot be subdivided for sale or by legally binding contracts made regarding individual ownership within the parcel. Technically, only those individuals whose names are on the deed have a legal interest in the land. Since marriage and the form of family is so experimental, however, all sorts of verbal agreements, which have little standing in court, are entered into on the basis of fictive kinship or some other social arrangement that has no official standing.

Most marriages are what would, in states other than California, be called common-law marriages. They are functional, of long standing, and may have produced children. A legal spouse married to a landowner, but whose names do not appear on land deeds are somewhat protected from losing their interest in the land by community property and inheritance laws. However, since California does not recognize common-law marriage, a long-term spouse equivalent and co-parent who has no legal standing with regard to the land may be in fact living on it, helping to pay for it, and investing labor and love in it, on the basis of trust in the legal owner to uphold a verbal agreement about the land. The "paper" situation may reflect partnership between certain individuals, while the actual functional situation is partnership between idiosyncratically defined families. Obviously, when changes are made in the social agreement, there is a great potential for the non-legal individuals to lose any right to the land. Sometimes they do and sometimes they don't. It all depends on the degree to which those involved "really" have broken with Amerikan law. This situation is one of the greatest sources of conflict in Mateel, particularly between sexes.

The land partnership, then, may be defined legally as being between named individuals, between sets of married couples and their children, or any combination of those two. Socially, however, there may well be members of fictive families operating as economic units who are considered land partners by the persons whose names are on the deed, who so consider themselves, and who are seen as being in the land partner relationship socially by the rest of the community. Social consequences of the land partnership are that a certain amount of co-operation is necessary in allocating building sites, water access, road access, use of timber, gravel, or firewood resources, environmental impact such as erosion from overgrazing or indiscriminate use of tractors, etc., use of meadows, location of orchards, gates, fences, and, most importantly, making land payments. In recent times a central decision involving land partners is whether or not to grow marijuana, an activity that renders all of the partners on the land liable to arrest, harassment, rip-offs, and/or confiscation of land. At least one long-term, otherwise idyllic, land partnership has been dissolved over this question.

All of the above factors create limitations on individual decisions about land and tend to make ownership ambiguous. This situation would seem incomprehensible to many Amerikans, to whom private ownership is a basic value and words on paper the only means of protecting it. Partners approach the necessary co-operation in various ways. Some arrive at a use agreement between themselves, one that has no legal status, effectively dividing the land in terms of authority. One partner could, for instance, sell timber from her/his portion of the land without consulting partners or sharing the profit, or instigate a lot-line adjustment on her/his end of the land. Water sources may be clearly allocated into "my spring" and "your creek."

It is, however, extremely difficult to arrange a land partnership in which the partners never have to arrive at mutual decisions, even in situations where this is greatly desired. It is therefore more common to find a greater degree of cooperation, sharing of water tanks, planting of communal gardens and orchards, cooperation on building projects of mutual benefit such as barns, fences, ponds and gates. Partners with communal experience are better prepared for cooperative decision making and agreements with no legal status than those without. Those without learn communal assumptions from those with greater experience, so that a more flexible attitude towards ownership and use rights to land prevails than in an ordinary Amerikan rural area.

Land partners are seen by the community at large as being in a special kind of relationship. This is in spite of the fact that the land partner relationship in question may be in a state of imminent dissolution. "Who's your partner?" is a common "small talk" question along with "Where's your land?" and "How long have you been here?" One of the disadvantages of land partnership is that the community tends to see partners as being to some degree responsible for each other as if they were kin, regardless of how the partners themselves have defined the relationship. For instance, one informant's land partner made an abrupt departure to "get a job in the city," making totally inadequate provisions for her livestock. When her horses began to wander into neighboring pastures, her partners were held responsible for them by the neighbors. The partners protested that they had no responsibility for the horses, that the neighbors were free to sell them, call the humane society or shoot them. They were, in the end however, forced by social pressure to retrieve the horses and vent their wrath on the errant land partner.

Given the obvious disadvantages of land partnership, most Mateelians would prefer to do without them. It is the financial fact that without a partner, few Mateelians can afford to buy a forty-acre parcel, even given the low land prices in the 1970s. Many Mateelians have experienced more than one partnership and the unpleasant experience of dissolving it. Their accounts of this experience suggest that the dissolution of a land partnership is an experience similar to divorce. In those cases where the land partners are also long-term sexual partners, perhaps co-parents who are not legally married, which fact deprives them of the advantages of a legal divorce, negotiations over the land may be the only aspect of the relationship that lends itself to settlement in the courts. Many land partnerships grew from communes or self-defined "extended families" of individuals who may have rearranged themselves as sexual couples several times over the years. The joint ownership of land, viewed from a social rather than a purely legal perspective, may therefore become complicated. The folklore thus advises prospective buyers of land to choose their land partners perhaps even more carefully than they would choose a spouse.

It is a testament to the determination of Mateelians to change their Amerikan assumptions about private ownership in order to live on The Land that any land partnerships work. That there are so many partnerships of long standing in which the partners define themselves as family in spite of years of wrangling, re-arrangement of sexual relationships, marriages and divorces, and re-arrangement of residence, is further evidence of both the desire to stay with the back-to-the-land dream and the willingness of the individual to painfully limit her/his ego in order to work out social arrangements that will make the dream possible. It is also evidence of the influence of the communal experience and the failure of the private ownership principle to completely re-assert itself.

The communal ideal and the enormous "hassle" Mateelians are willing to put up with in their efforts to sustain it is demonstrated by a situation in which one piece of land was owned by no less than twelve separate partners. This particular piece is located on the county road and consists of an ordinary Amerikan-built farmhouse, barn, and several outbuildings usable as art studios, workshops, etc. Rooms in the large house were rented out to several different people at different times. When a dispute ensued between earlier tenants and later tenants over just how many people could live in the farmhouse and who they were going to be, the multiple owners of the land had to attempt to settle it. There were factions within this group that supported each of the different tenants' points of view. Meetings were held involving no less than twelve owners and seven to ten persons claiming a right to live in the house. That a settlement was reached is a monument to the tenacity of the communal ideal in the face of incredible difficulties in implementing it.

The institution of the "free box" is another example of a social adaptation that functions to enable Mateelians to live on less. A free box is simply a box full of items that are free. One contributes items no longer needed and takes items one can use. It is usually, but not necessarily, located centrally wherever its presence is tolerated by the owner of the location. They are sometimes elaborate wooden bins with lids, maintained by a school, a co-op, or a private business, but may also be a cardboard box in the laundromat or on someone's back porch. Economically it is simply another recycling method, but as a social adaptation it is a paradigm of how redefining cultural assumptions makes more ecologically sound economics possible.

One informant describes how the free box acts as a symbolic bonding mechanism:

> When my first baby outgrew the first dress I ever made her, I decided not to keep it—it seemed a little too sentimental. So I threw it in the Co-op free box. Three years later, I happened to walk by that same free box and there it was, right on top. It was faded and threadbare and you could see it had been worn and washed over and over. I took it out and took it home and still have it. I love the idea that other community babies wore it, got use out of it, and when it was ready to retire, it came back to me to be a keepsake.

The nostalgic value of a baby's dress is enhanced, not diminished, by the fact that so many community babies wore it. This is a complete reversal of the Amerikan stigma on "hand-me-downs." It is a common learning experience for Mateelian children to decide that they have outgrown some favorite garment and to put it in the free box knowing that they may see another child wearing it. If they simultaneously choose something from the free box, charity becomes reciprocity. The children may well talk to each other about their free box "scores," but the implication that the recipient is somehow of lower status than the giver is precluded by the knowledge that everyone uses the free box. Children, and adults, may in fact be delighted to find a long-coveted item formerly belonging to someone in their social environment is now theirs for free or that a good friend is now the custodian of an item they donated with reluctance to the free box. The free box for young children is an education in interdependence, community, and thrift. The free box is also a fashion challenge. The famous "layered-look" that was high fashion in 1980, was well presaged and perhaps even inspired by hippies simply trying to keep warm and exercise a little creativity with the resources of the free box.

The free box has almost disappeared in Mateel in recent years, the last bastion of freeboxing being, logically, the recycling center located at the county dump. The reason many people give for this is that marijuana money made it possible for Mateelians to buy their clothes new and reduced the economic basis for free boxes. I have some reservations about this explanation. For one thing, marijuana economy has not at all reduced the total number of people who might need a free box. It has only created, re-created, a stratification based on money, while locally inflating prices for ordinary consumer items. Meanwhile, hundreds of landless seasonal farm workers, as well as unsuccessful marijuana farmers and the more or less steady percentage of single mothers who cannot sue marijuana farmers for child support are placed in an economic position quite similar to that of the earlier Mateelians.

The demise of the free box may be ascribed to other factors. They require a certain amount of upkeep, removing items that really are beyond the threshold of usefulness, preventing unsightly overflow, and keeping them out of the rain. The institutions that formerly kept them up have either become defunct for one reason or another or have been swamped with other duties because the marijuana caused population explosion has inundated the community with persons inexperienced in community responsibility. Another reason is the incessant pressure of capitalism. One informant stopped contributing because she too often found her contributions on the rack of second-hand clothing stores or at flea markets with price tags on them. All the social functions of the free box are subverted when capitalists make a profit on items intended to be free.

Still another factor is that the closer the community became socially, the more possible it was for potential contributors to connect with potential receivers and simply short-circuit the public free box. The spirit of the free box became defined in terms of more closely related people than in terms of, probably transient, needy people at large. If donated items are taken out of the area, the feedback of seeing them in continued use is precluded, so that the symbolic communication aspect of the free box is lost. The staggering influx of non-Mateelians as a result of the marijuana boom thus diluted the value of the free box as a community bonding institution.

Bartering is standard procedure in economic relations between members of the community. Many people maintain their own junk yards not only as a source of parts for equipment repairs and funky creations, but in order to have something to barter. Garden vegetables, eggs, fruit, nuts, livestock, poultry, fish, and dairy products may be exchanged through barter or as part of the generalized reciprocity that prevails in Mateel in exactly the same way that it does in primitive and peasant societies. Work exchanges are frequent, either exchanging work for work, or work for goods, or, again, as generalized reciprocity in the form of work parties called to side a residence, raise a redwood water tank, or pour a concrete foundation, for either individual or community projects.

Consumer co-ops have been a part of the economic scene almost from the start of the Mateel community. One began as a "food conspiracy" in which consumers ordered food in bulk together and volunteered labor to distribute it. This group eventually, under the guidance of the Consumer's Co-operative of Arcata, California, bought a store and attempted to develop into a cooperative along the lines of the well-established Consumer Co-ops in large cities in California. As a retail store, the Ruby Valley Warehouse Co-op was never able to really become self-sustaining, in spite of years of effort to make it so. It did, however, spawn another co-op retail store in another location that survived for several years.

The failure of the first retail store has been taken by many as a signal that the co-operative spirit of Mateel is either an illusion or has been subverted by a marijuana based economy. An enormous amount of bad feeling accompanied its failure, with blame being fixed on bad management and lack of public support. The original conspirators assume that the purchase of property and the attempt to expand is the only explanation. A more general analysis, however, is that increasing competition from local mainstream supermarkets simply made the original Co-op uncompetitive in its location too near to the mainstream supermarkets. One factor that greatly increased this competition was when the largest supermarket, only two miles from the Co-op, was sold by the family that had owned it for many years to an enterprising newcomer. The new owner had the good business sense to see that catering to Mateelian consumption patterns was more profitable than resisting them because of anti-hippie prejudice. He actually sent representatives to study the inventory at the Co-op, duplicated it, and improved on it.

When one could only obtain particular items like locally produced tofu or local organically grown tomatoes at the Co-op, there was an advantage to shopping there beyond the philosophical one of supporting "creeping socialism" (from a 1960s bumper sticker advertising the establishment of the Consumer's Cooperatives in Berkeley). While one was buying the tofu, one might as well support creeping socialism and local producers and get everything else possible at the Co-op. However, when it became possible to buy locally produced tofu and organic tomatoes at the supermarket, the Co-op's economic "hook" was lost, and shopping there became a matter of philosophy only. Behaving in an economically irrational manner in order to "make" an economic philosophy work seemed silly to people so experienced in surviving at low cost by use of their economic wits. The Co-op movement in Mateel lived on by planting its seed in a more rational location and allowing the parent store to die a natural death.

Like primitive and peasant societies the world over, and to a much greater degree than in Amerikan communities, reciprocity is a big part of the economic scene. This reciprocity takes the form of work exchanges and work parties, potlucks, hitchhiking, the exchange of gifts of crafts, services and recycled items, house and animal sitting, tool-sharing and the exchange of other kinds of favors. A prominent feature of Mateelian reciprocity is shared knowledge. Mateelians are eager to share what they have learned in such areas as gardening, cooking, crafts, dancing, music, arts, home building, water systems, vehicle repair, child-rearing, and sexual relations. People who are experts in any area often will donate large amounts of time for the pleasure of teaching an eager student. Experience is also shared for its informational value. Whereas malicious gossip is ideally avoided, most Mateelians are open to the exchange of life experiences, recognizing that everything is so experimental in Mateel that sharing experience is of great value in avoiding mistakes already made by someone else.

One particularly dramatic form of generalized reciprocity has been in the area of funerals, a subject described in more detail elsewhere.[2] I have witnessed two situations and heard of some others, in which the family of a deceased person found it unnecessary to purchase some of the most expensive services of an undertaker because friends donated those services. Beautiful handcrafted coffins were built by neighbors with donated materials, the graves were dug by the community in the local cemetery, remains were transported by friends using pick-up trucks, flowers and services were provided by the community. In one case, the friends washed and dressed the body, using the deceased's own clothing, rather than clothes bought specially from the undertaker. One may see these community efforts as both economic and symbolic, expressing an openness to interdependence difficult to find in Amerika.

An especially poignant example of the contrast between Amerikan and Mateelian economic philosophy occurred when friends of the deceased, who had built a lovely coffin with donated materials, took it to Eureka to get the body from the mortuary. (This was during a brief period when there was no local mortuary). So impressed was the Eureka businessman with the coffin that he attempted to order some more from the friends, who then had to patiently explain that they were not in the coffin-making business, but were a group of loving people honoring their deceased friend. The undertaker, I am told, accepted this explanation, eventually, with wonder and good grace.

Redistribution is also a factor in Mateelian economic behavior, with particular individuals who for one reason or another are wealthier than average being placed under social pressure to contribute to community causes. Such Mateelian "big men" and "big women" are generally also greatly respected and wield a certain amount of political power simply by virtue of their donations. They differ from Amerikan philanthropists and corporate funding agents and resemble their primitive counterparts in that many of their donations are to causes that are not tax write-offs, they are in a personal relationship with their beneficiaries, and they are constrained in the exercise of power by public opinion.

Becoming Producers

It is my impression that few Mateelians ever expected to produce everything they needed, the informant quoted earlier being an exception. This is regarded as a somewhat extreme, though laudable, goal in Mateel. The interest in home production of goods, however, has always been amazingly high. At any Mateelian gathering, conversation is going to center around two major topics—

economic activity and gossip. The economic activity topic, unlike such conversations in Amerika, will consist much more of experiments tried in production and recycling than it will of consumer items purchased or to be purchased. A rigorous quantitative study of the economics of Mateel is beyond the scope of this work. However, simple observations reveal much that is in contrast to Amerika.

Organic vegetable gardens abound in Mateel. Most Mateelian homes have some home-grown, home preserved food in the pantry. Even before breaking ground to build a residence, Mateelians are likely to build a chicken coop and plant fruit and nut trees. The barn, coop, goat shed or greenhouse has often been instantaneously converted into a "temporary" residence when the first rainy season caught new Mateelians with roofs over their plants and animals, but none over themselves.

Livestock experiments have yielded unclear results. Goats are the most consistently found livestock, since they are adapted to steep terrain and, like the early Mateelians, can exist largely on what would otherwise be defined as "garbage." Horses are problematic because of the steep terrain, which is easily overgrazed and is eroded by metal horse shoes. Many people have managed to maintain a few head of cattle, both for beef and dairy products. Cattle, again, are not especially appropriate for steep terrain. Some local ranchers keep small herds at the tops of ridges, but cattle have not been tried on a large scale by Mateelians. Sheep are often kept by persons whose craft is weaving, knitting, or crochet, but aside from this situation, they are not especially economical. Swine are rarely kept. My guess is that this reflects both the dietary preferences of many Mateelians who do not eat red meat, and the special effort required to keep swine and to process pork. Poultry—chickens, turkeys, and ducks—are common and fairly easy to keep, protecting them from predators being the central problem. Livestock and poultry are considered desirable not only for producing protein, but for producing fertilizer for the gardens. A person who is able to maintain a horse or a cow has an excellent product to barter or offer in generalized reciprocity, whether the horse is ridden or the cow produces milk or not.

A more impressive indication of the continuing effort towards self-reliance is the prevalence of the owner-built home in Mateelian society. Of twenty-six respondents to the HEBQ, only two were not residing in homes they themselves had built. One of these had only been in the area for two years, which more than likely explains why she was still living in a trailer. The building of one's own residence saves all of the labor costs in construction. It also places one under the less-stringent "Code K" category of the state building code. Building one's own home also makes it possible to avoid the building code altogether. An indication of the prevalence of the owner-built home is the fact that the Code K category was established as the direct result of the lobbying of countercultural rural residents in Humboldt and Mendocino counties.[3]

Mateelians do not have an exclusive claim to owner-building, since it is a logical move for any rural resident. However, I would guess from observation that a much higher proportion of Mateelian residents of Humboldt County produce their own shelter than non-Mateelian residents of Humboldt County do. Statistics to support this would be difficult to obtain, since the stupefying red tape and extra expense involved in getting a building permit insure that vast numbers of owner-builders never do. However, the importance of owner-building as an economic strategy was thrown into high relief in February of 1988, when an attempt was made to drastically increase the power of the building department to enforce the building code on owner-builders.

The public outcry was unprecedented. No less than four public hearings were held in Eureka to receive public input. Mainstream and Mateelian owner-builders attended these hearings in droves, many driving as much as five hours round trip on a weekday evening, an incredible inconvenience for those with ordinary jobs. The ratio of persons who, judging from their dress and remarks, appeared to be following a Mateelian cultural pattern, to persons who appeared to be following a mainstream cultural pattern, was about fifty-fifty. This indicates that the Planning Department inadvertently succeeded in producing a political coalition where twenty years of conscious attempts by political strategists had failed. Owner-building was the issue that crossed the "hippie" vs. "straight" line in Humboldt County for the first time.

Owner-building has, in addition to its economic importance, a great deal of symbolic significance. It is a clear statement of intention to remain in the area in spite of the economic difficulties of doing so, a physical manifestation of the rejection of Amerikan career-related mobility. It is a supreme statement of independence from the need for Amerikan experts. For the many women who have built their own homes, it is a statement of independence from the need for men to provide shelter. It is an artistic production exemplifying for many people their whole personal philosophy of life. It is a concrete rendering of their assumptions, expectations, goals, hopes and dreams. Building a residence, even someone else's, was for some people a spiritual exercise that served to break their tie to the life they might have expected to lead as an Amerikan and it taught them, simply, how good it feels to produce one's own needs:

> During the summer, I got terribly bored. . . . I thought I was just going to take a few drugs, and be wise. You know, read my psychology books, and work on my insides, and be wise. I found out it didn't work that way. So I actually, just left the beach and went up to help my friend build his house. And I was much more connected then. The real change is when I moved off the beach and I felt the joy of creation. And moved from this wise man image into acting, and then it was something I just had to do. I couldn't even change a light bulb, coming out of New York City, you know, these apartment children. . . . And I figured the way I can handle this is if I build a house. Then I know I can do things. So I came up with a bunch of students [from San Francisco] for one month and we built a cabin. In one month, with them from beginning to end, and it wasn't very creative. I modeled it after the cabin we were staying in, made some adjustments for size and things, made a few improvements, but basically the whole process was from the ground up. I did some things like, in the beginning I knew you were supposed to level off things, so I would level off the springers. But I had no idea that you could turn the level on its edge and see if something was upright. So all the poles were leaning every which way and I had to go back later in the summer and put a whole new row of posts in. But I built the cabin and it's tight and it's still there today. It's still usable 15 years later. The carpentry was abysmal, but the idea is good, the structure is good, and it works.

For those who cannot actually build their own home, the ability to live in anything, to produce their own shelter in some way, may serve the same symbolic and psychological purpose of establishing self-sufficiency as a component of self-definition. A female informant who lived in a plywood tool shed for two-and-a-half years with her baby, describes this experience as a watershed in her personal development:

> My father always attempted to control my actions by saying, "As long as your two feet are under my table, you'll do as I say." So, at age 16, I got a job as a waitress, boarded at a friend's house and, as far as I was concerned, got my feet out from under his table. Much later, when I left my baby's father and was able to remain independent of him because I could live in a tool shed, I felt I had my feet out from under his table, too. His male friends thought I couldn't do it, that I would be forced to return to him because I couldn't make it on my own in the country, but they underestimated what a determined woman can do, whether she builds or not. I was on welfare, but I consider that wages for mothering. Now I have built a home jointly with my new husband and if my feet are under his table, his feet are also under mine, and our four feet are under no one else's.

No statistics are available on the amount of clothing produced at home. Several observations may be made, however, which support a statement that less clothing is purchased by Mateelians than by Amerikans in general. They do not wear polyester and other synthetic fabrics because they are uncomfortably hot without air conditioning, much more difficult to clean by hand or in the laundromat, irritating and uncomfortable for active people who are unusually conscious of their bodies, and aesthetically unpleasing to people who value natural materials. Environmentalists reject synthetic fibers, in addition, because they are made from fossil fuel. The rejection of synthetic fibers alone restricts the amount of clothing available to Mateelians in stores. Mateelians do purchase clothing items they cannot make at home such as underwear, shoes, and jeans. Some percentage of these items are bought new, some at thrift stores, flea markets and rummage sales. The recycling function of the free box has been discussed.

I would guess that the Mateel community home-produces at least triple the amount of clothing that a similar size Amerikan community does. This speculation is based on observation—the number of handmade items I see Mateelians wearing, the presence of treadle sewing machines in Mateelian homes and the traffic in them evidenced by bulletin board and classified ads, the number of women who carry around their knitting, spinning, weaving, crocheting, and sewing, the expansion of the fabric department at the local department store after the influx of countercultural people in 1970, the length of time an additional fabric store was able to stay in business, and the prevalence of clothing that could only have been designed by the wearer.

It is reasonable to state that Mateelians choose long-term quality over either quantity or current fashion in their consumption of clothing. They might spend more, for instance, on an imported Guatemalan poncho than an Amerikan would on a fashionable new coat, but it is with the anticipation of wearing the poncho for the next twenty years, rather than buying a new coat in two years when the fashion is passé. Mateelians generally do not buy clothes according to the dictates of mainstream fashion, but according to the dictates of their own fashion. Some statistics on income and home production of food and shelter, derived from the HEBQ, are summarized in Table 3.

Producing one's own needs is, of course, dependent on learning the skills involved and this was a major undertaking for urban people raised on television. Many of my informants have, in retrospect, wondered if they would have been able to do what they did if they had realized at the beginning just how little they knew. What they don't realize is that the economic strategies here described are as much a function of deep-seated psychological tinkering as they are of learning specific production skills. The redefinition of needs applied also to learning to use what could be produced. If one cannot produce a house, one learns to use an available shed. If one cannot produce potatoes, one learns to like Jerusalem artichokes. If one cannot raise a steer, one becomes a vegetarian. The flexibility that resulted from discontinuity had its effects in the economic aspects of the new culture as well as in the purely philosophical and social.

History of a Commune

The economic history of one commune illustrates the way in which the four strategies discussed, lowering consumption, scavenging, adaptive institutions, and producing, as well as communal ideals and experience, made the transition from a commune to a smaller economic unit of partners practicing small-scale capitalism. It also

	HEBQ (1985)	Gbv (1980)	Frn (1980)	Hum (1980)
Mean Annual Income		$14,719	$19,429	$15,184
-$5,000	12%	23%	16%	
5-9,999	7	22	21	
10-14,999	19	14	12	
15-24,999	12	23	23	
25-49,999	38	15	20	
50,000+	3	.02	.4	
Median Income		$11,332	$14,590	
Per Capita Income		5,909	7,342	
Households w/ earnings	38%	79.3%	80.0%	
Public Funds	7	32	34	
Crafts/Services:	50			
% of income from craft or service	43			
Cash Crop:	50			
% of households w/ single source of income:	34			
cash crop	22			
craft/service	22			
earnings	44			
% persons below poverty level		21.8	14.8	
Per Cent 75% below		15.2	9.7	
125% below		28.4	19.6	
150% below		35.5	27.0	
200% below		45.1	35.9	

HEBQ=Household Energy Budget Questionnaire (see Methodology)
Gbv=Garberville Census District, includes Mateelians and non-Mateelians
Frn=Ferndale Census District, adjacent to Garberville Census District
Hum=Humboldt County as a whole, includes Garberville and Ferndale Census Districts
Note: Differences between Ferndale and Garberville in percentage figures probably reflect the presence of the Mateel community.

Table 3. Financial Status

provides some sense of how the four strategies integrate with each other and communal values and how the economic behavior of Mateelians evolved over time. It should be noted that, in contrast to the communes of the nineteenth century, and late twentieth century communal cults such as the People's Temple or the followers of Bagwhan Sri Rajneesh, there was never a central leader or much structure of any kind in this commune. Everything was done in compliance with the dictates of magical anarchy.

The commune began in Minnesota as a loosely associated group with no more structured a plan than an agreement to "be a commune." The group, which varied in number, but was usually about ten people, started out as a rock band and light show. They lived in one large house, shared rent, food expenses, labor and profits from performances. Individuals generally retained personal possessions, in contrast to rigidly structured communes that require that all personal possessions go into a common pool. When personal possessions were donated to the commune, it was voluntary. One member sold his motorcycle in order to buy a school bus to transport the band.

When a group decision was made to leave Minnesota, the commune held a large rummage sale in order to reduce the number of items to be hauled in the bus and to generate travelling money. Proceeds from the sale of individual possessions went into the general travelling fund. The commune ended up, after an eventful journey, in an old bunkhouse on a ranch near Miranda, California. The rent was paid in labor on the ranch. Food came from a communal garden, food stamps, barter, and donations. The number of people fluctuated widely, and was often swelled to the breaking point by travellers who exchanged labor for a safe place to stay. The location of the bunkhouse immediately off a freeway exit did nothing to slow up the flow of visitors.

During this period of time the core members of the commune established a relationship with the ranch owners that was common in the early days of the Mateel community and is still to be found today. The preceding decade of general economic decline had disrupted the intergenerational continuity of the local mainstream population as local young people abandoned the area in search of a better economic scene. Ranching tended to be an enterprise characteristic of older people. Many local ranchers initially perceived the urban refugees as simpletons who would buy worthless land foolishly thinking they could make a living on it. They soon found that their farming and ranching experience, which may have been considered outdated and of little value by their own children, partly because it related to organic methods, was considered by the newcomers to be a great source of wisdom. Many discovered, perhaps in spite of themselves, that if they were bewildered by the strange appearance, social arrangements and sexual behavior of the newcomers, they had to admire their persistence and eagerness to learn the old techniques.

The commune, with the aid of the Miranda ranching couple, was soon learning the basics of organic gardening, poultry raising, goat and dairy cattle raising, carpentry and food preservation. The commune survived a total of six years, from Minnesota to Miranda. Gradually however, it began to disintegrate by attrition. The membership fluctuated widely during the California period, sometimes as many as twenty or thirty people were staying in the bunkhouse, with its addition built from recycled redwood, or around the yard in buses, vans, and campers. An indication of the relative poverty experienced by the group is that at one point some of the original members, discouraged by the lack of cash, returned to Minnesota in the school bus. They hoped to work for a year and return with savings, perhaps to invest in land. The move was not successful, and the returnees came back to California after a year, minus some who stayed in Minnesota. They were as poor as they had started.

The commune gradually was reduced to four partners, two couples, living in the bunkhouse. Their economic status was fairly typical of pre-marijuana Mateelians. Income was derived from a cash crop of organically grown corn and tomatoes, sold to local retail stores and co-ops. Spare parts and junk from the junk pile created by the hundreds of visiting travellers from the commune days was also bartered and sold. The partnership made candles and sold them at fairs and to retail stores located as far as 100 miles away. Outside sources of income included food stamps and MediCal (California State Medical Insurance), but there were no other outside inputs. Rent was still paid with labor. Overhead was kept low through continuing redefinition of needs. Appliance and automobile repairs were either done at home or without. Electricity from public utilities was used sparingly, for light and refrigeration but not for heating either water or space. These were both heated with wood, as was the cook stove. Food not produced was purchased in bulk from food co-operatives. Cigarette smokers rolled their own. Baking soda was used for toothpaste. Clothing came from the free box; furnishings, from the dump.

A certain amount of input came from what one might loosely call hunting and gathering. Huckleberry sprigs were gathered from the ranch and sold to a middleman for use by florists—an enterprise tried by many early Mateelians. Firewood was gathered on the ranch as part of the rental arrangement and sawed by hand. Protein intake was sometimes enhanced by the collection of road-kill deer from the nearby freeway, although no one had the skill or equipment to actually go hunting. Fish, a common item of exchange, were obtainable from the nearby Eel River. Generalized reciprocity also helped hold down the overhead. Travellers still exchanged labor, food, tools, and sometimes cash for a safe place to stay. Hitchhiking was easy because of the location near the freeway. Exchanges of garden vegetables, eggs, fish and crafts were common, the latter filling aesthetic needs and maintaining the spirit of reciprocity with other Mateelians and craftspeople in general. Only two items were ever stolen, and then from large institutions—toilet paper and light bulbs.[4]

The partnership lasted for another two years and then broke down into separate nuclear families who subsequently became allied with other nuclear families in the land partnership arrangement. The evolution from communes to nuclear families allied in a land partnership seems to be a common fate for communes in Mateel. Lamented by many as a loss of communal ideals, this process can be interpreted as the natural outcome of the incompatibility between the two values of individualism and communism. The kind of tribal communism so admired by Mateelians is just too difficult to achieve in one generation by people so heavily enculturated with values that directly oppose it. Communal values are painstakingly taught to children, however, and the possibility of a rise in communalism in the next generation should not be dismissed.

Amerika

The Mateelian economic system differs from the Amerikan in the kind of unit involved. The Amerikan economic unit used to be the nuclear family, which included a reproductive couple and their offspring and had a clear division of labor between the sexes. In recent times, this economic unit has increasingly become a single working parent and her/his offspring, and the sexual division of labor has become less clear-cut. Nevertheless, the one or two parent nuclear family is still overwhelmingly the Amerikan norm.

The Mateelian economic unit is experimental. Nuclear families abound, but may be in a more or less communal or co-operative relationship with each other as land partners. Extended families, fictive and otherwise, are on the increase as retired parents move into Mateel and become more or less co-operatively involved with their children and grandchildren, and as children grow up and marry but stay economically involved with the parent's farm. This extended or nuclear family may include any number of unrelated individuals, foster children, current lovers of unmarried adolescents, or single landless adults who exchange labor for the right to build a cabin or camp out on the land. There are several households composed of unrelated people who define themselves as family. This arrangement has special advantages for male and female homosexuals and for single parents. The Mateelian sexual division of labor is based purely on physiological limitations and personal preferences rather than on traditional expectations. Families where the male supports the family through his job or profession and the woman cares for children and produces and processes food, appear to be in the minority.

Another possible way in which the Mateelian economic system differs from the Amerikan is that Mateelians rely much less on credit spending. This is perhaps because of the strong urge to self-reliance and the perceived connection between economic dependency and personal freedom, but it may also be because most Mateelians are precluded from getting credit by the fact that they cannot show a definite source of income. Amerikan credit is based on numbers on paper—wages, dividends, income tax returns. The economic system here described is nearly impossible to translate into terms understandable to the computers of Amerikan bureaucracies, even if there were no illegal cash crops involved.

Credit spending has been described as present oriented, in the Amerikan sense that the distant future is unreal, whereas savings are future oriented.[5] The economic behavior of Mateelians inclines to neither credit nor savings, but to investment in the home system. Mateelians buy land on credit because they have no choice. They recognize that land may be their only means of survival given the terminal quality of the physical environment in general. Improvements and farm equipment tend to be paid for with cash and surplus cash to be quickly invested in these tangible items rather than in savings accounts, or in stocks in non-local businesses. This tendency expresses a perception of the American economy as unstable because it is based on constant growth, a reluctance to be involved in large, remote institutions, and a refusal to support interests that are seen as probably exploiting third world peoples and destroying the environment.

Local credit, however, is often extended by owners of local businesses, mainstream and Mateelian, on the basis of personal reputation. Mateelian organizations do not extend credit, even to their own founders, because they must deal with all comers on an egalitarian basis. It is truly an ironic consequence of the Mateelian love of fairness and equality that long standing committed members of the community are not extended credit on the basis of the reputations they established by founding Mateelian institutions. This inability to socially reward community service by accepting personal reputation over Amerikan computer-based credit ratings is one example of the way impersonal Amerikan premises preclude community solidarity. It is reassuring on this score, however, that the high level of reciprocity and personal credit from local businesses replaces Amerikan credit as much as it appears to.

Ecotopia

The economic behavior of Mateelians increasingly approximates Ecotopian standards. There is an emphasis on local self-sufficiency, even though Mateelians, like anyone else, will purchase items in Eureka if they can cut the distribution costs added to non-local items. It is my impression that Mateelians would rather deal with other Mateelians, if only because they can get local credit and because they have the ultimate sanction of public opinion if the quality of goods or services comes into question.

Experimentation is in full-force for local economic bases. Resistance is well-organized and vocal against the introduction of large industries, chain retailers or any corporate entity likely to operate on Amerikan economic principles that might endanger the environment, be questionable aesthetically, or send more money out of the area than wages from these entities might bring in. Interest in planning the future of southern Humboldt County is rapidly rising among Mateelians and the main area of contrast between them and local Amerikans is their differing conceptions of the economic future of the area. Mateelians are becoming aware of the limitations imposed on their collective environmental and economic planning by their subordinate political position. Mateelians will be able to implement Ecotopian economic strategies, including the development of locally owned, environmentally sound industries and services, to the degree that they are able to develop a political strategy compatible with their ideals.

Summary

The Mateelian economic unit may be anything from a nuclear family to an extended family with many fictive members, to land partnerships with varying degrees of economic co-operation to actual small communes. Large communes or communes with rigid structures tend to be incompatible with the Mateelian context and to leave after a few years. Small communes tend to break down or redefine themselves as extended families in partnership, after a period of residence in Mateel. The economic base of these units tends to be diverse and to vary widely in the percentage of income derived from wages, cash crops, crafts, services and outside sources. Four major social adaptations enable Mateelians to live on less than their Amerikan counterparts: lowering consumption, scavenging, developing more adaptive social institutions, and becoming producers.

These adaptations were made possible by the change in consciousness that accompanied the philosophical and economic dropout. They resemble in some ways the economic adaptations of primitive societies and involve the primitive economic characteristics of reciprocity and redistribution.

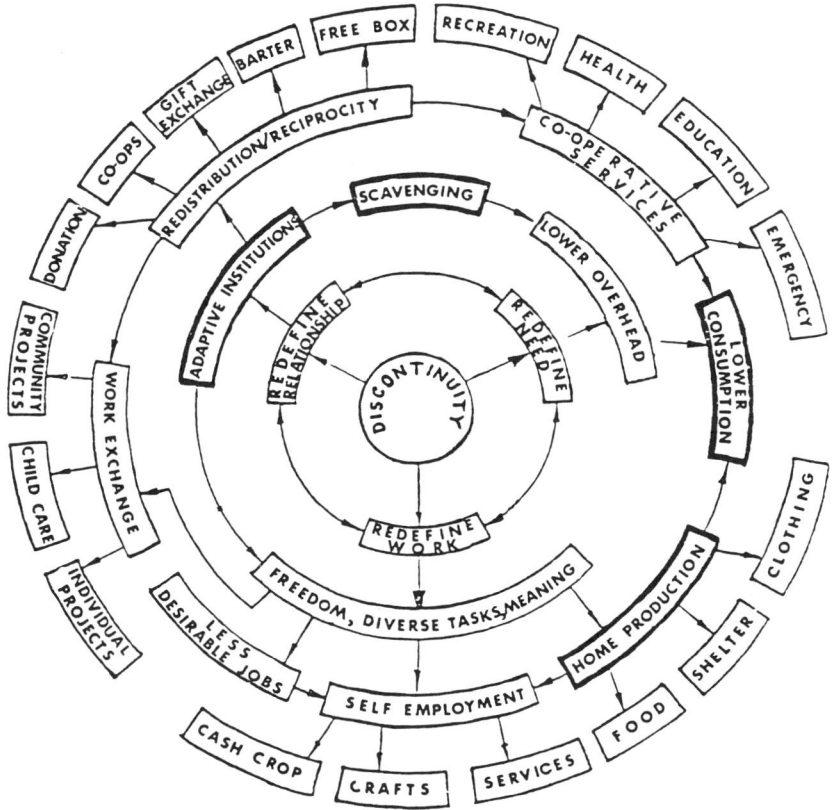

Figure 7. Mateelian Economic Relationships

The relationships between the redefinitions involved in the discontinuity experience, the four strategies, and their implementation are diagrammed in Figure 7. Causality originates in the center with the philosophical and economic aspects of the discontinuity experience. Each circle represents a step in the sequence of events leading to current economic behavior. Arrows represent lines of causality. Because of the discontinuity experience, Amerikan conceptions of what constitutes work, needs and relationships were redefined. Because of the redefinition of need, overhead is reduced. As status is redefined, the motivation to accept a high status but meaningless, dull and rigidly scheduled job is lowered, and the possibility of using recycled items is raised. Redefinition of status also eliminates status maintenance from social interaction, which raises the effectiveness of reciprocity and redistribution and opens up the possibilities of scavenging and recycling. Redefining work to include activities that are necessary to survival but do not produce cash, opens up the possibility of economic diversity based on combinations of low status jobs, self-employment, home production and work exchanges. The three major redefinitions all involve each other. If you need less, you can earn less money. If you no longer care about status in relationships, you can change your conception of work. Changing the conception of work creates a status system based on usefulness. For relationships based on such a status system one does not need status symbols, and so on.

Given the great publicity that has been devoted to marijuana cultivation in Humboldt County in the last decade, it would be misleading to paint a picture of Mateelian economic behavior without explaining how the description given here relates to the marijuana boom. Although various cash crops have been tried in Mateel, including gourds, garlic, tomatoes, fir trees and grapes, the inflated price of marijuana, which is due to its illegality, has insured that other possible cash crops cannot approach the potential profit of marijuana. Mateelians, however, incorporated marijuana into their already existing economic diversity, using the profits to build houses, to expand needed community services, and to improve or buy land. Such land is often purchased for no other reason than to preserve it from the ravages of logging or marijuana agribusiness or to have complete control over who will move in next door. This latter is not bigotry but survival instinct, since the marijuana boom has drawn so many violent outsiders to the area. To the degree that it can be assumed that land prices will continue to rise, these purchases of land could be considered financial investments. However, the assumption of continuing rise in land value is risky, since it is based on marijuana-caused inflation.

Aside from the wild spending that accompanied some families' first crop or two, marijuana money has generally been seen by Mateelians as a source of capital for investment into the continuing development of diverse economic bases. The profit from marijuana has financed water and irrigation systems to be used for food production, as well as barns, fences, housing, farm vehicles, livestock, solar and water twelve-volt electrical systems, fruit and nut trees, seeds, improved roads, trout ponds, numerous economic experiments, and community projects. Medical needs such as contact lenses, dental work, physical therapy, and psychological treatment, simply unmet before, were also purchased. Many income-producing businesses, crafts and professional educations were financed in part by marijuana. A shift to monocropping of marijuana has never been seen as a permanent economic solution by most Mateelians, but as a chance to get capital to finance their experimental life-style, to help establish alternative service institutions and to finance political—largely environmental—causes.

It is true that individual families and persons were diverted from other economic pursuits for their first few harvests, some even losing it all in wild spending on cocaine, vacations and motel rooms in town. It is my observation, however, that this was always a minority of resident Mateelians, that the media contributed greatly to the misconception of this behavior as typical of Mateelians by failing to discriminate between the countercultural and other growers. Steve Chapple's 1984 book, *Outlaws in Babylon*, is an example of this unfortunate confusion.[6] For the vast majority of Mateelians who were diverted from other economic pursuits by sudden money, it was a temporary distraction from which they soon recovered.

The post-marijuana economy, resulting from an increase in available capital, has resulted in a proliferation of small businesses and of services. Full-time employment at traditional nine to five jobs is still almost unheard of. Part-time, temporary, and self-employment, however, rise and fall with the availability of circulating money. At present, the negative social consequences of marijuana growing such as CAMP, locked gates, inflation and the influx of violent non-

Mateelians, have prompted widespread reduction in dependence on marijuana, re-establishment of food-producing efforts and a surge in efforts to find a better economic base for the area, as well as efforts to legalize marijuana. One new enterprise is wine making from the products of grapevines planted a decade ago. Locally produced wines have won prizes at the Humboldt County fair and are sold in local liquor stores. Some persons have also begun an alternative tourist industry, guiding tourists on local pack or canoe trips, one group complete with llamas imported from Peru. Health related services have soared. Many small Mateelian businesses have become stable and expect to remain in business indefinitely.

A disturbing economic trend accompanying marijuana cultivation is the shift towards a peasant economy complete with absentee landlords, tenant farmers, and stratification based on money. The inflation that accompanied the marijuana boom exacerbated the lingering Amerikan tendency toward stratification based on money, re-creating many of the social problems that accompany such inequality. Mateelians, differing from the early descriptions of the counterculture as middle class, derive from all classes and ethnic backgrounds. They had just begun to really tackle the basics of stratification within themselves, such as differential class-based cultural perceptions, when the boom hit. A curious reversal of Amerikan stratification resulted.

For a while the formerly middle-class, who had deliberately become the "nouveau poor," were not sympathetic with the eagerness of the formerly working class to become "nouveau riche." The sudden influx of money had revealed the old class lines in reverse. A certain spiritual snobbery appeared, with formerly middle-class non-growers castigating the "greed" displayed by formerly working class growers who, they maintained, were destroying the community by growing marijuana. The formerly working class growers pointed out that the only way they could hope to get land for the implementation of a new, improved life-style was by growing marijuana, since they had no inheritances, educations, professions, or savings to use. It made for a complex picture with regard to the implementation of the ideal of equality, resembling somewhat the position of Amerikan environmentalists *vis á vis* Amerikan labor or development in the

Third World. It was not long, however, before most of the "nouveau poor" were also growing, putting them in an untenable position to discuss greed. The clouding of the stratification picture produced by the marijuana boom makes it difficult to say if progress will continue toward the elimination of class-based biases.

In the case of resident Mateelians, this shift towards a peasant economy and its attendant stratification appears to have slowed, with the basic preferences for equality, diversity and self-reliance usually overriding the temptation to set up a plantation-like situation complete with low-status and/or immigrant workers. Nevertheless, enough resident Mateelians have gone in this direction, there has been a sufficient influx of non-resident growers and enough "locals" are growing to raise the possibility that southern Humboldt County may make itself vulnerable to all of the disadvantages of a peasant economy.

Mateelians, through their four economic strategies, have greatly diversified the number of ways to meet needs. They scavenge, hunt and gather, and produce, in addition to variations on the standard work-for-cash exchange. This pattern of diversity has every indication of stabilizing and continuing to move slowly in the direction of home production of needs. Whereas individual economic units are unlikely to achieve the complete economic self-sufficiency of the primitive band, the community as a whole will be able to become increasingly self-sufficient to the degree that economic diversity is preserved and the four economic strategies remain in force.

A Mateelian owner-builder inside his home.

Chapter Nine

Social Interaction

Don't let the past remind you of what you are not now.

—*Crosby, Stills, Nash, and Young*

Society may be seen as a sort of drama in which the actors have been taught from infancy to play their several roles. This learning process, called enculturation, is the result of learning by example from "role models." It is also the result of formal education, which instructs children in the ideal tradition of the culture. More subtly, the learning of roles takes place in ridicule, punishment, or failure to be recognized as a legitimate claimant to the role. The more traditional the society, the more roles complement each other. If a wife is expected to grow yams for the family, then her husband is expected to provide meat. If one is expected to be obedient, the other is expected to command.

By adulthood, most people in any society have acquired deep seated assumptions about the proper behavior for a mother, son, teacher, or leader, and individuals are expected to play their roles properly or accept the consequences. The expectations and assumptions accruing to each role have become so habitual, or unconscious, or internalized, that most individuals play their roles properly without thinking about it, displaying personal characteristics only within the limits of the role they are playing at the time. It is only when personal deviations become noticeable to others that the limits of the role become conscious to the actor. A question such as, "what kind of mother are you," then serves as a reprimand to bring the deviant back into line.

In complex, rapidly changing societies, there are many more roles, there is less agreement on how they are to be played, and they complement each other less. Yet, even industrialized societies, depending on how strongly their citizens cling to tradition, are composed of interlocking roles and the expectations that go along with them. Change in any society necessarily involves changing the conscious and subconscious assumptions that define its roles. Either the expectations change in response to economic or historical forces or the actors become conscious of the limitations of the roles, refuse to play them as expected, and are indifferent to the consequences of their actions.

The counterculture was a massive exercise in refusal of social roles. Women refused to be wives, men refused to be soldiers, college students refused to become professionals, and everyone refused to be anything without redefining it. "Hell no, we won't go" applied to more than potential draftees. It defined the very essence of "dropping out." It should be remembered that, what here is called the discontinuity experience consists of individual psychological changes, usually induced by mind-altering substances, and physical actions involved in dropping out.[1]

To understand the characteristic Mateelian form of social interaction, which is at the heart of all Mateel's institutions, it is necessary to examine the discontinuity experience. Although it has been widely perceived in the mainstream culture as a destructive process, it has in fact cleared the way for individuals to recreate their conceptions of themselves or, in psychological terms, of the self. Most Mateelians were originally enculturated as Amerikans. When they began to experience discontinuity, they had been as influenced as anyone else by whatever forces in Amerikan society shape personality.

One of the forces mentioned frequently by writers on the American character is conformity. That conformity exists side by side with the high value placed on individuality is one of the most instructive paradoxes of Amerikan culture. One social scientist, Francis

Hsu, explains this paradox as follows: the extreme of individualism is self reliance, the belief that "every individual is his own master, in control of his own destiny, and will advance and regress in society only according to his own efforts." The more this view is accepted, the more the importance of other individuals is denied, except insofar as they affect one's advancement. Widespread insecurity is the result, and this becomes the source of perpetual competition, conformity, and submission to authority in order to get ahead. Hsu also sees self-reliance as the source of racism and classism, which are efforts to put others down in order to keep one's own position in society stable.[2]

Charles Reich's description of the early counterculture, in *The Greening of America*, includes an illuminating discussion of American conformity, one that rings true in Mateel. He sees the conformist personality as fitting neatly into the technocracy as consumer and worker. This personality type is produced by an education that ignores huge chunks of individual potential and demands the abandonment of aspects of Self "that are of no utility for production or consumption in the Corporate State." The resulting self-image is based primarily on occupation, and as in his analysis, life is seen as the maintenance of a position on a scale of relative positions rather than as living-in-process. Such things as aesthetic sense, love of nature, passion for music, desire for reflection, or strongly marked independence are discouraged, especially in public elementary and secondary schools, where much of the personality is formed.[3] This view of the role of education in producing conformist, authority-following, incomplete personalities is supported by the findings of many social scientists who have studied the American school system. Reich calls the result a "role-self" or "substitute self."[5] Slater calls it a "false-self" which is schizoid, promoted by technological culture "even in the absence of individual pathology," and unavoidable, given the current educational philosophy.[6]

Characteristic of this false-self personality is its reliance on factors external to the individual. Citizens of the technological society ". . . eat, sleep, awaken, work and stop work when mechanical contrivances tell them it is time to do so." Objects are evaluated in terms of their relationship to money and status, rather than their uniqueness or usefulness.[7] Jules Henry, in speaking of education, remarks that Americans "do not cultivate a Self but rather a living standard." In the absence of a stable personal community, he observes, there is no way to evaluate oneself except by external criteria such as material possessions or school grades.[8] Slater makes a point particularly relevant to the discussion of externalities. He claims that no adult relationships can be experienced that have not been "previewed and rehearsed" in the media, an observation one assumes applies particularly to the television generation, part of which became the counterculture.[9]

Sociologist Erving Goffman has written on how these false identities are maintained in everyday interaction. His book, *Stigma*, deals with how social interaction is affected by deeply discrediting attributes that make individuals different from others.[10] These stigmas may be visible or invisible. Visible stigmas include handicaps, race, nationality and religion. Invisible stigmas are inferred from known records of mental disorders, imprisonment, addiction, alcoholism, homosexuality, unemployment, suicide attempts, and radical political behavior. Both kinds require the stigmatized person to employ particular interactional strategies that serve to manage the tension resulting from visible stigmas and to conceal invisible ones.

Marijuana use is considered an addiction in the mainstream view. Therefore this one characteristic places virtually everyone who participates in the Mateelian cultural system into Goffman's definition of the stigmatized. For most Mateelians, however, marijuana use was not the only stigma they found it necessary to deal with and, in fact, many may have originally started using marijuana in an attempt to deal with some other stigma. Many were non-conformist enough to be unemployed and unemployable even before they experienced marijuana. Many had already been defined by their families or high school peer groups as "crazy," because of some radical political stance, such as being pro-integration or against nuclear weapons. Freethinking women engaged in destroying the sexual double standard may have been defined as "whores." Deviations from sexual roles, such as female assertiveness or male sensitivity, then and now, may be considered evidence for homosexuality. Given the emphasis on conformity in Amerika, any high school student who tried to retain those aspects of personality Reich lists as excluded was and is likely to be called a misfit.

Stigmas are relative; everyone deviates from role expectations to some extent. Therefore Goffman's games for the stigmatized are sooner or later played by everyone. These games lead to shame, acceptance of a "resident alien" self, and self-destroying inner conflict over whether to reveal the stigma or to identify with others with the same stigma. At the very least, they inspire ambivalence about one's Self.[11] A major game strategy used by the stigmatized is separation of the social world into different groups to which one reveals or from which one conceals the stigma.[12] Another strategy is to break complete with conventional "reality," redefine the stigma, and give it an unconventional interpretation.

Stating the Stigma

One of the major complaints of the counterculture against Amerikan culture was hypocrisy.[14] To participants in the counterculture, the hiding of stigmas, the playing of self-negating games, was a major flaw in Amerikan culture. An early phase in the discontinuity experience was to perceive the self-hatred one had nurtured by accepting the games. The next step was to learn to love one's complete Self and retrieve the lost and atrophied psychological parts in order to create a Self one could love. The first step in doing this was "coming out of the closet"—stating the stigma. The lyrics of many popular songs of the 1960s reflect this theme:

> "Everybody's got something to hide, but me and my monkey"
> —the Beatles

> "Eleanor Rigby wearing the face that she keeps in a jar by the door"
> —the Beatles

> "One thing you can't hide, is when you're crippled inside"
> —the Beatles

> "Even the president of the United States sometimes must have to stand naked"—Bob Dylan

Reich's rejected personality potentials may be read as a list of stigmas revealed in Mateelian culture. Everywhere there are artists, musicians, independent thinkers, introspective hermits, and passionate lovers of nature whose society not only gives them free rein to retrieve these parts of themselves. What infuriated Amerika about the counterculture, and still infuriates some local Amerikans about Mateelians, is that they flamboyantly state their personal identity in everything they do. They adamantly refuse to return to a self-hating mode of interaction by concealing anything short of what is required for survival in a non-Mateelian world.

For so many individuals to attain this degree of psychological insight is remarkable. Historical factors, such as the Vietnam War, the Civil Rights Movement, and the nuclear threat surely set the stage for it. The fact that it occurred in a modern industrial society, where massive scale and rapid change had made social roles vague and anonymity easy certainly played a role.[15] Nevertheless, without widespread use of psychedelics and marijuana, the counterculture world might not have grown, as it did, from the deepest levels of consciousness. In terms of identity, what these substances did was:

1. to reveal with preverbal clarity one's stigma and one's strategies to conceal it
2. to provide an instant stigma to anyone short on them
3. to provide, because of the necessity of obtaining illegal substances from friends to avoid arrest, an instant support group of people sharing the same stigma.

The "false-Self," "substitute Self," stigma-managing Self, and alien resident Self became, for many, too unwieldy to maintain after the discontinuity experience. To understand why, it is necessary to look more closely at the particulars of the psychedelic and marijuana experience.

In 1968, psychologist Charles Tart conducted a study that broke with previous research on psychedelic and marijuana use. Operating on the hypothesis that the effects of these substances were greatly influenced by the factors of context, environment and degree of experience in using them, he sought out experienced marijuana users and used a questionnaire to solicit descriptions of their experiences. Tart made no effort to establish anything clinical about the marijuana experience, relying completely on users' descriptions. In addition to that strategy, what makes his study unique is that he only studied people who had learned to use the herb and who used it in a setting completely under their own control.[16] These aspects of

Tart's research make it particularly useful in the present context. Most people who use marijuana or psychedelics do not do so in rigidly controlled scientific laboratory settings which clearly influence the experience of the subject. How marijuana may have affected the everyday lives of long-term regular users and how it may have affected the culture they created are sociological questions. To answer them, Tart's sociological approach elicited the most applicable information.

Tart's sample consisted of 150 predominantly young, highly educated and idealistic California college students and professionals. They had a high interest in self improvement, considerable experience with other psychedelics and little with narcotics. They all used marijuana once a week or more.[17]

The implied goal of Mateelian society is the exploration and maintenance of higher consciousness. The perceptive changes described by Tart's informants are important in understanding Mateel because they formed the basis for this conception. A collective image of higher consciousness in turn affects social relations because it is the primary value around which interaction is oriented. Not only did marijuana assist Mateelians in stating the stigma, but it influenced the form of social interaction in general. The state of consciousness attained through the use of psychedelics and marijuana was seen as preferable to ordinary consciousness. Social relations should, therefore, encourage and support the individual in finding ways to remain in this state of consciousness as much as possible, with or without the use of these substances.

The use of mind-altering substances established this basic principle of interaction, that the obligations of a relationship should sustain, rather than resist, spiritual growth. Also important to the formation of Mateelian interaction were basic changes in the perception of Self and relationships with others. That part of the marijuana experience reported by Tart's informants in which one is incapable of small talk was incorporated into Mateelian assumptions about relationship as a high value on honesty, or real statements about one's Self.[18] Mateelian small talk exists, but tends to move quickly beyond the trivial. What Tart's informants reported about the effect of marijuana on their sense of identity reverses directly stigma concealment strategies, as well as the struggle for relative position on the social ladder.[19] At low levels of intoxication marijuana users reported a "childlike openness to experience in contrast to the classification of people and events by their importance to us." At higher levels, the individual may lose the sense of identity altogether and feel that the individual ego is replaced by archetypal feelings of oneness with the world.[20]

Attitudes toward one's body are important to concept of Self.[21] One common experience of Tart's informants was a changed perception of their bodies. Unless they employed techniques to focus attention on the body, it seemed that they had left it completely. However, if attention was focused properly, they reported the perception of internal workings of their organs, which would normally be inaccessible. If they moved around, they felt much more graceful, beautiful and in control. These effects were so widespread and profound that Tart sees them as potentially important "to psychosomatic medicine and the study of the relationship of identity to the body."[22]

Mateelians did not wait for scientific studies, but accepted their own knowledge in this area of psychedelics and incorporated it into their theories of medicine. In fact, folk medicine plays an important part in the life of Mateelians. For instance, they attach enormous importance to natural childbirth, home births, and midwifery. This is directly related to the belief in personal access to "involuntary" bodily processes. One of the original reasons for the establishment of the Redwoods Rural Health Center in Redway was to incorporate therapeutics based on this belief into an otherwise standard program. Two of the original members of the Board of Directors were the parents of a child born with a defective heart and given less than a week to live by the mainstream doctors who examined him. Defying the experts, the parents kept the child alive for four years, helping to start the RRHC while they did it, in response to the negative and purely technical attitude of the mainstream medical establishment.

A holistic conception of the body as one part of a system that includes mind and spirit is common in Mateel, as one may ascertain by simply looking at a Mateelian bulletin board. There are always classes being given in such Eastern methods of body consciousness training as Hatha Yoga, T'ai Chi, Tai Kwan Do, and Aikido, as well as in psychic healing, hypnotherapy, massage, Lamaze childbirth, and visualizing. Experts in acupuncture, acupressure, polarity therapy, rolfing and rebirthing abound. The presence of a college in Mateel with curriculum that is entirely composed of courses in such alternative healing methods partly explains this abundance of alternative healers. Whether the presence of the Mateel community had anything to do with the location of Heartwood College in southern Humboldt County is difficult to ascertain. However, when marijuana money made it possible for Mateelians to pursue educational matters, many went directly to Heartwood College to learn these skills, indicating the high value placed on them by many members of the community.

Dancing is also a route to body-knowledge. Every kind of dance is taught in Mateel—aerobics, jazz, African traditional, folk, Middle Eastern, classical ballet, square, and contra dancing. Mateelian dances or "boogies" are minimally structured, so that any person of any age, sexual orientation, or marital status can dance in any style or in any kind of grouping. This lack of formal structure maximizes the potential for individuals to experiment with body movement unrestrained by such conventions as the need for a partner, the kind of dance one "does" to a particular kind of music, or the assumption that a person dancing alone is necessarily transmitting a sexual message.

Charles Tart reports that for most of his informants, this apparent increase in perception of the body greatly influenced the sex act. Most people reported a feeling of merging with the lover in an experience of archetypal significance. In Tart's words:

> Instead of John Smith and Mary Jones making it in John's apartment in California on a particular night, Man and Woman Blend Together, in Now and Eternity, Here and Everywhere, an integral part of the Blending of Maleness and Femaleness of the Universe.[23]

For women, especially, a changed perception of and attitude toward the body was important to a changed Self-identity. Coming to terms with sexual freedom and its implications to the female self-images was for many Mateelian women the largest part of learning to accept and love themselves as women. One overwhelming fact governs female experience that does not govern male experience, even in the age of technological miracles, and that is that women have babies. The "sixties" woman who pursued individual freedom first had to deal with sexual freedom. The sexual double standard had to be questioned in the individual female life. Her first step toward self-realization was to take back from men the right to control her own reproductive activities. Modern birth control made this enterprise somewhat less risky than it had been in the past, but it did not come near making women as free as men to rediscover sexuality. They still were forced by biological reality to face basic social necessities, such as who is going to make a home for the children.

The fact that no birth control method except abstinence is perfect or without risk, turned out to be inescapable. This fact, combined with the countercultural distrust of modern technology and scientific experts, made many methods of birth control unacceptable to women who sought a more natural life. The desire to live a life as naturally as possible meant that countercultural females rapidly became mothers, and mothering conflicts directly with the kind of existential, on-the-road freedom at that time being touted by men. There arose a basic difference in male and female conceptions of freedom, freedom being an essential part of changing one's self-image. The newborn crying baby who just emerged from one's body cannot be left behind, as pregnant women can, for existential adventures on-the-road.

Two things happened to interaction as a result of this. Fathers were forced to look closely at their individualistic "freedom" and what it implied for the mothers of their children. Motherhood, which starts at conception, is highly social and dependent, and requires a modicum of permanence and security. Some Mateelian men at this point incorporated child rearing, stability, and homemaking into their conception of the proper male role. Others continued to see parenthood as confinement and women as people who could never really understand freedom. Women gradually recognized that existentialist freedom was a male concept and eliminated the necessity of it from their self image. It was only when women could see themselves as both mothering and free, rather than as a burden to male-defined freedom, that the stigma of being female could be stated. Carole King's lyrics said it well: "One more song about moving along the highway can't say much of anything that's new."

Trained by their Amerikan experience to compete with each other for men, women now found that many Mateelian males were on-the-road being free—if not literally then figuratively. That is when women spontaneously recognized their need for each other. Forced by motherhood to recognize their dependency, they could relate to each other from more tribal self images. The rise of female self-acceptance, solidarity and "consciousness" in Mateel is phenomenal. The bonds created by women helping each other give birth and mother, organizing play groups, schools, and child care exchanges to share the responsibility and provide early social training for children, are among the strongest unifying forces in Mateel.

The psychological process just described is by no means an accomplished fact for everyone. The social confusion caused by women breaking free from both mainstream and male countercultural role expectations is one of the strongest tensions in Mateelian society. This tension is evidenced by the diversity of female role models available and by the need for some women to go to apparent extremes to rid themselves of the last vestiges of a female role created to meet male needs. For some women, the hazards of relinquishing male-defined freedom and seeking a holistic self-image incorporating femaleness are so great that it can only be done by forfeiting, temporarily or forever, all intimate contact with men. The Lesbian community is active, open, and extremely supportive to women whose personal journey has led them from men. For those who have not come to this point, other female networks have developed that express the value of female solidarity and the ideal of a society in which male and female values are more balanced. Exclusively female religious, dance and music groups find that this kind of female non-verbal communication fulfills a female social need without necessitating a break from men. Women's therapy or "consciousness-raising" groups also serve this purpose.

The female exploration of and redefinition of Self, then, is an especially dramatic illustration of the changed self-image. Another example of the changed self-image as reflected in changed attitudes toward the body is provided by an informant, who when asked at a popular swimming hole why she lived in Mateel, replied "Are you kidding? Where else could I take off my clothes, smoke a joint and go swimming with my friends?" One of Raphael's informants echoes these sentiments:

> I can . . . walk out my door in the middle of summer stark naked, smoking a doobie [marijuana cigarette], and walk two miles in any direction without running into anybody who's going to mind. That's my barometer of freedom![24]

Nudity and marijuana are both seen as symbols for freedom of personal expression and consciousness by Mateelians. The function of clothing in Mateel has to do with the physical environment and artistic expression more than with status or modesty. Removing it as an adjustment to heat or for swimming is considered natural. This is in definite contrast to the Amerikan concept of nudity as either a component of sex or something "weirdos" do in special camps created for that purpose. Given the enormous emphasis on sexiness and physical appearance in Amerikan culture, the enormous anxiety created by the advertising industry regarding personal appearance and the importance of one's body as a component of self-image, there could be no clearer statement of the reversal of Amerikan stigma-concealment than the acceptance of one's body expressed by group nudity. That swimming holes, hot tubs or social gatherings on a hot day include people in every stage of undress who are old, fat, thin, tattooed, disabled, gay, black, pregnant, menstruating, freckled, extremely hairy or badly scarred, is indication enough of the degree to which Mateelians have learned to accept and love themselves, reversing the shame and self-hatred of stigma concealment. That they are, in all probability, simultaneously experiencing the childlike openness described by Tart's informants because they are smoking marijuana is further evidence of that self-acceptance.[25]

It should be noted that this kind of self-acceptance and love is not the same thing Slater describes as narcissism typical of Amerikans because it happens in an emphatically social context.[26] Mateelians see self-love as being a first step toward real relations with others because, as they would say, "you can't really love someone else until you have learned to love yourself." In the Mateelian view, exploring the inner self leads inevitably to connection with others, the natural world and the universe. This concept militates against narcissism, as does the psychological sophistication of Mateelians which enables them to immediately spot any leaning toward narcissism and call it to the narcissist's attention.

The emotional force of a changed perception of Self is indicated by the common practice of changing one's name. Goffman's discussion of identity is useful in examining this practice. He lists three kinds of social identity. Virtual, actual, and felt.[27] Virtual identity is what we expect from an individual based on categories and assumptions provided by society. Actual identity is who the person turns out to be, which may or may not coincide with the virtual identity others have constructed. "Felt" identity is the subjective experience of an individual, who one thinks one is. Actual and virtual identity rely heavily on "identity pegs" such as name or occupation, which allow dossiers to be constructed and filled with information about one's social identity.[28] The contrast between a Mateelian conception of Self and an Amerikan one is thrown into clear relief by the difficulty Mateelians encounter when they must fill in a form listing such routine aspects of Amerikan identity as marital status, occupation, address or income. Stating one's name, in particular, presents difficulties for those whose felt identity has differed so profoundly from the virtual and actual identity contained in their files.

Adopting a new name is seen by Mateelians as a healthy part of dropping the false-self system, as saying good-bye to that construction developed through years of maintaining what the educational system calls "your permanent record." Changing one's name to correspond with one's felt identity is seen as "adopting an alias" by Amerikan culture and, with the exception of stage names for movie stars, is taken as an indication of great dishonesty. In Mateel, it is an act of supreme honesty, a relinquishing of a Self constructed for consumption by the technocracy and acceptance of a self that includes subjectivity and personal experience.

There is, in Mateel, a name taboo. Relative to such taboos in primitive societies, it is fairly weak, though it is strong enough that no names are used in this book that have not appeared in print elsewhere, thus becoming public. This taboo is reflected in the fact that last names are seldom included in introductions and asking one's last name may put a sudden coolness into a conversation. Introductions, in fact, tend to be self-introductions, with participants assuming the right to decide whether this relationship will be of a nature to require any names at all. The name taboo reflects the possibility that mentioning someone's name might in some way bring them danger from the past. It also indicates respect for one's right to control the amount of information available to the public. Most important to this discussion, however, it bespeaks the right to break with one's past.

Names are not generally considered essential to interaction, and are frequently offered only after a period of conversation has established the nature of the relationship. One may know hundreds of people with whom one feels a strong tie through some shared experience, such as fighting a fire, attending a birth, or riding to Eureka in the back of the same pick-up truck, but not know that person's name. The community often generates a name to serve as a last name when a distinction needs to be made between two persons with the same first name. That name is likely to be based on some personal attribute, skill, or place of residence. Thus, instead of Jane Smith and Jane Jones, there may be Crazy Jane, Big Jane, Black Jane, Fiddler Jane, Dancer Jane, Midwife Jane, Redway Jane, Sister Jane or China Creek Jane. These are generally "third person" names, used only in the absence of the referent, although it is not known whether a third person name was adopted by the referent as a chosen name.

That these names include some that could be considered derogatory is not necessarily an indication of cruelty on the part of the Mateelians who use them. More likely, it is a reflection of the assumption that referents have made their peace with their set of attributes, and one need not sanctimoniously avoid the most obvious way to distinguish one person from another with the same name.[29] Thus a person may know that he is referred to in the third person as "one-armed David," and may experience some negative feeling as a result of that, but understand that those who use it give him credit for having made the adjustment to his "stigma." The existence of the "third person" naming custom, then, is an adjustment to the need to distinguish between persons with the same first name, an acknowledgement of the individual's right to not have a last name, and an implied general statement that individuals are secure enough in themselves that they will not be offended by statements of the obvious, or that they should not be offended.[30]

One of the major ways accepting the Self is accomplished is through Erving Goffman's strategy of reinterpreting the stigma in an unconventional manner.[31] All marijuana users must sooner or later reinterpret the stigma of being a user or accept the Amerikan view that they are "pot heads." For Mateelians, this reinterpretation ranges from the belief that marijuana is a harmless herb whose illegality is an error on the part of lawmakers to a more comprehensive view that marijuana is a sacred herb provided by the Great Spirit to aid humans seeking higher consciousness.

Those who ascribe to the latter reinterpretation may see cultivation and distribution of marijuana as their sacred duty and privilege. Many marijuana farmers found in herb farming the first meaningful, functional and authority-free occupation of their lives. When the Amerikan form asks for occupation, they often prefer to state "farmer" over "unemployed" because of the implications of these answers to self-definition. This positive value placed on a self-definition as "farmer" is clearly observable anytime someone suggests, sometimes jokingly, sometimes seriously, that if the federal government really wanted to stop the domestic marijuana industry, it should pay marijuana farmers to not grow marijuana in the same way it pays corn farmers not to grow corn. There is always at least one person in every crowd who responds to this suggestion with the remark "you couldn't pay me not to grow marijuana."

Relationships

Relationships are the result of interactions. The nature of the relationship is a function of the number and quality of interactions between the individuals involved. If the interactions are carried out in response to traditional rules, by persons concerned to stay within traditional role expectations, then the relationship will also continue to be traditional. Since changing society cannot be accomplished without changing the relationships of which it is comprised, and relationships are composed of interactions, changing the nature of interaction is crucial to changing society.

Charles Tart's informants reported a number of experiences that directly affected interaction by changing perception of themselves and others. For everyone, sociability was changed after smoking marijuana. Some people became more sociable, and some less. Those who became less sociable did so because they were more interested in exploring subjectivity. Those who became more sociable found that when interacting, ordinary social games seemed hollow and worthless. They felt that they had more insight into others and learned more about psychological processes when "stoned." They experienced a feeling of empathy that, depending on the level of intoxication, ranged from telepathy to a sensation of merging with the Other. At the highest levels, this became a merging with the world. When smoking in a group, they felt a part of some kind of larger unity rather than simply being in the presence of other people. This explains "these high level effects are greatly valued by users and are one of the important reasons why they consider marijuana intoxication a 'higher' state of consciousness."[32]

There is much in Mateelian culture that reflects these experiences of heightened responsiveness to others. Marijuana itself is a symbol both for relationship and higher consciousness. In the Pure Shmint play *Vibram Soul*, the main character is instructed to expand his consciousness through loving his woman. The spirit who instructs him is dressed in marijuana leaves because marijuana is understood as a symbol for higher consciousness that includes expanded relationship.

The persistence of the custom of "passing the joint" (marijuana cigarette) is an indication of the social symbolism of the herb itself. In order to get the effects, it is necessary to hold the smoke in the lungs as long as possible. To avoid wasting the smoke coming from the cigarette while an individual is doing this, it is passed around in a group, each person taking one puff or "toke" and handing it immediately to the next person. Failure to "pass the joint" is called "Bogarting" the joint, in reference to the inseparable relationship between the late movie actor, Humphrey Bogart, and his tobacco cigarette. Since this custom arose when marijuana was scarce, one might expect that in times of plenty, when each person could easily afford an individual joint, the custom would disappear. Such is not the case. No matter what the availability of marijuana, in times of plenty as well as times of scarcity, the joint is passed. At any community gathering, circles form around a joint and it is carefully passed after each toke. The explanation for this lies in its value as symbolism for the social experience Tart calls "group unity."

"Passing the joint" is part of a Goffmanesque strategy widely employed by the discreditable. This is to divide the world into a large group to which nothing is revealed about the stigma and a smaller group to which all is told and on whose help the stigmatized individual relies.[33] Part of the discontinuity experience was to simply drop the larger group from one's world and concentrate on the smaller group, the group with whom one "passes the joint."

A metaphor from the Zen tradition illustrates this strategy. A Zen master who holds a stick over the head of the student saying "If this stick is real, I will hit you with it. If it is not real, I will hit you with it. If you don't say anything, I will hit you with it." A response acceptable to the Zen master is for the student to reach up and take away the stick, indicating detachment from the relationship with the master. Gregory Bateson uses the Zen stick story in discussing the schizophrenia-producing double bind, another phenomenon important to the psychological saga of Mateelians. A double-bind is a situation in which individuals receive conflicting double messages from persons important to them. For example, a common Amerikan double-bind message is a spoken "I love you" from a parent who indicates the opposite by body language or non-verbal messages. The victim cannot escape the situation and is, in addition, forbidden to speak of it. If it continues over time, schizophrenia is generated as a defense.[34]

The stigmatized person receives the message from culture in general. The spoken message "I accept you," is received at one level but the stigmatized person knows that the stigma is not accepted and that speaking of this discrepancy is taboo. Rather than accepting the schizophrenic defenses this double-bind situation tends to produce, Mateelians took the stick away from the master by seeking out a group to whom the stigma could be revealed and be accepted.

Time and Interaction

One way in which Mateelian interaction differs from Amerikan interaction involves the perception of time. The emphasis on Sacred and other kinds of time as part of the Mateelian worldview has been discussed. The experiential basis for this differing perception is revealed by Tart's informants. At lower levels of intoxication, they experienced increased attention to the present at the expense of the past and future. At higher levels, time stopped:

> The user may experience archetypal time, where he is part of a pattern that man has always been part of, or . . . [lose] consciousness of the ordinary space/time framework altogether.[35]

One Mateelian described an LSD experience of archetypal time:

> I was stalking, me and my wife at the time, we were stalking and sort of pretending. I picked up a stick, and I went and looked over this rock. . . . I pretended to see something. And I threw the stick and it went in this perfect spiral, you know, just like a spear is supposed to go, and I had a flash at that moment, of being at this end of a spear before. I remembered seeing that spear go out. It was incredible *deja vu*. Since then I have often tried to pick up a stick and throw it like a spear, but the drug really cued me into that. I could throw the spear and I could see it and I could connect with other things about feeling my own roots.

The implications of this experience for social relations is a complete involvement with the present situation and present companions, another aspect of the "be here now" philosophy. Goffman describes the opposite, a way of interacting typical of Amerika that he calls "alienation from interaction." In this situation, people never really focus on the present situation but are constantly thinking about some other past, future, or hypothetical interaction.[36] This is not to imply that Mateelian interactions are insulated from the pressures of linear time, only that Mateelians consciously counteract that pressure with negative sanctions on inattention to the present social situation.

In the laundromat scene from *Vibram Soul*, it will be remembered that the two women, Spring and Loretta, dropped everything to interact fully with Jill in the present. The saying "be here now" implies full attention to the present scene and present companions, from one moment to the next. The flexibility of relationships, their lack of collective (as opposed to individual) definition is a function of the be-here-now philosophy. Sexual relations, especially, are resistant to traditional definitions that imply stages of commitment related to culturally understood time periods, such as "seeing each other," "engagement," and "marriage." One of the funniest lines in the Pure Shmint play "Growing Pains," which is set in the "Old Growers Home" for Mateelian Senior Citizens, is when "Blue" proposes to "Ruby," with whom he has been a land and sexual partner for forty years. He says, "Ruby, let's get married. I'm finally ready to make a commmi-mi-mi-mi-mitment."

The blank on the Amerikan form that asks for "marital status" is as potentially confusing for Mateelians as the blank that asks for a "name," since marriage is conceived of more as a continuum than an absolute state. Four slots labelled Married, Divorced, Widowed, or Single are simply insufficient to describe such relationships. Many Mateelians feel a sense of great dishonesty in selecting one of these choices and often refuse to answer the question unless some reason is given as to why it should be answered. Some feel that what Amerikans call marital status is irrelevant in most of the situations in which it is asked.

The general repugnance for such definitions as "husband" and "wife," the reluctance to apply any label to oneself or someone else reflects the belief that identity and consequently, relationship, should be based on feeling-in-the-moment rather than on roles, with their attendant expectations and assumptions. So widely held was this ideal at one time that at least one couple was secretly married for years, but never told their friends for fear of being considered "uncool." As the evolution of the cultural system became more visible and tolerance for individual diversity became a more important value, they eventually dropped the pretense. This does not imply, of course, that there are no assumptions or expectations in Mateelian relationships. One doubts if such a completely existential relationship is possible. It is just that expectations and assumptions are specific to a particular relationship and its particular history rather than based on traditional expectations for that relationship. They are the result of spoken and unspoken high-context "negotiations" more often in Mateel than would appear to be the case in Amerika.

The interval between the appearance of a conflict and its resolution is another time-related factor in interaction. E. T. Hall estimates that, for Western cultures it may be three to six months between the time an interactional problem appears and the time it is addressed. He contrasts this to Latin cultures, where feedback is instantaneous, perhaps overly so in terms of violence.[37] Everything in Mateelian culture reinforces immediate honest feedback and deplores a situation where unspoken problems are allowed to go on indefinitely, poisoning all relationships around them.

Time influences interaction in a more general way because of the sedentary orientation of Mateelians, most of whom expect to spend the rest of their lives in Mateel. Philip Slater speculates that a characteristic of the "temporary" society he saw embarking in the sixties would be the ability to form deep relationships in a short time. In the 1960s, the saying "if you can't be with the one you love, then love the one you're with," made into song lyrics by Crosby, Stills, Nash and Young, expressed the value placed on these kinds of relationships. Mateelians, then, are adept at this kind of interaction and do value it. In Mateel, however, it may be seen side-by-side with a growing appreciation for the value of lifetime relationships.[38]

Slater speaks of the small stable community as precluding escape from undesirable encounters. Mateelians realize that this is true and often joke about it. Because they also expect to be neighbors and friends over a long period of time, they invest more effort into reaching a stability with others that is compatible with their conceptions of honesty in social relations. As Slater predicts, because people must work with people they might otherwise choose to avoid, they are forced to develop parts of themselves they could have ignored in a large-scale situation. In an ordinary small town in Amerika, this superficial "co-operation" mode of interaction might be achieved by the increase of false-self production, an increase in nicety. In an urban situation, it may be achieved by an increase in impersonal interaction, by a professionalism in which people relate exclusively from their occupational roles.

In Mateel, the positive value of honesty, of revealing the stigma, and the negative value against hypocrisy forces the stability to come from honesty, tolerance and compassion rather than from additional layers of secrecy. The assumption that everyone is going to be around for a long time provides the motivation for achieving an honest interactional stability. Whereas this constant funky, "be here now," situational attitude toward relationship can become frustrating for those who need a little more predictability in their lives, it is seen by Mateelians as being healthier in the long run. It prevents the development of the schizophrenic defenses characteristic of double-binds and it releases individual growth from the restraints of a need to both role expectations and any need to be consistent, thus expediting social experimentation.

Psychological Savvy

Another difference between Amerikan and Mateelian interaction relates to psychological sophistication. Tart's informants state that when intoxicated they experienced a feeling of increased insight into others, an increased awareness of psychological processes. Those who do not become more sociable, tend to become more interested in their own internal experiences, a phenomenon that surely must raise comprehension of the subjectivity of others. Those who do become more sociable are much more aware of the social process. On the rare occasions when a "freak-out" occurred, a situation where negative psychological effects became overwhelming, the freaked out person is reported in all but one case to have been "talked down" by others on the scene.[39]

Probably as a result of their experiences with psychedelics and marijuana, Mateelians display enormous interest in psychology and great skill in aiding each other in psychological development and administering psychological first aid. There was at one time an active co-counseling group in which particular members were assigned to help each other psychologically in emergencies and ongoing situations. Different kinds of therapy groups, consciousness raising and support groups abound for such a small community. Dream analysis, communications skills, assertiveness and other self-help workshops are constantly being held at Heartland College, the health center, community schools, or private houses. Much marijuana money has been spent by successful growers wishing to learn these kinds of skills, for self-help or to help others.

Other evidence of this interest in subjectivity, psychological process, and mutual aid is linguistic. Tart, as well as most other researchers on psychedelics, reports that informants feel that their experiences are "beyond words," that is, that language is an insufficient means of communication by which to convey the experience.[40] The counterculture developed special jargon in an attempt to remedy the inadequacy of the English language to discuss subjectivity. This language is now passé in mainstream culture because, for those who did not attempt to implement the psychedelic experience, it was merely slang. For Mateelians this special vocabulary has become an integral feature of the language because it reflects ongoing experience. Such phrases as "where I'm at," "up front," "where I'm coming from," "space it out," "blissed out," "freaked out," "shine me on," or "far-out" express well known subjective phenomena for which there are no comparable phrases in conventional English.

Comparisons

The basic difference between interaction in Mateel and Amerika relates to the difference in the way people see and present themselves. Put briefly, Amerikan culture discourages the fulfillment of one's total potential and the exploration and expression of subjective experience. When Amerikans interact with one another, they do so within the confines of rigidly defined conventional roles. Mateelian culture, on the other hand, encourages development of complete personal potential, acceptance and revelation of stigmas, and mutual psychological aid. It promotes an individualism best expressed through relationship and flexibility in role, situation, and relationship definitions consistent with the "be here now" philosophy.

Because of the great diversity of primitive cultures, only the grossest generalizations about social interaction and conceptions of Self can be made. These, however, are helpful in understanding the degree to which Mateelian culture resembles the Primitive model in function, if not in specifics. One fairly safe generalization is that tribal individuals conceive of themselves in terms of their relationship to the tribe rather than, as Amerikans do, in terms of personal attributes. The more tribal the culture, the more that statement applies. In traditional societies, the roles that exist are clearly defined, with expectations, assumptions, and obligations known to all. There is little room for disagreement on what constitutes the perfect nephew, say, because, unless the culture is under pressure from outside it to change, opportunities for divergent ideas, or alternative role definitions is limited. In addition, the small-scale and technological simplicity of primitive societies results in a smaller absolute number of roles available. Further, the audience for each role is likely to overlap, so that one plays husband, grandson, shaman, before the same group. The possibility of radically changing one's character with each scene or role is not as available to a tribal person as it is to the compartmentalized Amerikan, whose various roles may never be played before the same audience. This factor would, presumably, limit the development of the schizoid personality some see as typical of Amerika.

Mateel is similar to the Primitive model in this smallness of scale. There, too, the audience for different roles often overlaps. Escaping a role or an interaction is probably easier than it is in most tribal societies, but harder in Mateel than in Amerika. Mateelians have reinvented the "avoidance" relationship found frequently in primitive societies. In primitive societies, these relationships are formalized and mandated. For instance, in many societies where a man goes to live with his wife's family at marriage, sons-in-law and mothers-in-law are forbidden to speak directly to each other. In such societies, no allowances are made for the individuals playing the roles—the taboo applies to the roles, even if the individuals like each other. Anthropologists have generally interpreted these relationships as functioning to prevent conflict between persons who must live in close proximity, but whose relationship has a great potential for conflict.

In Mateel, there are no such formalized avoidance relationships, but tensions between certain complementary roles are acknowledged and the pressure that would otherwise be applied to the individuals to work it out may be tacitly suspended. This allows these persons to, in fact, avoid each other as long as they need to. Ex-spouses, for instance, often avoid each other as do current and ex-spouses of the same individual. Former land partners or best friends who have had a falling out may openly (as opposed to secretly) avoid each other for years. Open avoidance relationships, while tolerated, are seen as a sort of necessary evil, better than secret avoidance, constant feuding, or having someone leave Mateel because some interaction is too painful, but not as good as honest resolution. The ideal is to arrive at a stable relationship requiring no dishonesty or games. The avoidance relationship is an adjustment for the discrepancy between this ideal and the difficulty of realizing it. As long as everyone knows it exists, the degree to which it can cause tension in other relationships is limited. Secret avoidance would increase the danger that the "bad vibes" would spread. The avoidance relationship in Mateel, then, serves the same function that it does in primitive societies and exists for the same reasons—smallness of scale and a commitment to stay, prohibit escape, yet potential conflict threatens everyone. There the similarity stops, however, because of the Mateelian application of "funky" relationships. Role definitions are minimal, flexible, and few. Relationships are negotiated from scratch by individuals who know themselves well and are adept at assessing the personalities of others. Unlike either the Amerikan or Primitive models, Mateelian society values the individual more than the role, the negotiated definition of the relationship more than the default, traditional one. One escapes role expectations in Amerika by leaving the situation, hiding in anonymity, or devaluing the relationship. In Mateel, one redefines the role in terms of the situation rather than trying to escape it. It is only because the cultural system supports security in one's self-image, that this kind of ambiguous, situational role and relationship defining works.

What flexible roles, situational interactions, and negotiated relationships do in Mateel, many primitive cultures accomplish through ritual. The Iroquois custom of acting out dreams and Inuit shamanic ceremonies in which the breaking of taboos is publicly confessed and the consequences ritually rectified, are ways of clearing the psychological air. The Plains Indian custom of changing names in response to important personal experiences is a means of releasing the individual from the bondage of no longer accurate self-images. Much of shamanism involves ceremonies that are seen as purifying the soul from social infringements or poisoned relationships.

Bateson's description of the sex reversal ceremonies of the Iatmul of New Guinea is still a classic example of the ritualistic safety valve. In this ceremony, Iatmul men dress like women and Iatmul women dress as men for a day. They engage in ritualistic behavior reversing the roles, amid much tension releasing laughter. The slapstick "acting out" (in modern psychological jargon) takes place within well understood boundaries but within those boundaries, is enthusiastic, and according to Bateson, highly functional in releasing tensions deriving from the rigid male/female role definitions.[41]

If Ernest Callenbach's fictions can be taken as examples of what relationships might be like in Ecotopia, it is clear that in this area Mateel most resembles the Ecotopian model. For example, in one scenario, a customer at an Ecotopian restaurant has a complaint about the way his eggs are cooked. Rather rigidly defining the principals as the customer (as in "the customer is always right"), the waiter, the cook, and most of the standers-by, all of these persons step out of their respective roles in the "restaurant" situation, and resolve the matter to the satisfaction of all concerned. The complainer is validated in his complaint, the cook is validated as being in a state of overwork, and the customers all volunteer to come back to the kitchen and help her if she gets swamped again.[42] It could be an "only in Ecotopia scene" except that similar situations are common in Mateel.

A midwife shows off the baby she delivered earlier in the day at a Mateelian home.

Chapter Ten

Kinship

If you can't be with the one you love, honey, love the one you're with.

—*Crosby, Stills, Nash and Young*

Kinship has been the organizational basis of society from time immemorial, regulating everything from residential patterns to land tenure to relations with the supernatural. It is difficult for citizens of modern industrial society to comprehend the extent to which kinship influences every aspect of traditional societies. Modern societies have reorganized around other foci, and long enough ago that it seems natural to us that individual goals should take precedence over the goals of the nuclear family, let alone the extended family.[1] Nevertheless data from Mateel indicate that twenty years after the countercultural revolution, it is the general concept of kinship embodied in the ideals of extended family and tribe, which ultimately tie the community together.

When anthropologists begin the study of the kinship of a traditional group, they utilize systematic procedures based on a hundred years of studying kinship. Three anthropological concepts to be used in the following discussion are the kinship categories of consanguineal, "blood" or "biological" kin; affinal, or "in-law" kin; and "fictive," or adoptive kin. Some attention must be given to this nomenclature before the discussion can proceed. How to discuss affinal kin is particularly a problem because there is no clear point at which any given couple can be defined as married and there are no universally accepted terms in Mateel for the kinship roles ordinarily described by the words "husband" and "wife." Legality stopped being the definitive trait for marriage long ago, although legal marriages do exist and may be on the increase in Mateel. Commonly, committed long-term, co-residential relationships between men and women are indistinguishable from legal marriage until they end. At that point only legal marriages have access to formal divorce proceedings which protect each partner from the loss of property and children.

No perceivable a pattern in the way couples refer to each other has emerged, since legally married and non-legally married couples refer to each other by all sorts of names including "husband" and "wife," "old man" and "old lady" or "lady," "partner," and "mate," reflecting the ambiguity of the relationship. California does not recognize common-law marriages. In the following discussion, reluctantly, long-term sexual partners who live together but are not, to my knowledge (and it is sometimes a secret), legally married, will be referred to, reluctantly, as "spouse equivalents," or "S. E.'s." I am thereby eschewing the vernacular "old man" and "old lady" or "lady," which are now considered obsolete, at least in feminist circles. Couples who are, to my knowledge, legally married will be referred to as "husband" and "wife." "Spouse equivalent" simply indicates an absence of the legal contract. It includes a very wide spectrum of relationships that overlap in function and behavior, with legal marriages at one end and fades off into short term relationships of limited function at the other. In truth, so ambivalent are Mateelians about cross-sex relations that there is no one universally accepted term, which leaves the observer with no choice but to resort to sociological jargon.

Mateelian kinship could be described in the traditional way, emphasizing structure. However, the kind of description ethnographers usually produce for less fluid cultural situations would not be entirely appropriate to Mateel and would miss the point. What is most instructive about Mateelian kinship is the way it has redefined and expanded mainstream concepts in the light of individual feelings. In addition, Mateelian kinship customs have incorporated many of the trends that originally appeared to threaten the continuity of the Amerikan family, and still do in the mainstream culture, and have eliminated others as unworkable. These Mateelian kinship systems include having multiple sexual partners, rejection of legal marriage, group marriages, homosexuality, the ideal of a less possessive and more communal attitudes toward sexual partners and children, and the emphatic rejection of guidance from the next generation up. Before these trends may be discussed and the kinship system described structurally, some historical context must be provided.

The Generation Gap

Perhaps the most frightening feature of the counterculture for non-participants was the vehemence with which its adherents rejected their families. Margaret Mead uses the phrase "generation gap" frequently to describe that enormous break in understanding that occurred between the generation that came to adulthood during the Great Depression and World War II and the generation that came to adulthood in the 1960s. She describes it as a completely unique event, something that happened world-wide simultaneously and on a scale never seen before; not a generation gap, but The Generation Gap. Mead blames the acceleration of modern technology during that period, in general, and the atomic bomb, in particular, with changing the terms on which the different generations were to meet the world. So significant was the atomic bomb to her that when she heard the news that it had been dropped on Hiroshima, she took the manuscript she had been working on and burned it in the fireplace, knowing that nothing she had said would be applicable in a world so changed.[2]

The experience of Mateelian informants substantiates the importance of the generation gap. Indeed, in view of the life histories collected in Mateel, "gap" is far too superficial a word and might be better replaced by "chasm" or, as Mead suggests, "grand canyon."[3] Since so many Mateelians were too young or not yet born when The Bomb was dropped on Hiroshima and Nagasaki, only one informant expresses a conscious memory involving the atomic bomb. This one memory supports Mead's view of the role of nuclear weapons in creating the Generation Gap:

> I was about four and I was standing out in my front yard in Cleveland. I realize now that I must have heard my parents talk about "the big bomb" that fell when I was three, because I remember them using that phrase later. I knew what shape bombs were from having seen World War II movies. I saw something very strange in the sky, coming out from behind a house down the street. It was very slow, but I was fascinated, I had never seen anything like it. As its shape gradually became revealed, I realized that I was looking at a big bomb, a huge bomb, suspended in the sky and I knew, all of a sudden, that whoever we dropped "the big bomb" on, they were about to drop it on me. I ran screaming into the house in a state of complete terror. It turned out to be the Goodyear blimp, but try to tell that to my subconscious.

In spite of the depth and importance of the generation gap, the return to kinship as a positive value in Mateelian society makes sense in the wider historical framework of hominid history. The importance of kinship in all societies is clear testimony to some basic, perhaps instinctual, human urge. Primates are among the most social of mammals, and the human primate is no exception. The roots of the evolution of society are seen by primatologists in the nuclear family formed by the mother and her children. This is true whether this grouping is under the protection of a single powerful male, as in the case of gorillas, or a group of males, as in the case of chimpanzees.

The kinship principle of social organization continues throughout history, all over the world, becoming more and more complex right up until the Renaissance. Monarchies were the elaboration of chiefdoms, chiefdoms the elaboration of tribes, tribes the elaboration of large extended families joined together as clans. It was during the Renaissance in the West that this paradigm of social organization began to change as the family felt the impact of other organizing principles, such as the Guild, and social trends such as urbanization, secularization and imperialism. The predominant view among sociologists is that it was industrialism that placed the greatest stress on the extended family. The nuclear family was more compatible than the extended family with the major requirement of the factory—a concentration of workers unencumbered by the necessity to remain with the extended family on the farm. It is also clear that modernization had the effect of encouraging the nuclear family pattern and discouraging any tendency to return to an extended family pattern.

The nuclear family became well-established in western Europe and the modern United States as the economic and moral support unit. It should be noted, however, that the value placed on the maintenance of extended family varies widely within the complexity of industrialized society. There are surely still regional, ethnic, religious, and class-related pockets of people who would choose family over occupational requirements in making life decisions.

In reestablishing the importance of the extended family, Mateelians redefined and reinstated a highly traditional value which dated from preindustrial times. It had only been relegated to a position of low importance relatively recently in the history of Mateelian culture. Philip Slater examines the nuclear family at the point just before the occurrence of the counterculture, describing the relationship of the nuclear family to what he calls the "temporary society" being created by the demands of corporate Amerika. In the stable society characterized by the extended family, economic tasks had been spread out among an assortment of individuals of different ages, giving all a claim to economic usefulness and therefore personhood. Any individual had a choice of persons to whom to turn for emotional support at any given time and children had a variety of role models. As corporate industrialism replaces the stable society, compatible with the extended family, with the temporary society requiring mobile nuclear families, it places impossible demands on the nuclear family. All of the economic functions previously served by the large extended family group are taken over either by the corporation or state, while all of the emotional functions are concentrated into only two basic relationships, husband-wife and parent-child.[4]

The strain on the nuclear family will continue as the society becomes more temporary. As Slater states, "The family as a whole cannot be as easily included in the temporary system framework as the single individual." Corporations act ambivalently, providing therapeutic services for the isolated woman, but in the long run demanding that the husband's "organizational commitment always come first." If she chooses a career of her own, competing job requirements threaten the couple, unless, as Slater puts it, "she is willing to assume ancillary status." (Logically, one assumes, that is also the case unless he is willing to assume ancillary status.) If she chooses, as was the more common case when Slater was writing, to assume the homemaker role, she bears the entire burden of child-rearing and emotional support for everyone else and her entire self-esteem becomes wrapped up in the success of the child, a situation that leads to neurotic excesses in the mother-child relationship.[5]

The generation gap, then, occurred at a time when some of the functions of the extended family had been replaced by the state, others had been concentrated into the nuclear family and the strain on that institution was increasing. Judging from the life histories of my informants and the statements of other observers of the counter-culture, when many in the sixties generation abandoned the nuclear family, it was practically non-functional anyway, or at least from an emotional standpoint. Many Mateelians describe their families as being cold, shallow, hypocritical, and unfulfilling. Most informants have expressed a feeling of abandonment, of being ignored or considered irrelevant by their families. These life histories confirm the feeling, rampant in the counterculture, that parents had little use for their children beyond insuring that property would be inherited and the family name continued. It was clear to many of those who later became Mateelians that their needs and goals as persons were of no consequence when compared to the maintenance of the family image through conformity to rigid expectations. The popularity of the 1960s movie, *The Graduate*, was due to the way it showed a college-age protagonist being used by everyone as a pawn. Surrounded by material fulfillments and recently spewed out by the impersonal educational machine, he perceives that everyone has a plan for him but no one is interested in what he thinks or feels. It is no wonder the film struck such a harmonic chord in the general population of that generation.

For those who dropped out, the generation gap was a gut-level experience. It was hard to see, from the other side of the abyss, the historical trends that had led to it. The younger, run-away "flower children" were responding to their immediate experience of dehumanization by family and educational institutions. For them, those disillusionments culminated with the physical break from the family of birth. For those older dropouts who had already made a start on adult experience with careers, higher education, or a traditional marriage (made more to please the parents than the bride and groom), disillusionment with these experiences confirmed their earlier experiences of the Amerikan family and educational system. As one male informant asked, "What better indication of the indifference of the family to the individual could there be than parents who supported the draft?"

Seen from a historical perspective, the generation gap was a reaction to the failure of parents to perceive the unique societal pressures placed on their children to validate the magnitude of the implications of nuclear weapons, undeclared wars, covert military actions, increased assassinations. Whereas the parents were perceived as displaying coldness, lack of understanding, sympathy, or true interest in the development of the adolescent as an individual, the children displayed, eventually, disgust for their parents as unquestioning participants in The System.

Consanguineal Kin

Many social scientists, prematurely dismissing the counterculture as an emerging cultural system, stated that it was only one generation thick. The real test was whether it would be passed on intergenerationally. The generation gap seemed to be a statement against the whole concept of kinship, truly an end to the institution of the family. If there is no family, how can a culture be passed on? This question became moot as countercultural "families" began to emerge from communes and other kinds of groupings. Eventually, the two variables of parenthood and sedentism took over, adding definition and continuity to imaginary fictive "families." These two variables are related in that one major force for settling down was to create the best situation in which to raise existing or potential children.

As soon as sexual freedom began to produce mothers and fathers, the counterculture became two generations thick. Whereas there was some undeniable evidence that not much real parenting was going on, many countercultural refugees arrived in Mateel as dedicated and conscientious parents, with one or several children, some half-grown.[6]

There were both couples and single parents; the latter were mostly women by far. Their deep desire to establish a healthy, rural, stable situation for their children and to avoid in every way recreating those aspects of their childhood that had caused them such pain, was immediately made evident by the zeal with which they began to organize cooperative playgroups and preschools and to seek each other out for that purpose.

As the Mateel community became more established, it became clear to many of the parents of Mateelians that it was not a passing fancy. Their children and grandchildren were determined to stay. Many of them began to see Mateel as the obvious place for them to retire. They then invested in land, often becoming land partners with their children, and began to arrive, build their own retirement homes and generally explore how much of the new cultural system might be appropriate for them. There are even cases where it was the older generation who came to Mateel first, then became a contact point for their adult children to be drawn into the Mateel community. Ironically, some of these older Mateelians experienced the same negative reaction from their non-Mateelian children when they "dropped-out" after retirement as the younger ones did from their parents when they dropped out from careers. Further spreading of the generations is now occurring because the children of Mateelians are having their own children. I do not yet know of a biological extended Mateelian family that includes four generations, but that event will surely happen in the next few years.

Consanguineal kinship relations are important to Mateelian society, then, because retired parents moved to join children and grandchildren, adult children moved to join retired parents and then had their own children, and the children of Mateelians have now had children. All of these events contradict the "one-generation-thick" idea.

The Family and Tribe

Individualism is an ideal in Western society, but conformity is the practice. This paradox has now been discussed in several different contexts. It was suggested that individualism and conformity are best viewed analytically as poles in a "relevant continuum" rather than as mutually exclusive absolutes. Perhaps the epitome of the individualistic end of the continuum in Amerika was the beatnik era. The beatnik ideal was absolute individualism, freedom from familial restraints, complete security within the self, and no need for anyone else. What many hippies, particularly female ones, discovered, was that no matter what its relationship to freedom, this kind of individualism is too hard a burden to bear.

Mateelians discovered this in exactly the same way that they rediscovered and reinstituted items of modern technology—after first impoverishing themselves in order to find out what was really needed. What they did about it was attempt to find a way to have their individualism and their family, too. The "culturelessness" aspect of the psychedelic experience had its effect on social relations in the ideal of dropping all prior people classifications, sexual, racial, classist. The culmination of Western individualism in the existentialist search for freedom was the final break from all family ties, the dropping of the classification of people as kin or not. The funky mentality then began, as it had with all other culture-based conceptions, to ask just what is my relationship to people?

Everywhere in the counterculture, groups of individuals with no traditionally recognized relationship to each other arose spontaneously to insist that they were "family." They ranged from religious groups to communes to hobo camps to amorphous groups living in school buses to the notorious Manson family. In all of these situations, the "family" was composed of persons who first went through the experience of breaking with their original families and then being alone for a while. Their attempt at instant connection was an instinctive reversal of the industrial destruction of family and the isolated, atomized alienation that produced a feeling sociologists call "anomie." One informant described her experience of resurrection from anomie in the sudden urge to find a family:

> Once I had a potted cactus plant. I am ashamed to say that I swiped it out of the Arizona desert. It was right after a rain. Everything was in bloom and this plain old cactus had a beautiful purple flower on it. I was after the flower. Well, the flower faded soon enough and I put the pot in a lousy place for it on my second floor deck, where it got

knocked off and fell down to the first floor porch. The pot broke into a million pieces and the cactus just laid there in pile of dirt, roots sticking out for a long time. I kept walking by it, not having time to repot it, and thinking "Stupid thing, why doesn't it die? Doesn't it know there's no place for its roots?" Then one day I walked by it and there was the purple flower. I had to smile. "You're not even potted, your roots are sticking out into the air and there you go reproducing!" So I picked it up and repotted it. I was just like that cactus at one point in my life, just before I took LSD the first time. When I came down from that trip, I suddenly wanted to belong somewhere, I had hope for connection to people, in spite of everything that happened to me. Stupid me, don't I know I'm not planted anywhere, and here I am thinking about a tribe or a family? But I repotted myself anyway.

Charles Reich describes the countercultural idea of community as based on "respect for the uniqueness of the individual and the idea expressed by the word 'together.'" At the time when Reich was writing, communes were the most obvious form of social organization emerging from the idea of 'together'. Reich explains the communal idea as coming from the experience that "members of the same species who are related to each other and to all of nature by the underlying order of being . . . [felt] united in a community based on having their heads in the same place at the same time."[7] He is using the word "head" here, of course, in the vernacular meaning of consciousness, subjective experience, internal reality.

Members of communes often referred to themselves as being part of an "extended family" and their activities at Reich's writing were seen as amorphous; but, as he says, their existence "clearly reflects the belief of many . . . that once one has experienced being 'together' with people, conventional social relationships seem pointless and boring and the prospect of life separated from one's friends seems too barren to be accepted any longer." The type of interaction that developed in Mateel based on this conception was discussed in chapter nine. What is of interest here is the type of committed, long-term and functional social arrangements that developed from it.

The concepts of "family" and "tribe" are valued in the abstract. While maintenance of the extended and even sometimes the nuclear family in Amerika is routinely given a lower priority by both individuals and institutions than are career and financial considerations, Mateelians have busied themselves forming all kinds of groupings they designate as "extended families" or "tribes." They generally prioritize the maintenance of these relationships over their consanguineal relationship to persons outside Mateel and over financial considerations and career possibilities. A basic principle influencing perception of the degree of kinship is residence in Mateel.

Evidence for this is the frequently heard statement that someone turned down a good job in the city because they couldn't bear to leave "my family," meaning the commune, the land partnership, or the biological family extended to include fictive members. More compelling is the assumption that children should not be removed from Mateel if at all possible. This view is brought into focus whenever there is a death. It goes "if I die, how can I prevent my parents (or siblings or ex-spouse living elsewhere) from taking my children out of the community to raise them?" This is seen as a tragedy of major proportions, far transcending the child's lack of biological kin should he or she stay in Mateel and be raised by friends or fictive kin.

Many attempts have been made to insure that, in case of death, the children would be raised in Mateel. Close friends, fictive siblings or ex-spouses may make mutual promises to raise each other's children in that event. Unless the proposed foster parent is also close biological kin, however, no such arrangement can be made that will have status in court. The preferred legal guardian can be named, for the edification of the judge, but it has no legal standing regarding custody. One informant wept when she described her unsuccessful effort to insure that in case of her death her half-black child would be raised in Mateel by the mother's S. E., rather than in the East Oakland ghetto by the biological sisters of the biological father. She was told by her attorney that there was no legal way to make such an arrangement, even though she had obtained full legal custody of the child.

When left unfettered by legal intervention, however, the case may work out in a manner similar to the following example. A mother and her two sons were involved in a traffic accident away from Mateel. There was a third son, not in the car, who was grown and independent, living in Mateel. The youngest son's father lived in Mateel with his S.E., whose children were also grown and independent. The father of the older two boys lived out of Mateel in a city. The mother's current S.E. was not the father of any of her sons. The mother was killed in the accident. The middle boy was severely injured and the youngest boy was less severely injured.

While the middle boy was still in a hospital near the accident scene, Mateelians anxiously wondered what would happen to the children. I heard much of the speculation while standing in the long line that formed at the local hospital to donate blood for the middle boy. The middle boy would require months of care while he recuperated. The older boys' father had expressed a willingness to take the middle boy, but that was considered an imperfect solution because it would remove the middle boy from Mateel, his full brother, his half-brother, and his current "stepfather" (the mother's S.E.) and, just as bad, place him in a city. The youngest boy's father and his S.E. were willing to take him, but did not have the resources for the middle boy.

What happened was that the middle boy stayed with his father in the city, but only while he recovered. At that point, he moved in with the older brother, and both older boys were parented by an assortment of interested adults at various times, including the youngest boy's father and S.E., the man who was "stepfather" to all of the boys at the time of the mother's death and later, his new S.E., and the mother of the older boy's girlfriend. The younger boy's father and S.E. cultivated a close relationship with the boys' former "stepfather" and began to include him and his new S.E. into their extended family. The close relationship between the younger boy's father's family and the "stepfather's" new family continued even after the middle boy became independent and started his own biological nuclear family and after the "stepfather's" new marriage disintegrated.

This story illustrates several aspects of Mateelian kinship. The primary concern of everyone involved was that the necessity for the middle boy to be cared for physically not result in his permanent residence outside of Mateel and particularly in a city. Staying in Mateel is more important than maintaining ties to non-Mateelian kin. The focus of concern was on the well-being of the children more than it was the convenience of the adults. Mateelian kinship is children focussed, as is Mateelian childrearing. The welfare of the children is the basic principle, no matter what is going on with the adults, death, divorce, spiritual quests, affairs, or creative bursts.

Rather than the responsibility for the children being broken down into whose are legally whose, every effort was made to define the boys' family so that it included all interested parties. Mateelian kinship is inclusive rather than exclusive. Tensions will be resolved by including more people into an extended family rather than by drawing strict lines of responsibility that exclude interested parties. Everything about Mateelian conceptions of kin emphasizes arrangements that expand the number of people one considers kin. The reasons for this are both historical and functional. Historically, it goes back to the countercultural concept of community as described by Reich.[8] Functionally, it relates to the extreme importance of children and the perception that the first value is to maintain a support group for the children and keep them in Mateel no matter how often and in what manner the adults rearrange their relationships. The wider the definition of this support group, the more likely it is that the children will be able to remain in Mateel, no matter what happens.

Fictive Kin

There is probably no society that ever attempted to replace the biological and affinal ties so thoroughly with fictive kin as the counterculture did and this attempt carried over into the Mateelian cultural system. Fictive kinship is, essentially, adoption. It is not limited to the parent-child relationship, but applies to other relationships as well. It is simply a declaration, perhaps accompanied by a ceremony in some societies, that someone not related by traditional kinship rules shall henceforth be treated as some specific kin. The fictive relationships may be more or less similar to the traditional relationship it is declared to be. Fundamentalist churches in the South, for instance, routinely affix the title "Sister" or "Brother" to names of church members. How much the church members truly treat each other as sisters and brothers varies with the situation. The custom clearly represents the ideal that they should. In traditional white, Southern Baptist churches, the title was honorific and had little practical application. The followers of Jim Jones, on the other hand, placed themselves into a position where their "father" required them to die for their "sisters" and "brothers."

Fictive relationships in Mateel are equally variable and also express the ideal that the participants should treat each other as kin. I have witnessed relationships between people with no biological or affinal kin connection that displayed more emotional and practical mutual support than either of the participants ever expected from any of their non-Mateelian biological or affinal kin. Characterizing such a relationship as a friendship requires a very large expansion of the meaning of that word in Amerika. If participants in such a relationship are pressed to name it, they may or may not call it a friendship, they may or may not describe the other party as specific kin (if they do, it will be as a sibling), but they will surely refer to the other party as "family." At the other end of the spectrum is the honorific "Bro," a shortening of "brother," adopted by the counterculture from Blacks and used to recognize male others as actual or potential members of the group, in the same way Blacks used it.[9]

Tracing the history of fictive relationships will very likely lead to land, children, or a commune. The fictive kinspersons may be former land partners, legal or not. They may be former members of the same commune, landed or not. They may be members of an "extended family" with biological relationships at its core. Such a family may include relationships that would be traditionally considered "step" relationships, if legal marriage had been involved. If a marriage is not legal, the "step" relationships it creates are, logically, fictive "step" relationships. Given the low importance assigned to legality in Mateel, however, such non-legal step relationships are routinely called step relationships and in the case of "step" siblings, the fictive principle is carried further and the children are likely to simply define themselves as siblings, thereby becoming fictive siblings.

Many degrees of fictive sibling relationship are possible, in addition to the legal or non-legal step-sibling. A child may have biological half-siblings who are treated by the child and everyone else as full-siblings. The half-sibling relationship is a key relationship in terms of function. Not only can it come to be defined as a full sibling relationship, but it also maintains and reinforces the connections between families of ex-spouses and spouse equivalents who bear a relationship to the same children through half-sibling ties.

For instance, in the situation charted in Figure 8, married couple A produced two children, A and B, then broke up. Husband A took Woman B as S.E. She was already mother of Child C by her S.E., Man B, with whom she had just broken up. Children A, B, and C, while small, spent half of the time with each biological parent. Following the widespread customary pattern, all the biological parents remained in Mateel after the breakups so that the children would not be forced to go in and out of Mateel to have access to both biological parents. Having to adjust to the cultural extremes involved in that arrangement is generally considered a trauma to be avoided at all costs. None of the children was over four at the time when Husband A left Wife A and began his relationship with Woman B.

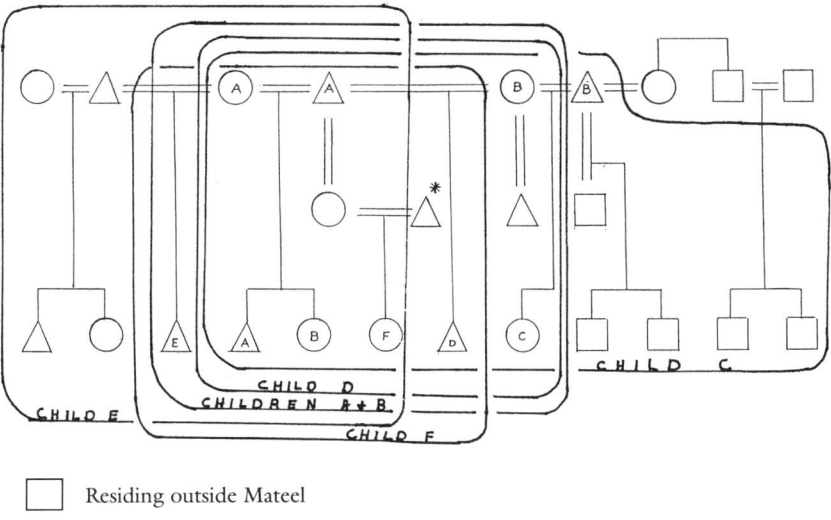

☐ Residing outside Mateel

═ Co-parents, not necessarily married

◯ Extended family from child's perspective

*The father of Child F lives outside Mateel and has virtually no contact with any individual on the chart. He is not considered kin, except by Child F in a purely genetic sense.

Figure 8. Child-Based Extended Family

Husband A and Woman B had a child, D, together. Children A and B are therefore half-sibling to Child D through their father and Child C is also half-sibling to Child D through her mother. The four children resided together half the time, when A and B were with their father and C was with her mother. The adults, Husband A and Woman B, Wife A, and Man B, representing three separate households, tried to time the alternations so that all four children would be together at the same time, in order to encourage the relationships between the children. The adults varied in their conceptions of the importance of encouraging the relationship between the four children, but all of them acknowledged it as some kind of priority. The four children consider themselves to be siblings and are treated as such by all of the adults in their lives. They are expected to be responsible for each other, even though Child C has no traditional relationship whatever to Children A and B, and even though, initially, only D resided in one home all of the time. Children C and D were frequent visitors at the home of Wife A when Children A and B were there. Although Child C had no biological relationship to A and B, she actually moved into Wife A's home for a short time when Child A vacated her room by going to college and Child C needed to live closer to her school and job than her mother did.

The story, however, is even more complex than that. Husband A and Woman B broke up when the children were all still dependent. Husband A took a second S.E., Woman C, who also had a child, E. Child D adopted the alternating residential pattern wherein he was with each biological parent half the time. Husband A and Woman C, to provide a time for D to be with his "siblings" A and B, attempted to time the stays of A, B, and D so that they would be at their father's home at the same time. This required the co-operation of both of Husband A's co-parents, Woman B and Wife A, both of whom placed the maintenance of the relationships between the children over whatever urges they might reasonably have had not to co-operate with Husband A. Children A and C, now adolescents, valued their "sister" relationship highly and frequently organized social events so that they would be together, either at one of A's biological parents' homes, or at the homes of mutual friends. Half-brothers B and D, who consider themselves no different from full siblings, also went to many social events together, in addition to living together half the time at their father's. From the point of view of the children, A, B, and D still spent the same amount of time together. Only C had been essentially cut out of a residential pattern that insured that she maintained contact with A and B. The fact that children A and C made special efforts to spend time together is an indication of their wish to maintain a fictive kinship no matter what the adults were doing.

D had no problem coordinating with C because by that time she lived permanently with her mother, Woman B, and he was there half the time. Child E and Child D, opposite sexes but near the same age, refer to each other as "my brother" and "my sister" even though their relationship is that of step-sibling, or would be if their parents were married. Beyond this, it is unclear the extent to which they conceive of themselves as siblings. Children A and B acquired a new half-sibling, much younger than themselves, when Wife A had another child, F. It is instructive that while A and B clearly conceive of F as their sibling, C and D feel no relationship to him beyond the general protectiveness older Mateelian children display towards younger Mateelian children. This would seem to indicate that the variables that made C as much a sibling to A and B as she is to D included the special effort of the adults to insure that they spent time together, and the closeness of their ages, as well as their mutual relationship to half-sibling D.

This complex pattern can be traced much further, following half-sibling relationships out from A and B through their half-sibling, F, to his half-siblings through his father or following half-sibling relationships out from C and her older half-siblings through her father. An interesting variable in C's case is that Man B, her father, never had any more children. His wife, however, cared for her sister's children for long periods of time, which created a fictive sibling relationship between C and her step-cousins.

The point here is that the half-siblings, through their relationships to each other and the fact that they spend half their lives in different households, effectively bind adults in a network of cooperation and mutual interest in the children. This is true even though one might reasonably expect these adults to avoid each other at all costs, especially since Husband A began each of his new serially "monogamous" relationships while still living with the preceding spouse or S.E. The value placed on providing a large kin group for the children, the small scale of the community, the value placed on honest communication and avoidance of ego trips, the ideal of non-possessiveness, the triumph of reason over jealousy and the assumption that everyone is going to stay in the area, are all instrumental in creating a context within which these child-focused serially monogamous extended families bond through half-siblings' relationships.

A second point, a corollary to the first, is that no matter what obligations and expectations the adults may recognize with regard to each other, from the point of view of the children, the biological and step-parents of their half-siblings are adults from whom they can expect aid. They are extended family in the sense that they provide a greater feeling of security to the children. A third aspect of the half-sibling extended families is that they join families in "chains" of obligation through the fact that a child they share is biologically related to children they don't share. The boundaries of such extended families are relative to their distance from any one half-sibling. This is shown on the chart by the circles indicating those relatives any particular ego in the bottom generation would include in her/his extended family.

The ramifications of this last observation have yet to be fully explored and Mateelian society has not been in existence long enough yet to determine how functional these half-sibling extended family chains might turn out to be in the long run. My guess is that these "chains" have the effect of strengthening the generalized sense of tribal and family feeling between those families most closely related in this manner. One piece of information supporting surmise is the fact that Mateelian children and adults can be frequently heard referring to step-relatives with phrases that stress a biological relationship or a fictive sibling relationship, rather than using phrases that stress broken relationships. One much more often hears "my sister's mother" (meaning, "my half-sister's or step-sister's mother"), "my daughter's brother" (meaning "my daughter's half-brother"), or "my son's father" than "my father's wife," "my ex's son" or "my ex," respectively. A first wife may refer to all of her husband's succeeding spouse equivalents and their children as "the family" and calling the most recent additions, "the babies," as if they were her grandchildren rather than her ex's children by his new young wife. (This tendency is also reminiscent of the attitude a senior wife might take in a polygamous society.)

Affinal Kin

The proliferation of lateral (within the same generation) relationships stems from the ambiguity of cross-sex relationships, which resulted from what many called the "sexual revolution" or "sexual freedom." Those phrases are placed in quotes to indicate that there is more to it than was readily obvious to those who invented them. Since the two criteria for kinship in all societies, "blood" and "marriage," are functions of sexual relations, it is reasonable to expect that a major change in sexual relations would affect conceptions of kinship. To understand the nature of kinship in Mateel, it is therefore necessary to consider what part the sexual revolution played in its history.

Although there certainly was some kind of a major deviation from the Amerikan pattern, and that deviation was shocking to Amerika, there is room for disagreement on just what the deviation was. As many informants have suggested, whereas their sexual behavior was seen to depart drastically from the traditional ideal, no one really knows how much it departed from the traditional reality. The most shocking departure for those who later moved to Mateel may have been more that they did not conceal whatever they were doing sexually than that they actually deviated so much from Amerikan practice. Promiscuity, adultery, homosexuality and bisexuality, and the whole array of techniques, in other words, were certainly present in traditional Amerikan culture and no one, not even Kinsey, can know how truthfully any of it was reported. Not knowing the extent to which informants on sexual surveys can be trusted to tell the truth, in fact, has turned out to be a major impediment to controlling the AIDS epidemic. That circumstance would seem to add support to the idea that countercultural "sexual freedom" may be as much a function of what came out of the closet as it was of what was in it to start with.

Whereas from the outside, sexual freedom was perceived as mere indulgence, along with the use of psychedelics and marijuana, from the inside, it was for many people an experiment in reconnection. Serial monogamy and divorce was becoming the mainstream marital pattern. Many Mateelians are from broken homes. Those who are not may yet have seen their unbroken families as being held together by nothing more than fear or, worse, inertia. For many adolescents who later became Mateelians, the only force for sexual commitment in the sixties seemed to be the fear of pregnancy, which appeared to have been rendered obsolete by "The Pill," or fear of gossip. Given the pain of anomie, why not accept the instant communication apparently offered by sex? In addition, Amerikan society was seen, with reason, as repressed and hypocritical about sex. Therefore, eliminating one's sexual inhibitions came to be considered almost a prerequisite to the establishment of a new social order. This idea was not lost, of course, on gurus from Manson to Rajneesh.

The point here is simply that the idea of "sexual revolution" looks different from the point of view of the participants than it did from the point of view of the observers. It was, like everything else, experimental, and that experiment continues for Mateelians, many of whom have modified the original direction to include insights gained from the women's movement and from watching the experiment for twenty years. Whereas all sorts of arrangements took place in the counterculture in general, "orgies" or group sex, group marriages, polygamy and polyandry, most Mateelians either passed through that phase quickly or were never involved in anything but heterosexual serial monogamy, legalized or not. It should be understood that, in the following discussion of heterosexual serial monogamy, the large, visible homosexual community in Mateel is not deliberately excluded. Within that community there are many stable couple relationships, some of which form the core of extended families and some of which are included in extended families of heterosexuals. However, simply because of time restraints on the research, no special effort was made to obtain kinship or sexual data from the homosexual community so that it is difficult to say how much of the following discussion applies.

Sexual relations in Mateel are confusing because the sexual couple is caught in a tug-of-war between opposing sets of ideas. The most obvious of these is the conflict between existential freedom on the one hand and the need for family on the other that was discussed in the last chapter in connection with the female self image. This conflict is brought into inescapable focus for women, for whom the immediate implication of sexual freedom is motherhood. Historically, it fell on women first to establish security and continuity for the children. They were, in a sense, re-inventing the wheel in discovering the function of the family in childrearing. How to re-invent the family without entrapping themselves in patriarchal expectations all over again became the major concern of many women's lives, affecting forever their relationships with men and causing, for many, a negative or ambivalent attitude toward the institution of marriage.

Another aspect of the sexual revolution that fed growing female suspicion was a nameless sense of sexual exploitation. A feminist leaflet circulating in Berkeley in the late sixties asserts that "we broke the bonds which made us private property only to find that we had become community property." The double standard had not been eliminated, merely redefined in terms every bit as exploitative. Neither the counterculture nor Mateelian culture has succeeded in reversing the double standard to the extent that women can assume their experimentation will not somehow result in their feeling like sexual objects. What Mateel offers is an emotionally supportive setting in which individual women can work on these ambivalent feelings, consider all options including promiscuity, homosexuality, or celibacy, without having to justify the endeavor.

Other tensions in the couple relationship derive from the ideal of non-possessiveness, a corollary of non-materialism. It is difficult to say how successful Mateelians have been in implementing this ideal. Certainly jealousy exists in Mateel to the same degree that it does in the mainstream society. If there is a difference, it is in the fact that the ideal of non-possessiveness is expressed unabashedly in Mateel, whereas it is considered ridiculously unrealistic in mainstream Amerika. Many informants have faulted themselves for their inability to eradicate possessiveness towards their significant others and much emotional agony relates to this subject. The ideal of constant personal and spiritual growth is a major factor in the dissolution of couple relationships. At least, that is the reason given to others. A couple may be having all sorts of difficulties that differ in no discernible way from the difficulties mainstream couples have, but when they finally dissolve the relationship they are very likely to explain it by saying "he/she was blocking my growth." This statement may, but does not always, indicate that the speaker's growth was dependent on a sexual relationship with someone else.

The couple, then, is caught between the search for individual freedom and the, perhaps instinctual, need for kinship; the pull of "being together" with others, made more intense by sexual experience, and the fear of all of the traditional expectations that go with an "up-front" marriage; the immediacy of parenthood; an "on the road" conception of individual freedom; the ideal of complete nonpossessiveness and the fact of jealousy; the ideal of continuing spiritual and intellectual growth and the problem of spiritually and intellectually outgrowing one's mate. What happens is an entirely situational attitude toward, and a gradient of commitment to, the sexual couple relationship. Every couple, in other words, is on their own, with only their observations and prior experiences to guide them. They are aided by the "be here now" philosophy, the general expectation of flexibility in social relations, and the high tolerance of the community for social ambiguity.

One determines what one wants to know about a couple largely from inference, a situation that may drive single newcomers wild as they try to ascertain who is "available" and who isn't. That so many relationships are "open" sexually, meaning no promises of sexual fidelity have been exchanged, does nothing to clarify the situation. Although observation reveals that the most likely economic and residential unit is the nuclear family, just as it is in Amerika, unless the couple decides to make their agreements explicit through a ceremony and/or through obtaining a license and becoming a legally married couple, one must rely on implicit guidelines to determine where any particular couple falls on a gradient of commitment, and therefore how the individuals wish to be related to as members of a couple:

How do they relate to each other in public? Do they model affection and commitment?

Do the parties live in the same residence?

Do they function as parents to the same children?

Are they land partners? Do they jointly own a home?

Do they drive each other's cars?

Are they partners in some economic enterprise?

Any one of these questions, by itself, does not necessarily imply a relationship resembling a traditional marriage. Taken together, however, they provide some clue as to how the individuals within the couple wish to be treated with regard to the relationship. The whole cross-sex subject is surrounded with humor and non-malicious gossip, exchanged eagerly by way of collective thinking on the problem. One informant suggested this idea for possible inclusion in the laundromat scene from *Vibram Soul*. One can infer levels of commitment within a couple relationship by watching how they do their laundry. If two people arrive at the laundromat in the same vehicle, but place their laundry in separate machines, that is a low level of commitment. If the clothes are pooled, then sorted by laundry categories rather than by ownership, something is cooking. If the clothes are pooled, sorted, and then the couple co-operates in folding sheets, there soon may be diapers in the laundry. The punch line would be, "Yes, but do they unroll each others dirty socks?" Another, half-serious suggestion was to ask couples who recently moved in together and refuse to define their relationship if they have inter-filed their record, tape, and book collections. Interested parties can, and often do, simply ask, "what's going on between you two?" but if they do, they must be prepared for a vague facial expression in lieu of verbal explanation. Of all the social relationships Mateelians are reluctant to define, the cross-sex relationship is vaguest.

Some marital data can be inferred from weddings. A couple living together may or may not have had either a public or a private ceremony establishing a permanent relationship, and may or may not have filed a license at the County Courthouse rendering their relationship susceptible to Amerikan laws. Regardless of legalities, if a public ceremony is performed, it is the one sure indication that the couple wishes to be considered by the community as a social unit. Ceremonies are highly eclectic, again, situational, may or may not invoke a deity, and may or may not involve a religious specialist. If they do not, they will probably be conducted by a friend who acts as temporary minister. To be legal, the license need only be signed by an ordained minister and many Mateelians joined the mail order Universal Life Church specifically to be able to sign marriage licenses for their friends.

If the wedding ceremony is so eclectic and the relationship it attempts to make explicit so ambiguous, one might well wonder what is the purpose of the ceremony? As a Universal Life Church Minister, that is the first question I ask in the pre-nuptial interview. From this data and from observation of dozens of Mateelian weddings, I can offer only one reason, one that is well within the range of anthropological expectation. Weddings are performed as rites-of-passage asking the friends and relatives of the couple to consider their relationship as something special. Some couples express a vague hope that if everyone else treats them as a social unit, they will find it easier to maintain that unit. Beyond this, one may only take each wedding on its own merit to discover what else is intended. The joke is always made, "Well, it's a great excuse for a party."

Traditionally, affinal relationships other than "husband" and "wife" are considered to be the "in-law" relationships created by a marriage. In Mateel, this category of traditional relationships is not especially relevant, because of the ambiguity of cross-sex relations, and because most legal "in-laws" live outside Mateel, which automatically lowers their importance. The only affinal relationship is the central one of the marriage or marriage-like relationship itself. If explicit marriages become the pattern in the next generation, affinal relationships could then become important.

One advantage of becoming legal is that when the relationship ends, one can file for a legal divorce rather than relying on good will to work out the intricacies of community property and child custody. This may be seen as a tacit acknowledgement of one of the central failings of Mateelian society, which is that there has never developed an accepted, effective, and reliably just way to resolve conflict. There are numerous strategies for the prevention of conflict and there is much in Mateelian culture that precludes certain kinds of conflict, but once the effectiveness of these has been surpassed, the general suspicion of mainstream authority limits access to mainstream law and there has evolved nothing to replace it. One of the most common of these situations is when a long-term couple relationship that has never been legalized comes to an end. Since common-law marriages have no status in California, community property laws do not apply. Even in cases where there is a legal agreement, either by way of a formal legal contract or a legal marriage, the fact that representatives of government agencies have been known to hang around civil courts looking for evidence of illegal activities, makes people reluctant to cast their lot with mainstream law. Agreements must be reached about the distribution of land, vehicles, savings (often buried in a jar out in the woods), dwellings, and children, by parties who are made as irrational by their emotions as people in similar situations everywhere.

What very frequently happens, in spite of communal and egalitarian idealism, is that property reverts to whoever happened to get a name on a paper and there is no recourse for the person whose name somehow did not get on the paper. This person is more likely to be female than male, although there are cases where it was the woman who had the down payment for the land. Mateel therefore abounds with disillusioned, embittered women who spent years of their lives making homes in the worst of conditions, wresting gardens out of rock piles, and doing the vast majority of child-related tasks, only to find ten years later that their partner in these enterprises is going to end up with the land, the house, and whatever is valuable. He often, perhaps usually, makes no arrangement to pay child support or to re-organize his life to include taking half the responsibility for his children. Many of the stories told by these women are indistinguishable from those of mainstream divorced women except that what little justice is available for the homemaker in the mainstream courts, was only available to those Mateelian women who got married. One female informant said in disgust, after telling how her child's father justified taking the land because he built the house and spent the most time on the cash crop, "That he could act like this and then turn around and call himself 'Sun Man' . . . !"

Given the number of women who are unlanded with the loss of their S.E., it is surprising that the ideal of "keeping it together for the kids" somehow prevails as often as it does. Men and women engaged in terminating a relationship that included children may go through unbelievable personal agonies to create or maintain as much continuity as possible for their children, while simultaneously attempting to gain as much financial advantage as possible from each other. One experiment commonly attempted is for both parties to build another house and attempt to remain on the same land. While requiring superhuman interactional effort, this solution has the advantage of providing the children with equal and spontaneous access to both parents. If they were legal land partners, this arrangement also solves the problem of dividing up the claim to the land. Usually, however, they are not, and this arrangement requires the non-legal partners to hand almost complete power over their lives to the legal partner, since he/she could order them off the land anytime. Nevertheless, many individuals, by far more of them female, accept that arrangement for the sake of the children, and there have been a handful of cases where it worked The most common arrangement, however, is that one co-parent leaves, reimbursed for her/his financial and emotional investment in the land or not, and remains in the community so as not to deprive the children of access to both parents and the community. Many informants have reported that when their relationship to the children's other parent ended they would have gone somewhere else, except for the children.

Children, then, ultimately bind the community together because the value of keeping them in Mateel so frequently overrides the value of seeking another life elsewhere. Children also bind the community by the fact that so many of the institutions were created for their benefit and as the result of individual parents attempting to create the best possible kind of life for them. The main impetus for the Redwoods Rural Health Center was to provide alternative childbirthing, believed to be the best for the children. The vigorously successful alternative schools were created by parents who could not bear the thought of abandoning the education of their children to the system that had so failed them. They bind the community through their fictive and real kinship ties to each other, which link adults who otherwise would not seek relationship. The kinship tie that has the most significance for Mateelian society is the one between parents and children as actual kin and that between children as half-siblings and fictive siblings. It is important, then, to examine these children, who bind the community together, and how they are raised.

Child Rearing

From a global perspective, the least environmentally responsible characteristic of Mateelian behavior is the widespread resistance to population control. Modern birth control is easily obtainable and is practiced, as are abortions, yet pregnant women, nursing mothers and children of all sizes are everywhere in Mateel and discussions of implementing zero population growth often fall on deaf ears. It is not environmental ignorance, as the same set of parents who have four or five children will religiously plant trees and food crops, control erosion, compost their organic garbage, and install solar panels. If one presses for an explanation of this apparent contradiction in values, one will be told that the problem is not overpopulation, but inequality, that if resources were distributed equally there would be no problem at all. Furthermore, the argument runs, Mateelian children are raised to be peaceful and environmentally conscious, therefore the more of them there are, the greater the probability that these ideas will gain power. Responding to these arguments with the obvious, that both inequality and overpopulation are factors in resource imbalance, and that the Nazis, too, thought their children were superior, is generally an exercise in futility.

One cannot avoid the impression that there is something about Mateel that inspires people to reproduce. The positive side is that most children who are born in Mateel are greatly desired. People who came to Mateel with children already grown and gone become inspired to start new families with new partners. Informants who had decided definitely never to have children, often because they saw the world so negatively that they hesitated to condemn another to life, change their minds drastically and start families in Mateel. Women whose education, intelligence and capabilities would have caused them to choose more career and less children had they remained in the mainstream, continue to have children into their forties in Mateel. It is not that, statistically, Mateelians are any worse in this respect than comparable communities, as the Ferndale census district reports more births per female than the Garberville census district.[10] It is that, given the ideal and actual environmental imperatives of Mateelian culture, the ease with which Mateelians produce more Americans to draw their disproportionate share of the world's resources seems incongruous.

It would be difficult to say how much this represents a biological imperative liberated from restrictions of rationality by psychedelics or more direct contact with the natural environment; how much it expresses the resurgence of hope for humanity encouraged by living in a hopeful, creative society; whether it is similar to the flower on the dying cactus, a last-ditch effort to keep the species extant on the part of people unusually sensitive to the possibility of extinction; or how much it is the lack of a birth control method that feels compatible with a return to a more natural state. Whatever the reason, Mateel abounds with children.

Negative pictures of countercultural childrearing have been presented in the literature. The accusation of neglect may also be heard in Mateel where it emanates from mainstream bureaucracies such as the public schools and welfare agencies, as well as from mainstream individuals who come into contact with countercultural children. This accusation is also leveled by Mateelians at each other in the course of collective educational efforts and in relations between neighbors. It would take a separate, systematic study to determine the extent of the validity of these allegations. Such a study would require careful definitions of words like "neglect," and "responsibility" and would have to carefully consider the frames of reference within which these words are used. There are many Mateelian children who, relative to three-quarters of the world's juvenile population, are not cold, hungry, frightened, or unloved, but have not recently had their noses wiped. These would have to be eliminated from any definition of child neglect appropriate to Mateel.[11]

Before continuing with a discussion of the negative aspects of childrearing in Mateel, it should be mentioned that one of the limitations of the present research is the fact that the sample may be somewhat biased toward the positive. During a large part of the research I was simultaneously raising my own two children. My observations are therefore overwhelmingly of children and parents encountered in the course of seeking the optimum conditions for my own children. No special effort was made to collect conflicting data in this area, although there clearly is a negative side to the picture. The following observations are based on the assumption that my experiences are in no major way dissimilar from those of other Mateelians who are also seeking optimum conditions for their children, but they admittedly do not present a complete picture.[12]

There are cases that could be called neglect and/or abuse by anyone's standard that take place within the six core watersheds and in residences that are Mateelian by the present definition. In one case, a clearly malnourished baby was removed from his alcoholic mother at her request by another Mateelian mother and cared for by her and other Mateelians for a period of six weeks before being returned. This child was later the focus of a prolonged legal case in which the Humboldt County Welfare Department sought to remove the child permanently from his mother. Individuals close to the case and the Mateelians who had once cared for the baby agonized over whether, if subpoenaed, they would testify for or against the removal of the child from its mother. They were torn between their deep love and respect for children and their intense suspicion of the methods and motives of the bureaucracy, which they perceive as already interfering overmuch in personal affairs. I have personally encountered two cases where children under eight were left in isolated cabins with no close neighbors or telephones for periods of days, and heard rumors of similar cases within Mateel.

My impression, unsupported by statistics, is that these cases are definitely exceptions among Mateelians. They could be interpreted as perversions of the attitude that children are much more naturally cautious than mainstream parents give them credit for and can and should be allowed to learn survival skills as early as possible. Because of the isolation of Mateelian residences with little access to telephones, ambulances, neighbors and sidewalks, it is believed that children need to learn early the consequences of their actions, such as what happens if you put your hand on a hot wood stove or play too near a cliff. They will never learn these lessons if they are protected and guarded at every turn. Many Mateelians have opined in my presence that mainstream children who are not allowed to learn survival skills suffer from neglect, since they would be totally helpless in the event of a major catastrophe that rendered modern technology useless and/or separated them from their parents.

The experience of one informant makes this comparison especially clear. She took her nuclear family to an extended family summer reunion in an Eastern suburb. Neighbors had loaned recreational vehicles and campers to the family and they had been parked all over the front and back yards. Sleeping arrangements had been made in advance by the suburban father of two teenage daughters, who apparently was operating on his own parental assumptions. When the informant discovered that she had been assigned to share a camper with her daughter rather than share a bed with her husband, she objected and asked why. The Mateelian family was amused and amazed that the organizer had assumed that the fourteen-year-old would be afraid to sleep by herself in a camper parked in the back yard. The daughter was an experienced wilderness backpacker who had slept, albeit in the company of other Mateelian children, on some of the most isolated beaches and mountaintops in the country from earliest childhood. A camper in the backyard of a suburban Amerikan home was, for her, tamer than her own bedroom, which had often been a tent in the woods.

The Hominid Child

In a quote used earlier, American civilization was described as "presenting more than anything else a test of the adaptive powers of the hominid child."[13] The author is contrasting modern America with older, simpler societies in terms of the social instability that results from modern technology. The image of the child being tested as an adapting faunal creature, a hominid, however, would be seen by Mateelians as fully applicable to the impersonal and detached way in which the infant is born and treated early in its life, also as the result of the social instability wrought by modern technology. Modern birthing is almost uniformly seen as presenting an incredible test for both the hominid child and the hominid mother, eliminating as it does all respect for mothering as a natural process.

A measure of the importance of preserving natural processes is the phenomenal emphasis on home births and natural childbirth. It was no small decision in the early days of Mateel to have one's baby in a cabin 20 or 30 miles over bad road from the nearest hospital and five miles from the nearest telephone. Yet enormous numbers of women with no preparation for it in their modern, urban backgrounds elected to do this in order to avoid what they perceived as technological interference, perpetrated overwhelmingly by men. It was not that childbirth in an isolated cabin without medical assistance had universal appeal in and of itself; it was just that at that time there were no in-between choices. Either the baby was born in a hospital, with the possibility of unnecessary and possibly harmful drugs, a mechanical ambiance, labor induced as often to serve the doctor's convenience as the health of mother and baby, unnecessary surgery, separation of mother and baby after birth, discouragement of nursing, and no room for family, midwife and friends, or it must be done at home, where these things could be avoided.

It was this extreme of choices that inspired potential and actual Mateelian parents to form the Redwoods Rural Health Center, raising funds for an office and equipment and bringing in sympathetic doctors and medical specialists. Several Mateelian women became licensed female hygiene workers in order to work at RRHC. One left Mateel to become a licensed Physician's Assistant, all in order to provide prenatal care oriented towards home births and natural births and to be able to legally assist doctors at births. The many lay midwives who continued to practice without licenses or formal training now had a sympathetic medical establishment to which to refer cases beyond their expertise. So successful was the RRHC that the local establishment hospital, originally vehemently opposed to home births, was forced to create a "birthing room" where midwives, family and fathers could be present at births, only calling on doctors and nurses if they were needed. At present in

Mateel a woman may choose from a wide range of possibilities in birthing and find complete support and help, whether she wishes to have a hospital birth or a home birth.

The respect for personal idiosyncrasy prohibits the social pressure for home and natural births from getting out of hand, although I have seen instances where the father placed pressure on the unwilling mother to have a home birth because it fit so neatly into his personal image of self-sufficiency and returning to nature. One of the functions of the midwife is understood to be counteracting this kind of pressure and reassuring the woman that whatever she chooses is valid. Midwifery did not increase the pressure on women for home births but has widened the options, so that the hospital birth does not present the technocratic specter it used to and women who might have chosen a home birth unwisely are not so reluctant to choose a hospital birth if that is more appropriate. What an alternative birthing establishment did do was make it more possible for babies to begin life with all the mammalian comforts to which every hominid child would seem to be entitled.

Unfortunately, the whole subject of childbirth and midwifery cannot be dealt with here in proportion to its significance to the development of Mateelian culture. However, there have been many books written on the subject of home and natural childbirth, addressing both the practical and the philosophical issues. A very enlightening recent publication and one that is especially relevant to Mateel is *Hearts Open Wide*, by Pam Wellish and Sandra Root, whose rural northern Californian informants appear to be in no way dissimilar from Mateelian informants in their views and the practical details of their lives.[14] Wellish and Root's informants are educated, articulate and obviously highly motivated, as are the majority of Mateelians. Their stories are models of the way in which Mateelian-type values are expressed so courageously by women willing to risk their lives and the lives of their children on the premise that birth is a natural process best left in the hands of women. Reading of the difficulties and near-misses described by their informants, one is struck by the strength of the desire to reclaim human experience for the individual. Everything about Mateel is an expression of that desire and nowhere is it more obvious than in childbirthing. However, home births, natural childbirth, and nursing were not invented by Mateel or the counterculture, although both may claim some credit in their resurgence.

Spock's Children

The blame for the counterculture has often been laid at the step of Dr. Benjamin Spock, who is said to have invented "permissiveness" as a childrearing method. In a lecture given at the "Conference on the Sixties" in San Francisco in 1987, and sponsored by the History Department at the University of California, Berkeley, Dr. Spock rejected the word "permissive" as an accurate description of his method and suggested the words "flexible" and "interactive" as more applicable.[15] He described his method as a reaction to the rigidity of science as applied to parenting and to the conception of the child as an automaton rather than an individual person with individual biological and emotional needs.

At the same conference, the longtime feminist Betty Friedan faulted Spock for helping to confine women to the home by placing such a burden of responsibility on them alone as parents. What Friedan and many feminists apparently do not realize is that Spock was inspired and influenced by an even earlier feminist, Margaret Mead, who selected Spock out of dozens of New York pediatrician/gynecologists because he was the only one willing to help her have her baby in a manner similar to the women she had just finished studying in Samoa. Margaret Mead was fifty years ahead of her time in arranging a natural childbirth and insisting on nursing her baby.[16]

The approach to childrearing exemplified by Spock and Mead is among the few ideas born in the technocracy and retained in the counterculture. This is because that approach is recognized as an early reaction to the technocracy. The later actions of Spock and Mead in opposing nuclear weapons and the Vietnam War confirmed to the next generation that they also viewed the technocracy with alarm and were willing to risk their careers to prove it. It was clear in Spock's 1987 lecture that he was not at all displeased with the way "his" children had turned out, which, no doubt, explains the standing ovation he received before and after his speech. Whereas

Spocks's original manual, *Baby and Child Care*, is now considered obsolete by many Mateelians, because it is generally geared even less towards working with natural stages of development than these Mateelians would prefer, the general trend it started is continued and expanded in Mateel.[17]

The Spock/Mead/Friedan trialogue is relevant to Mateel in that it typifies some Mateelian attitudes about childrearing. Mead's contribution to the thinking of Spock links the whole idea of the natural birthing and rearing of children in industrial society back to the preindustrial form of culture and back to women. Mead was inspired by a more natural and female-controlled way of having children and she inspired a sympathetic male doctor who then attempted to make those ideas applicable in a modern context. This is just exactly what happened in the history of Mateel with regard to having children. The acknowledgement of humans as part of nature took its most compelling form for women in the desire to have babies naturally. They enlisted sympathetic men into the effort to combine modern technology and knowledge with the urge toward harmony with nature, with the RRHC as a concrete result. Friedan's position expresses the conflict felt by many Mateelian women between this deep-seated acceptance of their biological nature and the quite realistic threat that it would somehow return them, against their will, to the kitchen and the nursery where they would face the responsibility of parenthood in isolation.

Be this conflict as it may, what is seen as good for the baby ultimately wins out in Mateel. From the moment of its birth and sometime even before then, the Mateelian baby is protected from treatment as a statistic and from neglect of its mammalian needs. Especially important is the biologically established bond between mother and child. Many Mateelians believe that their child is "bonded" to its mother at birth in the same way other species are, if it is born wide awake, kept by the mother's side and nursed immediately. Failure to meet these conditions will affect forever the relation between mother and child. Several informants have attributed problems with their hospital born children to the fact that they were prevented from experiencing birth naturally. Agnes Cereceda, one of Wellish and Root's informants, describes her birth experience in a Los Angeles hospital as taking place under "barbaric conditions." It was fourteen hours before she could see her baby and when he did not nurse immediately, he was removed back to the nursery. She was the only woman on a ward of twenty-five who even made the attempt. When she cried at his removal, she was given tranquilizers. She asks, "how can anyone bond under those circumstances?"[18]

Providing for the biological, social and emotional needs of the child as an individual human animal is a theme carried on throughout its entire childhood. Playgroups and preschools emphasize development at an individual rate, without competition with others, and in terms of the child's own potential. At Beginnings' two schools, Children's House and Skyfish, the environmentally oriented Montessori method has been adapted to rural conditions. In the home, the environment is made as safe as possible for the child, even though it may present some inconvenience to the parents, so that exploration, natural curiosity and a positive approach to the world will be thwarted as little as possible by the word "NO." Children are encouraged to be self-reliant, self-sufficient, independent and highly social. This is done first of all through interaction that stresses respect for the child.

Many a visiting grandparent or non-Mateelian visitor has described the Mateelian child as unsupervised, obnoxious, selfish and spoiled. Informal comparisons between Mateelian children and local mainstream children or visiting tourist children indicate that the Mateelian children are much more likely to expect to be both seen and heard. As older children they will certainly "question authority" (from a bumper sticker found commonly in Mateel) more. Alternative schools routinely take them on field trips to public hearings on nuclear power plants, offshore oil drilling, and spraying pesticides and herbicides specifically to teach them confidence in engaging in these democratic procedures. Manifestly, they are more at home in their bodies, more active, less restrained and nervous, and physically confident. The interpretation of this behavior as spoiled and obnoxious might well be made by persons accustomed to temerity in children. This is not to say that Mateelians do not sometimes also find their own and each other's children obnoxious, only that they make an exchange, believing that it is better to have a child who is pushy when young and confident when older than a child who never gains a healthy sense of Self even in adulthood.

It is largely the expectation of Mateelian children that they will be treated as persons, which brings about the criticism that they are spoiled. They have been encouraged in this expectation by the kind of interaction they receive from alternative teachers, their parents, and the parents of their friends. This interaction places the same value on their input as it does on adult input, and perhaps even more, since great patience is displayed in teaching them normal adult conversational rules. An ongoing adult conversation, for instance, will come to a screeching halt if a small child interrupts to speak to one of the adults. Everyone will stand by patiently until the child has been fully attended to. It is not until children are well established in their confidence and self-image that they will begin to be instructed about interrupting adults.

Another interactional factor is that adults refrain from the kind of interaction with the child that places words in her mouth or requires her to display false emotions. The kind of adult-child interaction in which the adult says to a completely uninterested child "Say 'My name is Carole.' Gimme a big smile and hug my neck. Go hug Aunt Zelda and tell her you love her. Say 'I'm too little to play baseball.'" and treats the child generally as if it were some kind of prop is rarely seen in Mateelian situations. Baby talk is generally avoided in favor of meaningful talk adjusted to the child's level of verbal development. These reversals of the common mainstream approach can be very frustrating to those who do not give the establishment of confidence in a small child top priority. The aim is to refrain from sending the child the interactive message that she is of no importance as a person, or is of importance only insofar as she can be "cute." The aim is also to reduce as much as possible the number of situations in which the child will feel powerless.

Adolescence

Most Beginnings parents agree that the themes of working with, rather than against, natural processes and stages of development, encouraging self-reliance, personal responsibility, confidence, and sociability, individualized education and treating the child with respect as a person have been implemented into a coherent program in the two existing schools. Parents of children in the other alternative schools generally express satisfaction with the progress in integrating these themes into school policy. Where parents find themselves most on their own is when the children reach adolescence. It is here that opinions become most divided on the best way to apply those ideas, that alternative education becomes least available and that non-Mateelian influences are least avoidable.

The Southern Humboldt Unified School District includes six elementary schools, one junior high school and one high school for all of the children in a 973 square-mile area. Whereas elementary schoolchildren are relatively close to their assigned public school, in order for junior high and high school students to attend these schools they may face school bus rides up to two hours long in each direction. The length of the ride alone makes some children reluctant to attend the public schools and their parents hesitant to force them. In addition, it is clear to many Mateelian parents that, although individual teachers are not necessarily opposed to Mateelian ideas about education and Mateelian teachers have increasingly been employed at the public schools, there is literally nothing that can be done to loosen up the structural inflexibilities of mass secondary education.

This is not perceived as so crucial a problem in the elementary years because Mateelian parents determined to avoid the problems of public schools have some alternatives, and because those who cannot or do not arrange for alternative schools for their children have more access to the less centralized public elementary schools than they do the distant junior high and high school in terms of parental input. In addition, parents have more control over the individual preschool and elementary school child and can compensate for perceived public school shortcomings at home. Also children this age are learning basic skills, not explicit political, social and philosophical concepts, so that differences between the mainstream and Mateelian families are not so highlighted as they become later.

In secondary school, the child has reached the developmental stage of social awareness. Social differences become obvious, peer groups all powerful, and conformity vs. non-conformity a crucial issue. Social questions require honest answers. Adolescents, it has been shown time and again, are more conservative than any other age group. The rigid structure of the public secondary schools, necessitated by mass education, may be experienced as unbearable for a certain percentage of Mateelian adolescents, particularly if their educational experience to date has been exclusively in alternative schools. Equally unbearable may be the demands of mainstream adolescent society, itself.

Numerous instances of harassment of Mateelian students by mainstream students have been reported. They are based on refusal to conform to the requirements of mainstream fashion, pacifist and environmentalist political views, an enormous difference in the freedom allowed to Mateelian adolescents by Mateelian parents, especially in the area of sexual activity, factors related to poverty, or irreverence for mainstream high school traditions. In short, the adolescent harassment cases are exactly like the adult harassment experiences except that for the secondary student, there is no escape. Mateelian parents, mindful of the cultural differences that they have the freedom to avoid and remembering their own, often painful experiences in the public high schools, are reluctant to advise their children to "grin and bear it."

The only options are the Independent Study Program, which allows course requirements for a General Equivalency Diploma to be completed at home, meeting with special teachers twice a week, or continuation school, designed for disciplinary cases who would otherwise drop out. Neither of these programs were intended for academically satisfactory or superior children, certainly not college-bound children, but both have tried to adapt to the influx of children who are miserable for social reasons in the standard program.

The three year existence of Briceland Community High School was an attempt to provide a secondary education compatible with the type of elementary and preschool experience of children who attended alternative schools. Operating under the umbrella of Beginnings and set up on community owned land, BCHS was nevertheless plagued from its inception by the inadequacy of its financial base. Parents who had succeeded in establishing pre-schools and elementary schools found that it took much more money to set up a secondary school, especially if they were to prepare students for college. For the first two years, BCHS received twenty percent of its budget from the Independent Study Program and included two teachers on the staff who held secondary teaching credentials and were paid by the Independent Study Program.

The remainder of the budget came from tuition and private donations, both of which sources were inadequate to start with and dried up with the establishment of the CAMP program. In the third year the shaky relationship between the school district and the alternative secondary school came to a head when a list of conditions was issued by the school superintendent under which Independent Study funds could continue. The clincher for the staff was the rule giving the district complete power to decide which district students would be permitted to attend BCHS. It was decided to forfeit the twenty percent of the budget by declaring the conditions unacceptable. The school folded that term.

Financial problems were not the only source of difficulty, however. Parents, students and staff were never able to achieve the most minimum level of consensus on basic issues of educational policy, structure, and discipline. The conflicts and tensions that arose in this collective effort to provide for adolescents is typical of the tensions that exist generally in the culture and affect not only the alternative schools, but the public schools and family life as well. There was disagreement as to the philosophy of the school. The principal founder, who did an enormous amount of fund-raising, research, and organizing and was the main person interacting with mainstream entities, often stated that he was inspired by Summerhill, the British experimental school founded in the 1920s by A. S. Neill.[19] Others on the staff saw this model as the source of some good ideas, but not entirely applicable, since Summerhill was essentially one man's experiment rather than a collective effort, was geared to the upper class, and died soon after Neill did.

It was never clear to parents, students or staff whether attendance in class was mandatory, elective, or necessary. Battles raged over just how open the campus was, how responsible the school was for students off campus during school hours, and who was authorized to remove the students for what reasons. One teacher complained bitterly when a parent appeared at the morning "circle" and invited the entire school to a spontaneous, basically unsupervised beach party, then failed to provide those who went with a safe ride back to the school. How much the students were part of the decision making was ambiguous. In line with the emphasis on early self-reliance and responsibility, some felt that no policy should be implemented without the consent of the students, while others felt that students should be incorporated into some appropriate decisions as they collectively displayed maturity. One problem in this area was that not all of the students had attended alternative elementary schools. Those who had only attended public schools had no other model to work from. Consequently, they were either interested only in reacting to their negative experience, using this opportunity to discharge a backlog of negative feelings, or they wanted to copy the public schools in every detail and balked at the slightest experimentation. The students had been told that they ran the school as much as the adults, but this policy turned out to be nearly impossible to implement in every situation. This resulted in many occasions when students felt either double-crossed because decisions were made without them or frustrated because they could not determine what was expected of them.

Discipline was impossibly complex. Under what circumstances could a student be suspended or expelled? Was the repeated refusal to do assigned chores or the lack of academic progress sufficient grounds? What was to be done about students who gathered in the abandoned building next door to smoke marijuana and then returned to campus? Had they broken the rule against marijuana on campus or not? The central problem here is one of the central problems of the entire cultural system, namely, the enormous reluctance on the part of responsible individuals to assume any authority. No one wanted to be in the position of "policing" the students. Everyone wanted to bring about voluntary compliance to general policies based on the students' sense of social responsibility. Everyone agreed that this was a worthy and viable long-term goal, but given that there were too many students in whom that sense was insufficiently developed, the immediate steps to be taken to achieve the goal were constantly under dispute.

No less ambiguous was the criteria for selection of students and staff. One negative ramification of the extreme tolerance of Mateelians is that individuals who drain collective resources or create unnecessary confusion cannot be restrained. No one is willing to advocate rejection, restriction, expulsion, eviction, firing, or punishment. Magical anarchy has no mechanism for preserving the integrity of the social system under threat, although it has many mechanisms for preventing the occurrence of conflicts. Unfortunately, these did not appear to work at BCHS, perhaps because so many members of the staff were new to the community and were unfamiliar with the history and subconscious culture of it. A very clear dichotomy developed between students who were committed to the survival of the school, understood its collective nature, faithfully performed their chores, worked well under the low-structure, flexible, individualized, and contractual program, on the one hand, and those who either were in the school because they were unacceptable elsewhere or who for some reason did not work well in a low-structure situation on the other. The inability of the adults to clearly demonstrate commitment to a disciplinary policy that encouraged responsibility and discouraged irresponsibility ultimately made cynics of some of the more committed students and frustrated parents and staff to the point of paralysis.

A major controversy was the degree to which the school should attempt to maintain public academic standards. Although the main attraction the school had to offer was a program tailored to the needs of the individual student, made possible by a very low student/teacher ratio (ten to one), it was impossible to completely eradicate the conception of age-based grades, derived from the public schools. If students were to be able to transfer into public schools at the grade appropriate to their ages, they had to have completed the required work. Also, students who had had any experience with the public schools were unable to conceive of doing work based on their abilities rather than their age and therefore their grade. Subjects were therefore taught to students in more or less the same grade, rather than in a similar range of development in that subject. There was such an extreme range of ability between students in the same class that the staff was hard put to keep the promise of individualized programs.

An eighth grade social science class might have students who were reading at college level and those barely capable of reading comic books. College-bound students worried that they would not be accepted even into the state university system, let alone higher quality private universities, because there were no facilities for laboratory courses, while non-academically oriented students and their parents questioned the necessity for a functioning school library.

All of these issues illustrate differences in the general approach to adolescence and questions of how much or how little structure is appropriate. When BCHS disbanded, students who transferred to the public high school, the continuation program, or independent study, generally made good adjustments. Some students who had not been ready for the lack of structure at BCHS suddenly improved in the public school programs. Some students simply took the GED (General Equivalency Diploma) exam and dropped out without graduating, and then "hung out" a year or so before attending community college. Other BCHS students simply dropped out of any educational program and with the approval of their parents, concentrated on learning practical survival skills such as building, farming, wilderness survival and crafts.

When BCHS disbanded, another alternative high school was organized at the geographical fringe of Mateel in Petrolia. This high school stands a good chance of avoiding some of the problems of BCHS. Its remote location requires that many of the students reside on campus, elevating solidarity and commitment to the school, and reducing distractions. The remote location also reduces friction with mainstream critics, since educational experiments are not so visible. Some students whose performance at BCHS had been mediocre, transferred to the new alternative high school and immediately bloomed, both academically and in terms of personal development, under the more cohesive and artistic regime there.

Some see a negative influence on Mateelian adolescents in marijuana cultivation. As a social science teacher, I many times was asked by my students why they should learn geography or history when these subjects had no bearing on their future as marijuana farmers. The cultivation option does not appear to adolescents as ephemeral as it does to their parents and many adolescents develop attitudes based on their marijuana cultivating that appear maladaptive and unrealistic to their more educated parents. Since they have not learned basic economics, they are unaware that the marijuana economy is a boom economy extremely liable to a bust phase. My answer to my students was that a knowledge of geography and history would help enable them to foresee major catastrophes that would affect their survival, such as a war into which they might be drafted, or an economic depression that would dry up the market for their crop. Another answer was that the less educated they are, the more vulnerable they would be to political and economic exploitation. Such a view, however, was sometimes too abstract for students and their parents, a circumstance that reflects the permissive anti-intellectual bias among Mateelian parents.

Despite the great variations in parental approaches to the adolescent, there is no evidence that Mateelian children are impacted any more negatively by their Mateelian childhoods than mainstream children are by theirs. There are indications that, individually, it has been a very good experience for many of them. For instance, in the South Fork High School class of 1987 the top three students were the children of parents who lived at one time or another, in one of the six core watersheds. One of the top social science students at South Fork was asked to look at the honor roll and the Dean's List, which are routinely published in the local mainstream newspaper, Redwood *Record,* and, using her knowledge of the individual students in the student body of 356 in 1988, to check the ones considered to be from "hippie" families. (Students at South Fork High have no difficulty at all deciding who is "straight" and who is "hip," as the harassment incidents mentioned earlier suggest.) Her list indicated that a third to a half (the difference consists of question marks) of the students on the Honor Roll and Dean's List are considered "hippies" by the other students. This statistic would be much more useful if there were some way to determine the proportion of "hippies" in the general population. As it stands, however, it is a rough indication that the commonly expressed fear of widespread brain damage in the children of the counterculture is not supported by that datum.

Additionally, in 1987 and 1988, the Humboldt County Office of Education coordinated an "Olympics of the Mind" at Humboldt State University in Arcata, to which all of the junior high schools in the county sent representatives, who competed in six areas of intellectual endeavor. At least half of the representatives from Miranda Junior High School live in one of the six core watersheds. They won by a mile in three areas and placed second in the other three, against urban schools three times their size. In 1988, at least five of the eight finalists to be chosen as Miranda representatives lived in one of the six watersheds. Again, these data are of limited use without a statistical context, but they would seem to contradict any notions of inferior academic achievement in Mateelian children and indicate that, even using traditional Amerikan standards, such as scholastic achievement, they have not been harmed by their Mateelian childhoods.

One striking difference about the Mateelian approach to child rearing is the release of the next generation from the sexual mores to which their parents found it necessary to rebel. Small children are never prevented from engaging in sexual play and are educated in sexual matters, including birth control, from the earliest possible moment. Children attend the births of their siblings and, beyond the common instruction "you have to wear pants to town," little attention is paid to modesty.[20] Children of opposite sexes sleep in proximity to each other on camping trips and at overnight parties without restriction. When they reach puberty, adults ideally take a practical approach to helping them with their new relationship to sexuality. The exception to this general statement is Mateelian fundamentalist Christians.

Teenagers' lovers are usually accepted into the extended family as fictive or potentially affinal kin. It is commonly accepted that when the adolescent is individually ready for it, he or she will bring a lover home for overnight visits. I have never heard of a case where this was discouraged, let alone forbidden. The adolescent couple may alternate the time they spend with each other's families. Eventually, if all goes well, the young man may simply move in with the young women's family on a permanent basis and become part of the economic unit. One such case resulted in a wanted pregnancy with the delighted grandparents welcoming their new common-law son-in-law into the home. The couple eventually moved into their own apartment. In one case, the young woman moved in with the young man's family, who then parented both teenagers, extending their help to the young woman, even after the couple broke up. It would be premature to attempt to read a pattern into these cases, since there has not yet been a sufficient number of Mateelian children to reach late adolescence to see how they will work out their matings. At present, however, there is no reason to suspect that they will revert to a mainstream pattern or deviate in particular from the mating behavior of their parents.

When girls reach their first menses, they are congratulated and generally treated with new respect by their families. Only two formalized first menstruation ceremonies are known to me. Girls are encouraged to go the Planned Parenthood clinic at RRHC soon after their first menses, or are taken there by their mothers. Boys often go for birth-control instruction at puberty. Both sexes may arrange to go together with a friend and Planned Parenthood workers report that the whole procedure has taken on the flavor of a *rite de passage*. Again, it is too early in the evolution of the cultural system to generalize very much as to how this positive attitude toward teenage sexual activity affects the teenagers, either immediately or later on, although it is a subject that cries out for further study.

Comparisons

If kinship is seen as a system for defining relatives, the only difference between Mateel and Amerika is that the Mateelian system includes a large number of fictive relatives by redefining individuals considered less related in the mainstream society as more related. These include individuals who would be considered "step" relatives if the connecting couple were legally married, individuals who share a half-sibling, and ex-spouses and spouse equivalents. They also include individuals who define themselves as related because of a shared historical relationship, such as being present or former land partners or present or former fellow communards. The Mateelian system is identical to the Amerikan system in the way consanguineal and affinal relatives are defined.

In terms of expectations and obligations that accrue to kinship roles, Mateelians generally prioritize Mateelian actual and fictive kin over non-Mateelian kin, except in the case of the children of Mateelians living outside Mateel. The result of this practice is that non-Mateelian kin are more likely to move into Mateel to be near their Mateelian kin than vice versa. Every effort will be made to keep Mateelian children in the community, reinforcing their enculturation in Mateelian culture and maximizing the viability of the cultural system. Mateelians, like Amerikans and perhaps more so, are child-oriented. The child-orientation of Mateelians makes children functionally important as bonding agents for the society, because parents breaking up with each other are reluctant to either remove children from Mateel or to leave them in Mateel while they go elsewhere. They therefore remain in Mateel and become linked in families of serially monogamous spouses and spouse equivalents related to the same children.

American kinship, relative to that of other cultures displays a characteristic that could be called "fuzziness," that is, relationships become more indefinite as one moves away from any particular individual on the kinship chart.[21] There is no formal, categorical limit to the range of kinsmen. Who is included is a function of several variables, including the achievements of the relative, the emotional attachment of the speaker to him or her, geographical distance, and whether the more distant relative is deceased. The emotional variable is defined by anthropologist David Schneider as "enduring diffuse solidarity,"[22] a definition of love many Mateelians would find a hilarious example of scientistic jargon. Schneider stresses that whether or not Americans will include an individual as kin will depend a great deal on whether ongoing interaction obtains. In this flexibility of definition of non-immediate relatives, Mateel is similar to Amerika, and, again, even more so because of the great expansion of the concept of fictive kinship in Mateel and because of the Mateelian vs. non-Mateelian kinship principle.

Affinal kin are probably not as important in Mateel as they are in Amerika in terms of practical and emotional support. Except for the spouses and spouse equivalents themselves, the main situation producing affinal kin is when non-Mateelian blood kin move to

Mateel, thereby becoming available as affines to Mateelian spouses and S.E.s. Parents may do this. In a few cases, children did it, but the most common such situation is a sibling moving to Mateel to join another close-age sibling. Quite a few of these sibling pairs have formed the consanguineal basis for very extended families. The other situation, so far fairly rare, but bound to increase, is when children of Mateelian parents choose mates from within Mateel. If that circumstance becomes commonplace, the affinal tie will become increasingly important in maintaining community solidarity.

Divorce, the cancelling of an affinal tie, has different implications for kinship in Mateel than it does in the mainstream culture. Because of the importance given to staying in Mateel and keeping children in Mateel, all of the parties involved are much more likely to stay in contact than they would be in the mainstream situation. The funky attitude toward roles and situations, discussed in the last chapter, makes this easier for Mateelians than it generally is for mainstream divorcees. Since children commonly move with ease from the household of one parent to the other, and serial monogamy creates a proliferation of step-relations and half-siblings, these households tend to become defined as extended family. This, in turn, increases the number of individuals available to each child for emotional support and as role models. Divorce, or breaking up, then, widens, rather than narrows the child's kin universe. It is a reasonable guess that this is a great departure from the Amerikan serial monogamy pattern, if only because of the mobility of Amerikans and the scale of most Amerikan communities. Both of these factors would tend to preclude the development of the serially monogamous extended family which remains cohesive over time.

The tendency of Amerikan society to isolate persons of the same age is strenuously counteracted in Mateel, although there are certain sources of it that cannot be resisted, such as the public school system. On an interactional level, children are truly listened to, rather than "talked at" through a filter of preconceptions about how one acts toward children of a certain age. This is believed to encourage children to mature at their own speed. Visitors frequently express amazement at the general precocity of Mateelian children in conversation. The preference for independent school work, which allows educational development at an individual rate, also discourages age grading. This can only be implemented in the alternative schools, however, or the independent study program, both of which serve a minority of Mateelian children. Activities that involve the whole school such as plays, field trips, and camping trips provide situations where older children are expected to help with younger children.

Mateelians generally delight in activities that are attended by all ages such as picnics, parties and dances. They take pride in the fact that a "boogie" is always attended by children, teenagers and adults who relate to it in their own ways. Adolescents may tend to bunch up and interact mainly with each other, but they do so in a heterogeneous context that includes all ages. This, too, appears to differ from the mainstream situation where adolescents attend school-sponsored dances often specific to the particular grade and adults attend functions intended to be separate. Mateelian adults disagree on the extent to which this should be the case, with some expressing frustration that there are so few exclusively adult functions, and others insisting on bringing the smallest children even to adult plays. Even if agreement were reached in principle, babysitting is fairly unworkable because of the lack of telephones and the isolation of most Mateelian houses. It thus becomes a matter of practicality as much as inclination with the "let's always bring the children" group arguing that if they did not bring the children, they could never go anywhere. One drama group finally began stipulating "no children" on the playbills for adult plays to reduce noisy interference, so routine is it that infants and small children go with the parents. Whatever the reason for being, children attending events as a family also works against age grading.

The reestablishment of the family as an economic unit including children as useful persons is an ideal highly compatible with that of economic self-sufficiency. It is impossible to generalize a statement from the data available as to whether Mateelian children are actually more or less useful economically than Amerikan children. The opportunity to make the family more of an economic unit would logically seem to be provided by the pattern of building one's own home and raising one's own food. Also, the emphasis on including the children into whatever adult activity is going on, counting work, would tend to raise the economic unity of the family. In the case of smaller children, I suspect that it is truer of Mateelian than Amerikan families, but I have seen no evidence that Mateelian adolescents continue to work within the family unit more than Amerikan adolescents and some evidence that in fact they are less likely to do so.

The one clear tendency toward re-establishing the family as an economic unit is the incorporation of children into marijuana cultivation. Older children and adolescents are often given their own patch and expected to raise their own plants from seedlings, water them, fertilize them, harvest and process them. They usually are not expected to sell their own crop until they are young adults, since this is the most dangerous phase of cultivation and requires the most experience. Alternatively, they may work for their parents or other farmers in exchange for a percentage of the harvest. The results of this custom are mixed. Some adolescents become successful growers as young adults, learn the value of hard work, the practical aspects of farming (which will stand them in good stead should they ever need to grow their own food to survive) and the basics of business. They become independent early, buy their own land or save up for college, build their own homes, have babies and generally become no different than the adults. Others are not motivated to become educated in any other way, since they assume they will be able to grow marijuana indefinitely. They are negatively influenced by money gained too easily and, to everyone's dismay, abandon the idealistic views of the next generation up. They consume cars, guns and drugs wildly, drive recklessly, remain near-illiterate, and display none of the positive Mateelian values. What percentage of Mateelian children are marijuana cultivators is unknown, as is the percentage of juvenile and adolescent growers who are either positively or negatively influenced by the experience.

One general statement about the difference between the Mateelian and Amerikan approach to kinship is the attempt of Mateelians to re-establish the importance of the kinship paradigm in relations, particularly *via* the concepts of "extended family" and "tribe." Schneider's "enduring diffuse solidarity" translates into a generalized feeling of loyalty towards Mateelians for each other as members of the tribe and becomes more intense and specific towards those regarded as "extended family," be they fictive or not. There is, of course, no way to measure love scientifically, except insofar as it is observable in non-verbal and verbal behavior. Sincerity, also, cannot be measured. Based purely on observations of non-verbal behavior and the explicit statements of both Mateelian and Amerikan informants, I would guess that Mateelian individuals are likely to receive more signals they interpret as indicating "enduring diffuse solidarity" over the course of, say, a month than does the average Amerikan. This is a frequent reason given by informants as to why they stay in Mateel.

In the area of kinship, the differences between Mateel and Amerika are probably less than the differences between Mateel and primitive societies in general. Mateelians like to think that their social organization is similar to that of tribal peoples and delight in what tribalistic characteristics they do display, but the true resemblance is really only in the general elevation of the concept of tribe and extended family over other priorities. Further study on this subject would require inclusion of the great diversity primitive peoples exhibit in their kinship systems. There is evidence to suggest that anthropologists studying kinship may have failed in some cases to allow for built-in flexibilities of those systems, which would make them more like both the Amerikan system and the Mateelian system.

There are tribal languages in which one word refers to the biological mother and her sisters or one word that refers to the biological father and his brothers. These languages will, conversely, have one word that refers to one's own children, as well as to one's sibling's children. The general tendency of Mateelians to spread the sense of responsibility for children beyond their own immediate offspring and the corresponding tendency of the children to conceive of classes of adults to whom they may turn for help is reminiscent of this. While it would be going too far to place that widened sense of responsibility above the biological relationship between parent and child, it is fair to say that Mateelians display more of this generalizing tendency than Amerikans do. In a functional sense, this tendency is consistent with the preference for keeping children in Mateel. The wider the group of individuals the child is accustomed to thinking of as parental and vice versa, the greater are the chances of keeping the child in Mateel should its biological parents be rendered nonfunctional.

The nearest Ecotopian writing comes to addressing kinship is in describing the Ecotopian family, which Toffler predicts will be less child-oriented, and more of an economic unit, perhaps with the help of computers, than modern families. It will be non-nuclear, but will take many diverse forms. Computers are becoming more prevalent in Mateel, opening up the possibility of the "electronic cottage" with children incorporated into the electronic home industry. The form of the family in Mateel is certainly diverse, but nuclear families are, nevertheless, the norm and they are even more child-oriented than in the mainstream. However, because of the great diversity of individuals and social forms and because of the tolerance toward social experimentation, it is quite possible that the child-orientation of consanguineally based, nuclear and extended families may not be true of other kinds of extended families or among groupings of singles.

The Ecotopian redefinition of marriage to include wanted children only in order to reduce population growth has come to pass only partially in Mateel. Whereas most Mateelian children are wanted, many of them do not appear to have been planned and little value is placed on population control. The Ecotopian elimination or reduction of sexual repression has more or less come to pass, but it may be questioned as to whether sexual equality has been any better achieved in Mateel than elsewhere, particularly as an ego-support to replace that provided by having children.

Comparative Child-rearing

The major difference between Amerikan and Mateelian child-rearing is in the Mateelian emphasis on natural processes and the natural development of the individual. From birth to death the child—and the adult—is viewed as a growing individual, developing at her/his own rate in response to natural processes. Although home-birthing and natural child-birthing experienced a mainstream surge in the 1970s, it never became the established pattern, whereas one of the most predictable statements one can make about a

Mateelian couple is that they will prefer the most natural possible form of childbirth appropriate to their circumstances. Similarly, the recognition of the child as an intelligent, mobile, individual mammal contrasts with the Amerikan attitude, embodied in the institutions of public education, that there is a timetable and a set of rigid expectations that must be met if the child is to be considered normal and is to be competitive in the economy.

In terms of childrearing, Mateel more clearly resembles primitive peoples. Natural childbirth and nursing are obvious similarities, to which can be added the emphasis on educating the child for survival and direct experience of the natural environment, unavoidable in primitive societies and actively encouraged in Mateel. One aspect of primitive societies that is lacking in Mateel but greatly desired is adolescent "rite of passage" ceremonies. The "rite of passage" is a ceremony that marks a change of status in the individual in relationship to kin and tribe. Mateelian culture has produced ceremonies to mark birth, marriage and death, but it has not yet become customary to stage a ceremony at some point in the adolescent's development to acknowledge arrival at adulthood.

The popularity and success of the Tai Kwan Do program at Beginnings may be partly that it helps to fulfill this perceived need, at least for boys. As they become more and more proficient, they are tested and publicly rewarded for their mastery and discipline. There is no corresponding situation for girls, except insofar as the first menses may be recognized within the family or between mother and daughter. Many Mateelian parents have toyed with the idea of creating adolescent rites of passage, but, without universal recognition among the adolescents, they fail to function and the nearest thing Mateelian adolescents have to a ceremony marking passage to adulthood is the receipt of their driver's license or high school diploma, as it is in Amerika.

One major difference between Mateelian child-rearing and Amerikan child-rearing, at least as it may be observed in mainstream situations in Mateel, is the attitude toward juvenile and adolescent sexuality. This subject comes to the fore at Miranda Junior High School and South Fork High School, where mainstream objections to sex education have been known to prevent visits from Planned

Parenthood for periods of up to five years. These classes were reinstated as the result of the demonstration of clear support from Mateelian parents of secondary students. Given the rapid fluctuations in attitudes toward sex in the mainstream culture, which is now apparently experiencing a fundamentalist backlash to the inroads made by the "sexual revolution" of the sixties and seventies, comparison to Amerika in this area would be risky. Suffice it to say that, with the exception of Mateelian fundamentalists, who are a minority within Mateel, the trajectory suggested by the sexual attitudes of countercultural individuals in the 1960s has continued and matured, with additions from the women's movement and the gay movement, and has been passed on to the next generation in a manner consistent with Mateelian culture.

Margaret Mead points out that American children are often seen as the hope of the family and are expected to achieve more than their parents.[23] This is only true in Mateel in a very general sense. Questions on the subject are generally met with expressions of mild disbelief, as if to ask, "you really want me to make some kind of statement about the future?" Asking a Mateelian about her/his children's future conflicts with "be here now" and with conceptions of karma. The child, says the Mateelian, will be whatever she/he is supposed to be. The idea of children achieving more than their parents in terms of money and status, however, is consciously avoided and parents will specifically state that they "don't want to lay that trip on them."

The hope for the children of Mateel only comes out reluctantly. It is that their unique upbringing will inspire them to actively work for a peaceful and environmentally sound world and that it will help them become happy, loving individuals who will not need to rebel as violently against their parents as their parents rebelled against their grandparents. This hope is, of course, expressed concretely by the incredible collective energy that has gone into constructing a culture that attempts to avoid what Mateelians perceive as their parents' mistakes. While it is too early to generalize as to the success or failure of this construction, the majority of informants with grown children express satisfaction and pride in them.

Acknowledging that a certain amount of adolescent rebellion is part of the natural process of maturation, first generation Mateelians generally reject the idea that the generation gap they experienced was merely an adolescent rebellion that will be repeated by their children. Mateelian parents almost uniformly express the hope for their children that they will be happy rather than the hope that they will be rich. Mateelians freely admit that their hopes for their children are hopelessly idealistic, which is one reason, no doubt, why they are reluctant to make them explicit. Whether the different ways Mateelians and Amerikans want their children to be an improvement over themselves has any effect on the way the children actually turn out remains to be seen. It is certain, however, that this difference in hopes for the children expresses something very profound about the way the two groups view the world.

Comparing Mateelian to primitive child-rearing is, again, difficult because of the great diversity of primitive cultures. Only very general statements may be made. Birthing and mothering in Mateel take place as naturally as possible, in the context of the family, as they tend to do in pre-industrial societies. Educational ideals include holism and practicality, learning in context and as much as possible by doing. These ideals are facts of life in primitive cultures, but fast disappearing as these cultures are brought under the influence of industrial cultures. The Mateelian child is encouraged to maturity and is minimally held back by rigid conceptions of development built into civilized educational structures. This corresponds to the educational philosophy of preindustrial cultures, where children have economic value.

In the area of child-rearing and education, the Mateel system compares well to the Ecotopian model. The relational, holistic, practical education that is cultivated rather than inputted has always been the goal of Mateelian alternative elementary and pre-schools. This goal has been largely met, or met as well as possible, given the restraints imposed from without by mainstream requirements. This kind of education was also the goal of the alternative high school, but the degree to which it was achieved would surely be a controversial subject among the participants. The type of personality described for Ecotopia, resulting from its educational and child-rearing methods, has a strong personal identity, clear aims and values, takes pride in individual and group achievement, is self-disciplined and self-realized, more likely to question authority, to work for incentives other than financial ones, and is most adaptable in general.

There is much to suggest that these personality traits are indeed exhibited by most Mateelian children, and are certainly the ideal that informs Mateelian education and child-rearing. Briceland Community High School's production of *West Side Story* was a case study in pride in group achievement. Three quarters of the student body was involved in the production for the final month of the school year. In spite of the fact that the school was at that time in the deepest throes of controversy, the performance of the students was remarkable. It would have been remarkable in a large, urban high school, let alone a tiny, rural, community-sponsored one. The value of the experience to the students in terms of personal development, learning cooperation and responsibility, interactional skills, and in the experience of creating a successful group production and being publicly acclaimed for it by parents and general community alike was undeniable. Such a production in a "normal" high school would not have been the same in terms of pride in group achievement because it would have been focussed around a drama class or club and accomplished by students with aspirations in drama. In this case, it was a school production, accomplished by students with no particular leaning in that direction, under conditions an ordinary drama teacher would have found primitive to say the least.

In terms of self-discipline and adaptability, one informant reports that when she took her two children with her to the university town where she hoped to complete graduate school, both of them were far behind their grade level academically. This was not surprising, since academic standards in an almost entirely university oriented school system could be expected to be higher than average. Both children had attended public schools and alternative schools in Mateel, with the alternative experience accounting for the main portion of their education. The mainstream teachers of both children independently remarked to their mother that they had never encountered students that far behind academically who were so confident, nonplussed, adaptable, and able to work independently to catch up.

One amazed teacher questioned the mother at length, trying to get more information on the kind of school that produced this independent child. Both children had caught up academically within the first semester and one was on the Honor Roll before the end of the term.

It is, surely, only one example, but it is completely in line with the observations of other mainstream teachers who deal with Mateelian children. It may be taken as an indication that the Ecotopian ideals incorporated into the alternative schools have met with at least some degree of success.

The diverse, self-sufficient orientation of the Mateelians allows parents, especially fathers, more time with their children than a mainstream nine-to-five job does.

Conclusion

We are star dust, we are golden
And we've got to get ourselves back to the garden.

—Joni Mitchell

This study of Mateel reveals a unique cultural phenomenon in its embryonic stages. I have tried to present this view as objectively as possible, given the fact that I have become a part of the culture in ways not generally recognized as traditional anthropological practice. However, value judgements are inherent in the way we organize ethnographic material, from our selected observations to the words we choose for our descriptive narrative. The best way to approach that problem is to state as clearly as possible the values of the ethnographer as part of the data. I have chosen and organized themes based on their potential for highlighting those aspects of industrial civilization that should be changed in order to restore ecological balance between people and their natural environment. In making the value judgement that such changes are required, I am joined by a growing number of people, scientists and non-scientists alike.

The second reason for studying Mateel was to evaluate its usefulness as a model for planning that cultural change. What, in other words, is Mateel good for beyond the personal satisfaction of the individuals who subscribe to it? Mateelians would say that is reason enough for the community's existence, and many have objected to these efforts to find any more reason for it. They deny any personal desire to influence others to live, think, or feel the way they do, thereby lending support to the contention that tolerance for individual diversity is a central value of their culture. Mateelians also question the arrogance implicit in the assumption that they are different than anyone else. Yet, one should not be led astray by the assertion of the "we-are-not-here syndrome." Viewed from the perspective of social science rather than from within the constraints of Mateelian humility, Mateel has great potential for influencing Amerikan society. They have demonstrated that, under the right circumstances, the citizens of industrialized civilizations can drastically change their expectations and behavior. A coherent, viable way of life can be collectively created by those sufficiently willing to change themselves.

The development of a cohesive cultural system from a minimally structured conglomeration of refugees came as a surprise to many of the participants. Operating on the experience gained during the late 1960s and early 1970s, anything seemed possible to them: from the destruction of civilization to isolated lives devoid of cultural supports, to the establishment of Ecotopia. The history of Mateel, in fact, turned out to consist of such a rapid reconstruction of social life and culture that it is difficult to find ways to describe it as it evolves. Cross-cultural relations have been a major force in its development, in terms of setting limits to experimentation, in terms of eliciting reactions that were incorporated into the cultural system, and in terms of the healthy exchange of ideas and cooperation in improving the general community.

The history of cross-cultural relations presents a complicated picture. At the beginning one could have diagrammed the situation by drawing a straight line with "hill people" (hippies) on one side and "locals" (rednecks) on the other. Twenty years of history has made that line wiggly in some places and blurred in others, as full of hairpin curves as the mountain roads of Mateel. While both groups have influenced changes in the other, and great strides have been made since the early days in mutual cooperation, tolerance, and understanding, increased contact has also generated polarization around certain issues, notably what kind of future to work for in southern Humboldt County.

One approach to describing the current situation is to distinguish between individual cross-cultural contact and collective cross-cultural contact. Early Mateelians generally met with negative reactions from individuals in the local mainstream population. Many were shot at, almost all were physically threatened and numerous wildfires in the vicinity of Mateelian homes were deemed cases of arson by Mateelian and impartial observers alike. There were, however, crucial and significant exceptions to the rule of negative contact. The first were those whose primary motivation was economic. Local ranchers who sold to the new people were surely originally motivated by economics. Yet at least one major seller and his wife were seen as more or less interested and sympathetic to the aspirations of the newcomers. Others with primarily economic motivations include junk dealers, heavy equipment operators who stood to profit from making access roads and building sites, and almost anyone who had something to sell. Many mainstream individuals, however, engaged in behavior that calls into serious doubt the purity of the economic motive and suggests that this reason may have been mixed with social and psychological ones, and may well have changed over years of contact with Mateelians.

One such social factor in the early days was discussed in the chapter on Economics. Whereas the practical knowledge of the old-timers did not render them high in status among members of the mainstream social structure, it did in the counterculture. The willingness of urban refugees to "cop to" their ignorance and turn loving and respectful faces to anyone who could help them cure the goat's mastitis must have been hard for some locals to resist. Eccentrics, too, and every small town in America has its share, were given high status by the newcomers; they enjoyed a degree of respect and attention they had never received from their mainstream neighbors. Lecherous old men also had their reasons for cultivating the friendships of female sexual revolutionaries.

It is possible to see a pattern of cross-cultural relations based on mainstream stratification that is entirely predictable sociologically. Those with the greatest status in the mainstream social structure had the most to gain by repelling threats to that structure. Those with the least status had the most to gain by welcoming threats to the social structure; there were more social rewards for them within the alternative culture, which valued them, than there were in the mainstream culture, which devalued them. On the other side, tolerance was a stated ideal among the newcomers and personal idiosyncrasy considered a plus. There was also the peacemaking image to maintain. So as long as political and moral questions could be avoided in conversation, quite an exercise for some of the dropouts, the original Mateelians and some of the "locals" were able to lower their defenses to interact with each other on an individual, situational basis, to their mutual benefit.

Over time, the influx of population into the area, including the new professionals, and the gradual relaxation of both groups from the need to bolster contrasting self-images through defensiveness, resulted in the abandonment of symbols and stances now unnecessary to individual self-definition. Thus, many mainstream individuals became involved in the less militant Mateelian peace and environmental organizations, and a certain number of beaded and befringed garments landed in the free box. The picture became more complicated when violent non-Mateelian marijuana growers arrived in their camouflage shirts, and then grew beards so that they would blend in with the hippies. This inspired many Mateelian men to shave their beards and cut their hair so as not to be confused with these new arrivals. There is presently a much larger number of individuals who could only be assigned to a cultural system on the basis of their own self-definition than there used to be.

The collective picture is somewhat different. Any evidence of organizational potential in Mateel has always been met with collective opposition by the local mainstream population. This dynamic was in evidence as early as 1970 and 1971. In an incident too complex to be detailed here, a collectively run garage and truck stop was "torched" by persons unknown after months of threats from its mainstream neighbors. It had originally been intended to be a stopping place for countercultural nomads to repair vehicles and rest. The founders had been altruistic organizers in the Haight-Ashbury. They came to Mateel when that experiment began to dissolve. Located next door to a small general store and post office run privately by Mateelians, the truck stop had gradually come under the *de facto* influence of a particularly militant nomadic commune, one that did not fix its vehicles and move on.

The appearance and behavior of those "hanging out" at the truck stop came to be resented, not only by the local mainstream population, but by the Mateelian population as well. Rip-offs, particularly of the general store, increased and Mateelians and locals began to fear the potential for further squatting in the area. The general disrespect for individual rights displayed by the squatters at the truck stop offended Mateelians and locals alike. The wrath of the local population, however, recognized no distinctions within the group they defined as "hippies." The absurdity of it all became clear when pacifistic Mateelians found themselves carrying rifles in their pickup trucks as protection against the locals who carried rifles in their pickup trucks. No one, however, had a peaceful solution.

It was never determined who was responsible for the truck stop arson, "locals," resident landowning "hippies," or the squatters themselves in vengeance, but the bad feelings generated against Mateelians by this incident made them extremely reluctant to present a collective face to the public for years afterward. Even organizers of children's play groups and car pools to school were warned against organizing too flagrantly. It was only when a sufficient number of even newer newcomers arrived, who did not have that incident in their memories, that a major undertaking such as Beginnings could be attempted. Even then it was against resistance from those who remembered the truck stop and feared a mainstream backlash.

The success of Beginnings, the Redwoods Rural Health Clinic, the Mateel Community Center and other Mateelian organizations is a monument to the diplomacy of individuals both Mateelian and mainstream who were able to patiently work around the potential conflict implied by the truck stop situation. The difficulty encountered by the MCC in attempting to rebuild its community hall, which was also "torched," is taken by most of its membership as an indication that this potential is still very much alive, if buried under layers of new arrivals and more recent history.[1]

Meanwhile, cross-cultural relations have been facilitated by the development of a number of unifying political issues, such as opposition to the CAMP program, which lumps both Mateelians and locals under the heading "marijuana cultivators." There has also been cross-cultural opposition to a county garbage tax, to a county building code enforcement program, and to the Department of Interior's proposed Lease Sale 91, allowing exploration for oil off the Humboldt and Mendocino coasts. Mateelians have proven themselves worthy cultural additions to the general community and locals of an artistic bent have enjoyed and joined in the renaissance of art, classical music, jazz, dance and drama sparked by the arrival of the talented refugees. The College of the Redwoods extension in Garberville has, for years, formed a sort of neutral ground wherein learning and personal development transcends cultural differences.

Some of the churches, similarly, provide a neutral ground with a transcending purpose. Whereas a certain number of Mateelians always were interested in the fundamentalist churches and were accepted, to the degree that they could approximate the required behavior and subscribe to the moral precepts of those churches, other churches are now drawing Mateelians. Mainstream informants within the Community Presbyterian Church in Garberville have described the process by which its young, socially conscious, folk-singing, co-minister couple was chosen. Attracting members from the Mateelian community was a conscious goal, one that departed from the church's attitude in the early 1970s, when more than one Mateelian family received a lukewarm welcome.

Mateelians have also begun to join established local organizations such as the Soroptomists and the Garberville Chamber of Commerce, further increasing opportunities for cross-cultural exchange. Most of these organizations have remained composed predominantly of individuals who would describe themselves as mainstream, but one experienced a gradual shift of power from mainstream control to Mateelian control. This is the dramatic case of Garberville Post 6354, Veterans of Foreign Wars. Over a period of five years Vietnam veterans, joining at first one by isolated one, then in groups, gradually came to outnumber the World War II and Korean veterans. They adopted "wage peace" as the official motto of the Post, began to sponsor monthly "wage peace" dances, generated state level resolutions against war in Central America and district level resolutions against offshore oil drilling, spraying of pesticides and herbicides by the BLM, and against the county code enforcement program. They also drew fire from other posts by sponsoring peace activist and VFW member S. Brian Willson to speak against aid to the Contras in Nicaragua.

These activities of the post resulted in doubling their membership two years in a row, for which they received awards, and in sparking the revival of the local American Legion, now also composed of mostly veterans from the last two decades. A third veterans group spawned by the VFW is the Veteran's Vietnam Restoration Project, which sent sixteen Vietnam veterans to Vietnam to build a rural health clinic. These activities illustrate the place of the Vietnam War in the history of Mateel. They indicate just how many Mateelians are Vietnam veterans who saw no future for themselves in mainstream Amerika on returning from combat and how these veterans have formed a philosophical and cultural alliance with many former peace activists whose experiences led them to Mateel.

One of the most hopeful indications of Mateelian viability is the organization, after years of struggle, of community-operated radio public station KMUD-FM in Garberville. Although Mateelians were and are prominently involved in its establishment, its programming and staff of volunteer announcers reflects a wide spectrum of social, artistic, and political interests. Its basic message is compatible with the Mateelian worldview and the station manager is the poet Deerhawk, but, as with all Mateelian originated organizations, it is committed to including in its operation the widest possible number of individuals who are willing to work. Most importantly, the existence of the station offers a way for members of each cultural system to exchange or simply listen to each other's views in a harmless, non-confrontational way. Diverse views are exchanged on the talk shows, often vehemently, but radio is a conversational format that limits violence or prolonged harangues, just by its nature. The potential of the radio station to transmit Mateelian culture as far as its signal goes is the most powerful force for change Mateelians have ever controlled, aside from the economic power deriving from the cultivation of marijuana.

Comparisons

It was said at an environmental gathering in 1970 that "you can't live an ecological life in America. That is not an option that is open to you."[2] Assuming from context that the speaker meant "ecologically sound" here, I would reply to this statement that you can certainly try. The existence of the community of Mateel and other similar communities is living proof that if one is willing to undergo the pain of changing culture at the level of the individual unconscious, where the basis for most of culture lies, and if there are others also trying, culture change in the direction of ecological balance is possible. As E. T. Hall observes:

> Our purpose should be to facilitate human interaction, to begin to turn ourselves around and to loosen the unconscious grip of culture so that instead of being controlled by the past, human beings can face the future in a quite new and more adaptive way.[3]

Hall's "should be" is a real process in Mateel.

Numerous Ecotopian writers have looked expectantly to the counterculture for signs of deep-seated culture change.[4] One spoke in 1972, of the hippie movement as drifting "rather self-consciously" in the right direction but qualified the statement by adding that "a deeper and more broadly appealing contact seems needed."[5] In 1988, it was possible to say that the appeal of the life-style represented in Mateel has broadened and deepened considerably. Judging from the reports of non-Mateelian countercultural informants, persons living in a manner similar to that of Mateelians are dispersed throughout rural areas in Northern California, Oregon, Washington, Idaho, West Virginia, Arkansas and British Columbia, at least. Mateel is obvious only because it has become so organized as a community. I do not know of a community where the life-style described here has attained as high a level of organization or self-awareness as it has in Mateel. However, in at least nine communities in the states mentioned, enough cohesion has been reached that these communities are known by name to one another.[6]

In 1978, Marvin Harris dismissed the counterculture as any sort of model for the future because of what he saw as an abandonment of rationality and a shortage of political force.[7] This characterization is demonstrably incorrect with regard to Mateel. The political consciousness and skill there is growing by leaps and bounds. More importantly, political action in Mateel probably reflects the "will of the people" in Mateel more than political action in Amerika reflects the "will of the people" of Amerika. Klein also dismissed the counterculture as being unable to escape the premises it most attempted to counter.[8] He, like Harris, conducted his autopsy much too soon and, like Harris, based it on no ethnographic data whatsoever. The Mateel community has radically changed many Amerikan premises, placed many in a new context, and is actively working on the rest.

In comparing Mateel to the three models, Amerika, Ecotopia, and Primitive, with regard to the most obvious changes and the new contexts, my perspective is objective ecological inquiry and my bias, is hope. I am not at all concerned to determine whether the Mateel cultural system has succeeded or failed to do something by some criterion derived from Amerikan premises. In Mateelian, this attitude would be described as "it is what it is what it is." Beyond this, few "conclusions" can be drawn.

Generally speaking, the greatest contrasts between Mateel and Amerika are in the areas of worldview, personality structure, values, interpersonal relations, social organization and political behavior. It is in these areas that the Mateelian cultural system is most comparable to the Ecotopian model. Economic behavior and material culture may be seen as transitional, with many contrasts to the Amerikan pattern, but incompletely comparable to the Ecotopian or the Primitive model. For instance, the widespread and rapidly increasing use of alternative technology is well-documented in Mateel, but the use of fossil fuel may be still be similar to that of Amerika. This is because the total home system, of which alternative technology systems are sub-systems, is still in the process of being developed to a point where the use of fossil fuel can be reduced. When food production is maximized, trips to town for supplies in automobiles can be reduced. When the houses, barns, and chicken coops are all finished, gasoline operated generators for power tools will be used less. When passive solar water heating systems are all installed, propane water heaters can be eliminated, and so on. The use of alternative energy is a good example of a value in a transitional state where statistics out of context may be misleading.

The Mateelian, Ecotopian and Primitive models are similar to each other in the area of worldview and contrast to Amerika in this aspect. In all three, the universe is not limited to what is perceived through the senses and their technological extensions, but allowance is made for non-rational input. What Bennett calls "a certain humility in the face of nature,"[9] which primitive people display because of their limited technology, is characteristic of Mateel because of a conscious recognition of the ecological limitations of modern technology. The view of the human as "an autocrat with complete power over a universe . . . made of physics and chemistry" is eliminated in Mateel as it would be in Ecotopia.[10]

In the Mateelian and in the Primitive worldviews, in contrast to Amerika, there is less distinction between the natural and the supernatural. These are seen more as a continuum, with mysterious and unknown power immanent in every part of nature, more in some places than others. This power is seen as accessible to humans who are willing to engage in internal explorations and perhaps psychological or physical danger to obtain it. The Ecotopian, Primitive and Mateelian worldviews, in contrast to Amerika, do not see a clear separation between humans and nature or between natural and Supernatural. Interdependence with a physical universe that includes the non-rational is a dominant theme.

Conceptions of time and space are comparable between the Mateelian and the Primitive worldviews, again in contrast to the Amerikan. In Amerika a linear, goal-oriented, compartmentalized conception of time supports the competitive, individualistic conception of Self.[11] In the Mateelian and Primitive worldview, past, present and future are conceived in some way other than linear and there is no goal but the goal of balance and harmony with the universe. Mateelian and Primitive conceptions of time and space thus incorporate environmental limitations, and progress in the materialistic Amerikan sense, forms little part of them. In this both Mateelian and Primitive culture resemble the Ecotopian model, which requires that religious and philosophical ideas incorporate environmental limits and long-range conceptions of past and future.

These fundamental conceptions about time, space and the place of the Self and humans in the universe carry over into human relationships and it is here that they begin to have an effect on physical reality. In the Mateelian worldview, as in the Primitive, humans are not as distinct from each other as they are in the Amerikan worldview. As in some primitive societies, human souls may merge with one another at certain times and a conception of economic, social and spiritual interdependence is developing that is in great contrast to the Amerikan philosophy of "none of your business." The saying "we are all one" may sound insipid and stupid when spoken on the floor of the stock exchange, but in the context of a circle of honest and dedicated people holding hands at a Spring Equinox ceremony, even the worst cynic might catch a glimpse of the hope it expresses.

The Amerikan concept of individualism and freedom is changed in Mateel by the recognition and acceptance of dependence on other humans and the environment and the acknowledgement of the unshakeable reality of environmental limits. This growing recognition of the limitations of individuality is a trait in transition, informed by the ideal of primitive tribalism, but also by a conception of freedom even more comprehensive than the Amerikan. A group of related ideas placed into a new context in Mateel, then, are individualism, self-reliance, freedom, and internal versus external control. Mateelian freedom includes the important ideas of freedom to explore one's complete potential, freedom to create one's Self, freedom of personal expression, freedom from rigid scheduling, freedom from rigidly defined roles and hierarchical statuses, freedom to adjust everyday behavior to personally experienced time and biorhythms, and freedom to fully explore the potential of relationships.

It is just because Mateelian individuality includes these kinds of freedoms that the limitations imposed by nature are not experienced as onerous and self-reliance does not conflict with interdependence. Mateelian freedom specifically does not include freedom to harm the environment, even that part of it that one "owns," or to exploit others. Whereas the Amerikan ideal of freedom as described in the Constitution does not exclude any of the Mateelian freedoms, the actual day-to-day experience of Amerikans is of conformity, rigid schedules, rigid expectations, and restrictions on the development of personal potential. Mateelians see the laws against cultivation and use of marijuana and the restrictions on the use of other mind-altering substances as direct limitations on the "pursuit of Happiness" guaranteed by the Constitution. Many consider their situation with regard to marijuana cultivation and use completely analogous to that of the Native American Church, which was finally granted the right to use the psychedelic cactus, peyote, ceremonially only after a long and bitter fight. If one asks in what aspect of Amerikan life Amerikans actually experience the most personal freedom, one is forced to conclude that it is the freedom to choose among consumer products. To many Mateelians, this kind of choice has little to do with freedom and much to do with oppression.

In terms of social organization, Mateel is transitional. It is hard to say whether the transition is toward a primitive pattern of villages, bands, extended families and clans organized around kinship principles or whether it will turn out to resemble the rural areas of Ecotopia, with scattered farms in between small, diverse cities. The watershed level of organization resembles the band or village in scale, and the land partnership is not unlike an extended family, but households only cluster physically as a function of the terrain. What type of organizational unit is to be found in any one residence will be anybody's guess, given Mateelian diversity of family form. Suprawatershed organizations operate on the ideal of tribalism and often refer to themselves as a tribe and to larger gatherings as "a gathering of tribes," but their structure is much more nebulous than the tribal social organization described by most ethnographers. Mateelian social organization is still evolving too rapidly for predictions as to the form in which it will stabilize.

Politically, again, the ideal is tribal, but the reality is a transition away from Amerika and toward an Ecotopian situation in which the will of the people is actively sought and hierarchy and centralization of power actively avoided. The matter of internal and external control is one being worked out in Mateel in response to both primitive-like pressures and Amerikan pressures. Philip Slater observes:

> Mobility and change [of temporary societies] rule out the efficacy of any permanent system of social control. *External controls* (italics Slater's) depend upon the permanent embeddedness of the individual in the same social unit—a condition that has largely vanished from the civilized world. *Internalized controls* of a fixed kind (italics Slater's) become irrelevant to a changing social environment.[12]

Mateelian political behavior suggests the development of internalized controls of a flexible kind, which would not be irrelevant to a changing social environment. This political behavior is only understandable in the context of a small scale stable social situation in which idealistic people hold key values in common and in which they are in maximal communication with each other. The Mateelian conception of ultimate oneness with everyone and everything and of expanding individual consciousness as a route to this oneness is the fundamental shared value. The shared experience of seeming to merge with others while in states of higher consciousness, the belief in the "contact high" and in the reality of parapsychological phenomena, the emphasis on so many activities in the culture that raise the ability of people to "sync" with each other, the values of honesty and emotional expression in verbal and non-verbal communication, all suggest that Mateelians are in maximal, high context, interaction with each other and their natural environment. They not only share common values, but, because of the real suffering involved in trying to preserve and implement those values—peace, freedom, equality, restoration of The Land, spiritual seeking—they are connected to each other in a way perhaps only comprehensible to certain tribal peoples. Their controls may be internal and flexible in a sense that social scientists are only now beginning to understand. In the area of political behavior, then, Mateel is re-establishing the high context, internal control characteristic of tribes, but with a flexibility that may be more adaptive in a modern, Ecotopian situation. Politically, they may be on the track of something new.

Economically, the Mateelian, Ecotopian and Primitive models are similar in their emphasis on home production, local production, organic methods, conservation of resources, diversity, recycling and material simplicity. Mateel and the Primitive model are especially similar in the incorporation of the ideas of reciprocity and redistribution. The Mateelian model is like the Amerikan, however, in that complete local self-sufficiency has not been accomplished and even minimally self-sufficient individual household units are extremely rare. Economic behavior is still in transition from the Amerikan pattern, with the effects of marijuana cultivation tending to mask underlying economic assumptions.

The material simplicity of Mateel is in decided contrast to the materialism of Amerika but some specifics of it, such as the number of vehicles *per capita*, need interpretation for that contrast to become clear. It is also in decided contrast to the material simplicity of primitive peoples and the lower classes of most third world nations. Even the poorest Mateelians, who may be living in a tin, plastic and cardboard shack not unlike those to be found in a Tijuana slum, have access to some modern medical technology through MediCal (California State Medical Insurance), to food supplies through the Food Stamp program and free food giveaways. Yet, given what most Mateelians might have expected in the way of material possessions had they accepted their places in mainstream Amerika, even the wealthiest Mateelians are unlike Amerikans in the way they make their economic choices. Again, the transition is away from Amerika and towards Ecotopia.

In the area of social relations, the Mateelian model differs from the Amerikan in a changed conception of Self that includes a holistic positive attitude toward the body, and relationships predicated on the assumption of personal development and interdependence. The Mateelian model, unlike the Amerikan, insists on revelation of and tolerance for what are in Amerika, stigmas. The Mateelian model is like the Primitive in those aspects that involve scale and stability of the personal community and unlike the Primitive in that role definitions are situational rather than traditional. The Mateelian model of social relations resembles closely those described in Callenbach's novel, *Ecotopia*, but aside from this one reference, there is little to go on in comparing Mateelian to Ecotopian social relations beyond the general idea of personal development and self-realized individuals.[13]

Systemics

The most general and the single most important aspect of Ecotopia relates to systemics. In addition to setting limits on such things as consumption of resources, environmental damage, population and the rate of technological innovation, it incorporates systemic features that insure continued stability of the system. Watt, *et al.* define system stability as that property of a body that causes it, when disturbed from a condition of equilibrium or steady motion, to develop forces that restore equilibrium. They list three specific causes of instability: limited diversity, too much complexity, and too much shock to the system from outside.[14] Limited diversity refers to economic diversity in social systems—one crop, one industry, one product—but the importance of diversity to any system is a basic idea in ecology. Genetic diversity within species, species diversity in a community, a diversity of ideas in a communication system, are all examples of diversity in homeostatic systems.

The Ecotopian model includes the ideas of local communities with diverse economic bases, diverse communities unlike each other, diverse, i.e., non-conformist, individuals, a diversity of things to do besides consume. The prevalence of arts and crafts implies diverse, unique, material goods. Mateel displays all these kinds of diversity. There is diversity between watersheds and in individual and household economic activity, religious and philosophical ideas, personalities, and ways of exploring consciousness. Whereas there was at one time a lack of racial, ethnic and age diversity in the population, that situation is rapidly reversing as more and more persons from other nations hear of Mateel and arrive from Guatemala, India, South Africa, Australia, Britain, France, Switzerland, Germany, and Canada and from ethnic enclaves within American cities. Age diversity increases as more and more parents of Mateelians retire in Mateel and as Mateelian children become parents.

The second cause of instability, too much complexity, refers to the size of the system and interconnection among components. If a system involves too wide a web of interdependent pathways and has an insufficient number of negative feedback mechanisms with a short response time, then a perturbation in one part of the system may be allowed to reach a value that causes disturbance throughout the system. The feedback time from the problem to the controlling mechanism, in other words, is too long. In common language, there is too much red tape and problems cannot be stopped before they are so large they affect everything in the system. This cause of systemic instability is one of the reasons why Ecotopian writers all call for political, economic and organizational de-centralization.

Community organizations in Mateel consciously choose de-centralization as much as possible. Decentralization also tends to occur, whether anyone chooses it or not, just because the physical environment dictates decentralization in the residence pattern. The fact that it is simply inconvenient to get to a central location in order to organize implies that unless there is an overriding need for a larger group, it is easier to organize at a watershed level than any other. When the Citizens Observation Group was formed in 1984 to monitor civil rights violations committed by law enforcement agents, observation teams were originally organized around days of the week. The "Tuesday" team, for instance, was responsible for observing police actions on Tuesday anywhere in Mateel. This required members of the team to meet at a central place in Mateel to get the necessary information. Rapidly a movement developed within the organization to have, in addition, "home" teams, organized at a watershed level, who would meet at a central location within a watershed currently under aerial surveillance or in which arrests were taking place. Persons in remote watersheds found this arrangement much more convenient and home teams soon became as common as day teams, illustrating the trend away from centralized arrangements.

Again, the Mateelian representatives on the School Board are always the advocates for re-opening schools closed when the District unified some years ago, and for supporting as much as possible, watershed level alternative schools, of which there are at least six. When a large women's consciousness raising group formed including women from several different watersheds, it soon broke down into smaller groups composed of women located in the same watershed. The community center was for a long time the most centralized organization, with active members from all over Mateel. When the building burned down, functions immediately returned to the watershed level, with classes, meetings, and dances held at smaller community buildings within the scattered watersheds.

The last cause of system instability listed by Watt, *et al.*, too big a shock to the system, is one against which the community has little defense, except its defenses against the other two, diversity and decentralization. It remains to be seen how large a shock it would take to destroy the Mateelian cultural system. The various attacks of mainstream society on the culture of Mateel via the building inspector, the internal revenue service, drug enforcement agencies, the media, and direct acts such as arson, violence and threats of violence, have so far failed.

The instability that derives from maximization of one variable at the expense of others in the system is of interest with regard to the Mateelian system. Bateson's discussion of "the ills of conscious purpose,"[15] which tend to overemphasize one variable and begin at the individual level, has been mentioned (see Amerika). According to Bateson, the more individuals have experiences involving the "whole" individual, as opposed to only the conscious mind, the more the collective effects of conscious purpose on eco-systems will be corrected. Such activities, which engage the unconscious as well as the conscious mind are: dreams, creativity of art, poetry, and "such things," and what Bateson calls "the best of religion," a phrase that is not as mystifying in Mateel as it is in Amerika. Recognizing the use of mind-altering drugs as an attempt to compensate for over-purposiveness, Bateson warns against substituting one partial view of the self for another and calls for a synthesis of the view derived from psychedelics and from the conscious mind.

I maintain that there is no better place to observe such a synthesis than in the community of Mateel. What Mateelians call "consciousness expansion" is not only becoming as conscious as possible of the influence of culture on the make-up of the individual mind, as Hall suggests,[16] but engaging in behavior that expresses the unconscious mind, as Bateson suggests. The holistic activities called for by Bateson and other Ecotopian writers, are everywhere the focus of Mateelian energy. In this regard, counteracting the systemic effects of conscious purpose through the engaging of individuals in holistic activities, Mateel is more like Ecotopia than the Ecotopian writers, with the exception of Callenbach, have so far imagined.

Lessons to be Learned from Mateel

Taylor predicts that in Ecotopia, "the most significant changes [may be] . . . in the way ordinary people choose to lead their daily lives." Anderson emphasizes the economic importance of "exercising control on day-to-day market decisions—whether to buy a little more gasoline or another packaged good, whether to throw away a jar or use it for canning." Slater observes that "change in America has come from. . . . day-to-day decisions made by millions of completely faceless individuals."[17]

The most important lesson to be learned from Mateel is the power of individual people to create culture through micro-decisions. The theoretical position of this work is that the relationship between ideals and behavior is based on a mutually causative feedback. Mateelians have demonstrated that changing "the inside of your head," changing one's worldview, assumptions, habits of thought, changes one's behavior with regard to other people and the environment.[18]

Slater states that:

> In times of change it is those who are most whole, . . who are in the best position to innovate creatively.[19]

If wholeness in this context may be assumed to be the acceptance of the entire self and the fulfilling of complete individual potential, then wholeness is clearly an ideal in Mateel. That the ideal is implemented is suggested by the numerous ways in which the cultural system is geared to encourage this acceptance and fulfillment. Mateelians have demonstrated the truth of Slater's statement by creating innovatively a whole new way of life.

Another lesson to be learned from Mateel, and a much more pragmatic one, is that the holistic anthropological conception of a close relationship between technology and the rest of culture is true. Mateelians are able to make successful use of multiple energy systems, to produce their own food, clothing, shelter, and community services only because they have made such progress in reversing Amerikan assumptions about needs, time and space, social relationships, and the nature of reality. In Mateel, a home is a system that interfaces directly with the environment. Keeping the home system and all of its various sub-systems running smoothly cannot be done by persons who can only operate on monochronic time because the human component of the system is the homeostatic control, and must be able to think systemically to perform this function.

The use of alternative energy works in Mateel because it is compatible with cultural ideas of decentralization, time, relationship to The Land, material simplicity. You cannot efficiently iron all your clothes using a twelve-volt electrical system, but redefining the value of ironing clothes enables you to be happy with un-ironed ones. You may not have solar heated water or solar electricity at all in the middle of a winter storm, but freedom from rigid work schedules, the flexibility of the concept of funky, the pragmatic understanding of household energy systems, the ability to think in relationships and a deep understanding of the immediate physical environment allows you to switch to wood-heated water and kerosene or propane lights without considering it a "hassle." Decentralizing Amerikan economic and energy systems is going to require basic shifts in Amerikan conceptions of time, space and relationship, but the existence of Mateel shows that it can be done and it can be fun.

A third lesson from Mateel is that much of what is Amerikan need not be reversed, only modified. Such ideas as freedom, individualism and self-reliance have not been re-invented by Mateelians, only resurrected from the Amerikan pioneer past and reinterpreted in the light of new knowledge. In these ways Mateelians may be said to be more American than Amerikan. They are American idealists who would die for the Bill of Rights but not a government composed of the rich and powerful. They are Americans who recognize intuitively the connection between limited American abundance and the ideals of freedom and equality—not in order to despair, but in order to find a way to preserve personal freedom while yielding to the laws of ecology. They are making progress in doing this by converting their American self-reliance into personal exploration of consciousness that leads them to acceptance of human interdependence.

It is not that the ideal of personal freedom is incompatible with preservation of the environment, but that freedom and equality do not necessarily coincide with material goods. It is freedom to pursue the happiness that comes from the fulfillment of creative and spiritual potential and the equal right to fulfill that potential—to be protected by the laws, to be educated, to gain access to the tools for the fulfilling of potential. This kind of freedom is made more possible by the curtailment of freedoms that endanger the existence of the entire species: freedom to reproduce irresponsibly, freedom to exploit the potential of other humans and the environment for the sake of personal aggrandizement.

Ecotopia or Bust

The planning problem presented by choosing a cultural over a technological route to change is to determine what cultural changes people will accept under what conditions. There has been a great reaction to anything that suggests "social engineering" ever since Hitler, and the kind of Utopia presented by B.F. Skinner,[20] based on the principles of behaviorism, is a nightmare to freethinkers. What I mean here by a cultural route to environmental planning is to be distinguished from social engineering by the fact that no coercion is involved. Ecotopian writers point out that unless some corrective measures are taken fast, coercion will be unavoidable. Population control measures taken in the Republic of China support this projection. Non-coercive cultural measures would aim at creating real alternatives and educating the populace as to the environmental and personal rewards to be gained from following them.

This systemic approach can be seen as being analogous to H. T. Odum's "ecological engineering" in which changes are made in the higher levels of a system, but details are worked out at the lower levels by the components themselves.[21] Real, fundamental changes in education such as those described by Perelman[22] are an example of what Odum's ecological engineering might look like applied to social planning. What we teach our children about learning to learn, about becoming responsible for changing themselves, about the relationships in their environment and in their social structure, about their personal responsibility as members of society, about what they really need as human beings and what fantastic potential they have to be something more than workers and consumers, may have more long term importance to what kind of new culture is created than any amount of oil exploration, development of nuclear energy, or totalitarian regulation of human behavior.

Anything done to encourage individuals to change that little microcosm of culture they bear inside their own minds is another application of ecological engineering to social planning. I am not and would not make an argument that everyone's route to Ecotopia is via the use of marijuana or psychedelics. The fact that situational and psychological variables are so fundamental to the marijuana experience, that experienced users need less and not more to achieve the same psychological state, the "contact high" phenomenon, and the fact that marijuana users can control subjective aspects of the experience through non-drug related techniques are all indications that it is not the use of the drug but the use of the knowledge gained from it that counts in changing both individuals and cultural habits. My argument here is that what Mateelians learned about changing themselves from their periods of marijuana and psychedelic use is one route to Ecotopia and that progress toward a society predicated on ecological principles will be slowed to the degree that individuals do not incorporate similar lessons into their life plans.

Mateelians began to make these changes as individuals using mind-altering substances in a social context that encouraged responsible self-examination, but the changes themselves do not necessarily require the use of any substances. What is required is the sincere motivation to learn introspection, honest evaluation of one's own actions and motivations, and courageous implementation of the lessons learned from this re-making of one's Self. Slater states:

> There can be no mechanical prescription for demechanization—any person, . . . can begin to experiment with his or her own circuitry in whatever sphere—personal, political or occupational, suggests itself.[23]

This self-directed experiment is made infinitely less painful if it takes place in a social situation that supports rather than hinders it. Collective political action that helps to create such a situation in terms of education, religion, self-help groups, healing and personal freedom as described here, is as important to the creation of an ecologically balanced cultural system as are direct attacks on the technological problems of environmental degradation.

Ecological engineering applied to social planning implies that much is decided implicitly through complete interaction by the persons most concerned and affected by immediate circumstances, before it ever reaches the point where an organizational hierarchy must decide. This is only possible in a small-scale social unit composed of people who see themselves as responsible for their own government, which is why planning should aim at small scale social groups.

Mateel is not Ecotopia. There are Mateelian environmentalists who despair of its potential when they see how polluted the lower watersheds become in summer, how much erosion occurs from road cuts in the winter, how tempting it is for marijuana growers to use chemical fertilizer, pesticides and rodent poison. I see this despair as a failure to acknowledge the tenacity of culture, the slowness of the pace at which it normally evolves. If the perspective is shifted from the environment itself, which will take dozens of years to heal at least, and to the people, there is plentiful room for hope. Everywhere there are individuals awakening to their responsibility for healing the Land. Everywhere there are people busily trying to create lives that balance need against resources. Everywhere there are individuals healing the psychological scars left from their experiences in Amerika and trying to avoid creating similar scars in their children. If there is hope anywhere, there is hope in Mateel, where the advice to the aspiring is "you start with yourself."

Appendix One

Note on Methodology

To date, there has been no ethnography of a large, clearly defined countercultural community. This work is as ethnographic as possible (in the traditional sense) despite the fact that the subject is untraditional. I used the standard ethnographic method of participant observation throughout my fifteen years of residence there. With the exception of one six month absence in 1975-1976 and three nine month absences in 1981-1982, 1982-1983, and 1985-1986, I was a resident of Mateel and accepted as a member of the community.

My methods of observation included:

1. my inability to divest myself of my training as an ethnographer, no matter how much I might have wished to in specific situations
2. the collection of hundreds of documents throughout that period relating to historical events, cultural events, philosophies, life histories, health, and education
3. the sporadic keeping of notes and journals, which became increasingly systematic as my children changed from toddlers needing my full attention to more independent school children
4. photographs taken throughout and
5. tapes made from 1976 onward of cultural productions, political meetings, and everyday conversations.

For three months in the summer of 1980, I camped in the backyard of a dwelling occupied by members of an improvisational drama group called "Pure Shmint." All of the group's members were Mateelians. Pure Shmint was, at that time, rehearsing the play *Vibram Soul* which, like most Pure Shmint productions, was aimed directly at a Mateelian audience.[1] The improvisational method used closely resembled psycho-drama and relied heavily on long, often philosophical discussions of Mateelian behavior and history. I assumed that an intensive ethnographic study of the group would yield information about Mateelian culture in a concentrated form. This turned out to be the case. For three months I lived and traveled with them, taping conversations, rehearsals, and interviews with group members. They defined my role as that of ethnographer and script person. I consider my work during this period to be typical in every way of traditional ethnographic research and have considered the play itself as a text amenable to analysis as folklore, after the manner of Claude Levi-Strauss.[2]

In 1985 I conducted the only quantitative research for this book. This research took the form of a six-page household energy budget questionnaire (HEBQ) distributed to a selected sample of Mateelians. Those who received the HEBQ were asked to return completed forms anonymously to a central location. Fifty forms were distributed; twenty-six were returned. Households included in the sampling were selected on the basis of three criteria:

1. residence in one of the six watersheds in Mateel with the highest density of countercultural individuals
2. my assessment of the likelihood that someone in the household would complete the form
3. my assessment of the ability of someone in the household to complete the form, given its emphasis on factual information. The survey was not sent to a representative sample of Mateelians. Instead it went out to a typical group of residents in six watersheds who were sufficiently sympathetic with my work to be motivated to add and subtract necessary to answer the questions. Various statistics from the HEBQ are mentioned throughout this book. However, statistics whose validity I questioned because of compilation errors were not included.

My most frequently used observational method was the compulsive questioning and observation of anyone I encountered in Mateel. In this, I was driven by curiosity about the obviously unusual social phenomena that was taking place all around me. I was incapable of attending any gathering without automatically doing a mental estimate of the number of persons there and the age structure of the group, gaging the emotional tone, and noting other perceptible patterns, such as which watersheds were represented, which interest groups or kin groups were represented, and the patterns of symbolic behavior, such as new language usages or fashions in clothing or art. Before 1976, I recorded only a small fraction (perhaps two percent) of these observations. After 1976 I began making extensive notes, usually within a day of the event being described, sometimes during it.

Throughout the fifteen-year period, I deliberately placed myself in situations where social behavior could best be observed—cafes and bars, meetings, parties, ceremonies, the laundromat, classes, births, work parties, waiting rooms. Any conversation was considered data and, within the constraints imposed by professional ethics, human compassion, and respect for privacy, I was not averse to deliberately manipulating conversations to elicit specific data. Informants are thus considered to be anyone and everyone with whom I interacted during the period of the study. They were my own family and friends, students, teachers, hitchhikers, people with whom I hitchhiked, and people sitting next to me in any of the situations mentioned. The information I gathered in this way became the basis for a more systematic approach adopted later when I focused my attention on six watersheds.

After 1976 I began separating information pertaining to these watersheds from more general information. Formal taped interviews were conducted with ten informants. Several of my friends acted as key informants throughout the study, deliberately gathering and reporting information they knew I could use. I considered the photographs, tapes, and documents to be *pure data*, not subject to personal bias, except insofar as my choice of what to preserve constitutes a bias. In situations where I called my objectivity into question, I often studied the records to see if they substantiated my thinking or if additional observations were necessary. Pure data served as a check against personal overinvolvement.

There are some reasonable objections that can be raised about my methodology. One is the apparent lack of a systematic approach during the early years of my observation; another is the degree to which I relied on general impressions and memory. I respond by pointing out that the length of time spent observing the community compensates for the absence of records in the initial stages, the time lag between observation and written record later, and for the shortage of quantification. Since I had time to collect an enormous volume of data, it was easy to check and recheck emerging patterns against my documents, photographs, tapes, and the observations of my key informants. Also the three months of formal observation of Pure Shmint was sufficiently systematic to form the basis for a cultural analysis on its own.

A second, perhaps more serious objection is the level of my objectivity, given my status as a member of the culture that I studied. There are several responses to this criticism. The first is obvious. Were I not considered a member of the Mateelian culture by others, most of the information presented here would have been inaccessible. Mateelians are keenly aware of their legal vulnerability and the resistance of mainstream society to their culture. Their experiences with the local mainstream society in the early days, when gunfire and arson were not uncommon features of everyday life, make them wary of strangers asking questions. Even given my credibility as a "hill person," I encountered a certain amount of suspicion, to which I deferred without question. In fact, some of the collected data cannot be reported for ethical reasons. It is my position, however, that the value of the data, in the context of environmental crisis and the need for cultural change, outweighs any problems presented by the fact that it was gathered from within the culture rather than from without.

It must be remembered that objectivity is a relative concept. Ethnographers are only objective observers to the extent that they are aware of themselves and the contents of their own minds. This is the only way they can know the degree to which their observations are determined by their parent cultures and their personal histories. Since most ethnographers receive no formal training in self-observation, they necessarily carry cultural and personal biases into the field with them. Some of these are conscious and can be stipulated as part of the data and dealt with in the field. Most, however, are unconscious. As a member of a cultural system that has as its highest value the exploration of personal consciousness, I have received intensive training in self-observation; I consider myself especially able to view social behavior with a clear awareness of the extent to which personal bias may affect what I see. In addition, other Mateelians, also trained in self-observation, were only too willing to point out to me possible sources of personal bias, a service for which I have always been grateful in direct proportion to the purity of their motives in doing so.

The least traditional aspect of my methodology was the inclusion of myself as an informant. But this practice is not without precedent for ethnographers who study their own culture; it is certainly what sociologists, economists, and political scientists do.[3] Traditionally, however, ethnographers have refrained from studying their own cultures for fear that they will not be objective and because they come from societies that are too complex and too large to be observed by a single participant observer. Given the urgency of the global environmental crisis caused by the very cultures which spawned anthropology, this reluctance is now inappropriate and unjustifiable. Western industrial civilization must be subjected to the same exhaustive, rigorous, and holistic study we have applied to non-Western and primitive societies in order to determine how to reverse its own destructive trends. If present anthropological methods are inadequate to the task, then they must be made adequate.

In the case of my research, I learned that a profound change of subjective experience of the individual Mateelian forms the very crux of the community's cultural system. It is impossible to understand Mateel's historical roots without understanding the emotional and spiritual forces that created it. What better way to understand the subjective experience of a culture than to be a member and to examine one's own subjective reality? The obvious danger is, of course, that one's experience might be unique and, therefore, no generalizations could be drawn from it. This risk has been minimized in the present instance by the long-term nature of the study. My experiences, subjective and objective, were validated again and again by comparison to the experiences of my neighbors in the course of fifteen years.

In addition, including one's self as an informant has specific advantages, especially in regard to those subconscious aspects of culture that E. T. Hall calls "covert." According to Hall, ethnographers may use themselves as instruments to get at the unconscious aspects of culture by monitoring personal reactions to cultural situations.⁴ If I ever suspected, as I sometimes did, that I invented Mateel as an elaborate justification for my own seemingly irrational choices, or if I ever believed Mateel existed only because I wanted it to, all I had to do was leave the community for a while. The resulting culture shock provided me with instant and plentiful insight into the hitherto unconscious differences between Mateelian and mainstream American culture. This experience of culture shock was verified for me on numerous occasions by informants who had just returned from visits to the "outside," by visitors from "outside," and by new emigrants to Mateel.

If a conflict exists between traditional ethnography and the kind of ethnography I have done here, it does not mean the two approaches are irreconcilable. Although they may yield different kinds of data, both kinds are useful. A year or two of participant-observation by an outside observer untrained in introspection and weighted heavily toward observation is useful in obtaining etic data. This approach is appropriate to the study of slowly changing, traditional cultures. On the other hand, a much longer period of participant-observation weighted heavily toward participation and carried out by an observer highly trained in introspection is more useful in obtaining emic data; it is better suited to the study of a rapidly evolving culture.

My final method was the highly traditional one called cross-cultural comparison. But, once again, I departed from the standard practice of comparing Mateel ethnography to more general and abstract models of conventional social entities. I constructed three models selectively, choosing for each those aspects most related to the problem of culture and the decline of our global environment. The community of Mateel is presented in more detail than the three models to which it is compared. This is because my purpose is to present primary data, as well as to elicit secondary data from comparison. The three models are included to contrast those elements which relate directly to environmental problems. All three are far too complex to be adequately presented as anything other than representations to be used for heuristic purposes.

Appendix Two

Song of Twelve

All Life
Being
Sacred:
tell me now,
where is there not Life?
where is not the Breath of Life?

i looked within the waterstone silence,
       to the very fireheart of stone
        whence songs of stone arise,
where the red earthstone takes voice
       repeating our questions
           as through a white cloud:
"where is there not life?" was the refrain,
"where is not the Breath of Life?"

i turned to the sisterhood of meadow grasses,
     asking, "All Life Being Sacred,
       where is there not Life,
       where is not the Breath of Life?"
and their wind-formed dance told tales
       of beginnings and of endings
but nowhere told of anywhere
       there is not Breath of Life.

and the standing ones who witness,
    a family called oak and madrone,
        redwood, pine, fir,
    a people of a thousand names, roots and branches
        agreed as one, saying,
"nowhere is there not the Breath of Life."

then i thought to ask the totem clans
    —Chejauk the Crane who guides the People;
Kineu the Eagle who sees for the People;
Noka the Bear who heals and defends the People;
Wawashkaesh the Deer who feeds the People;
Mizi the Fish who instructs the People;
Mukukee the Frog who cures the People—
i thought to ask these and all our relatives
but somewhere in the watershed mountains of Mateel
    the question dissolved, was washed away,
        for our world is loud with the busyness of being,
            and in Being is All Answer.

        so that
    All Life Being Sacred,
      tell me now
what songs shall we sing?
which dances shall we dance

        with gifts of thread and yarn and clay,
        with the blessings of wood, stone,
            metal and glass,
        with the blaze of creation in brush
            and paint
        with all of our bodies and
            minds and breath,
toward what star shall flow our art
    as we, being sacred children,
        walk upon our Earth Mother?

        * * * *

i sing a song of years,
       years by the dozen,
              of a dozen years ago today:

where were you then, what did we say, what did we do?
where were you, what did you say, what did you do?
                       and who are *we*?
                       and who are *you*?

Surely you remember the tunes of yet another dirty little war,
      well-reasoned for your television considered consent
        that gave the G-R-E-A-T AMERICAN PEOPLE an economy
      booming like the bastard Congress and traitor President,
      looming paper dollars like incoming artillery rounds
              shattering you or your dumb honky brother grunt
               and all his dope-depressed true-believer dreams
               that will always recall the smell of
                        Saigon brothels
               and country children dismembered with a studied M-16

a mere dozen years ago today,
       Amerika choosing suicide Vietnam genocide
         a debauch of murder on all sides
and not so very far from stylish Benbow Lodge—
not nearly far enough for that angry mixed blood Briceland boy
             who returned sealed in an aluminum box,
                him and those other cubs from South
                      Fork High.
no, not nearly far enough for the beautiful black sons of
                        Harlem and Detroit,
          the proud brown boys from East L.A.
          the brave red lads of Paha Sapa, Flagstaff and
            Hoopa,
          the betrayed white trash kids from Jersey,
                 Bakersfield and Alabam'
and those saffron weeping people of Mekong and long-remembered
                           My Lai.

"we will wage a war on Po-ver-ty," LBJ declared,
    and the Pentagon warlocks smiles to share
        promotions and blood money profits
           with technocratic lords of corporate boards
        whose body-count tallied
           the poor souls of Schizophrenic Amerika.

i ask,
    toward what star shall flow our art,
        as we bring sacred children,
        all walk upon Mother Earth?

a dozen years ago—
    who were we then, what did we do?
        dodge the draft?
           chant for peace?
               stone and fire of the b. of a.?
                  off the pig, or was it the slope?
                    play the game, pay
                  the price?

decide, which side am i on, lord,
    which side are you on:
down in Selma, Alabama, which side are you on?
or in Desperate Nicaragua, which side are you on?
up in filthy Chi-town, which side are you on?
and here in the grace of Mateel land
    which side are you on, tell the truth,
    which side are you on?

never forget, brothers and sisters,
        fathers, mothers, friends, foes,
the sacred tribe here growing, evolving now,
        celebrating today on the banks of the Sinkyoko Eeeel River
            dwelling here in the grace of Mateel
                was forming in madness a dozen years ago
              today,

        was coalescing in the sun bright white light
            that dissolved the doubt of being
            that renewed the opening hearts
            hungry
                for Love's dominion,
                      starved for Aquarius!

    * * * *

a dozen years ago today,
in downtown beefaholic Garberville
        (a town i know and truly love),
that man of real estate said to me,
"Son, you may be a Haight-Ashbury long-haired
        peace freak nigger hippie, and probably queer,
but my client, a well-respected and much be-hated man hereabouts,
has seen the truth of your generous down payment
and has graciously accepted your blind faith offer
to purchase what's left of a piece of his kingdom
that will no longer profitably support his cattle or his sheep
and that has been brutally plundered of all marketable
        standing timber;
mind you, he retains all mineral rights
    (meaning he owns everything 18 inches below the surface—
        but don't you worry about that. . . .
        worry about that the day you see the oil wells
            in Briceland, har, har).

ya know," he said to me, "this property was once owned by a
            homesteading family.

        the old man got hisself killed
            and the survivors forfeited their deed to the
            bank;
and before that, ya know, this here was a campsite for a bunch
        of ignorant miserable digger injuns

>   who all of a sudden died off real fast
>   or were placed as slaves—I mean to say
>   "apprentices"—
>   in good Christian homes;
>   even my old great aunt Ethel had one.

aw hell, i don't know why I'm telling you all this,
maybe it's because you look like jesus christ behind them
                                        granny glasses

but goddamit,
i ain't prejudiced
and six thousand cash is six thousand cash!
sign on the dotted line, jim."
a dozen years ago today
that man of real estate realized, and told his friends,
"ya know, there's probably other kids like him
            and a hundred dollars an acre might not be too much
                                        to ask after all."
then began my payment my payment of dues to this land,
            dues to this territory where many bones lay
                  among the standing people's forest skeletons
                        on one as yet could sell to the mill.

then it was the deer and hawks and fire-scorched fir
            hear *me* announce, "this is *my* land!"
                  there was no dispute, but the silence sickened.
sickened in Mateel's memories of *ten* dozen years ago
            when the ancestor's people
                  of Mattole, Sinkyone, Nongatl, Lassik, Wailaki, Cahto
            who had known harmony with All Life Being Sacred
                  fell to frontier genocide Humboldt-Vietnam suicide
                  fell to ragged self-righteous outlaw troops of empire.

i say the dues must be paid
            and thence flows our art!

i praise and celebrate you,
    you who play your part,
    you who will share your art,
        All Life Being Sacred.

            * * * *

o'grandmother, grandfather spirits—
o'all you invisible ancient ones here with us today.
        this year
        this now:
see that a people is reborn again,
see that the circle is returning.
see that the hoop is truly prayed for—
    let it open and rejoin to contain all who assent
        "All Life Being Sacred"

hear the people say
    truly we do not own this land
    truly we cannot buy and sell our Mother
    truly we are her children!
hear this song of the one who had forgotten,
hear his longing for his People—
approve the change-filled, difficult labors of this People
approve and forgive as we learn to daily live the good medicine way,
approve and help as we heal our Earth Mother,
    as we heal ourselves
    as we nurture All Life Being Sacred.

with honor to the East, whence shines Illumination,
with honor to the South, whence comes Faith,
with honor to the West, whence comes Self-Knowledge,
with honor to the North, whence comes Wisdom,

with thanksgiving for the abundance of our Earth Mother
with all praise to the One Great Spirit

o'Earth People
in every direction of our lives let us live

ALL LIFE
ALL BEING
ALL SACRED.

(Sung by Deerhawk, drums by Sunsong,
for the Third Annual Summer Arts Festival,
Aries/Taurus Moon, Virgo Sun, 1979
Sinkyoko Eel River, Mateel Territory)
Mateel is a name offered for that region lately called
Southern Humboldt County, California.
The Mateel is roughly described by the
watersheds of the Mattole and Eel rivers.

This poem is dedicated to all the newcomers in Mateel,
remembering that the true oldtimers were here
at least five thousand years ago.

Appendix 3

Explanation of Mateelian Names

Spirtiual values not directly associated with the Land

Rama—Hindu god.
Yang—Taoist concept.
Om—Sacred syllable, used for meditation in several Eastern religions.
Pilar—Persian, pillar of the temple.
Tao—Baxic concept in Taoism.
Sita—Hindu goddess.
Freya—Germanic goddess of love.
Shantidavi—Hindu goddess of peace.
Damara—Corruption of "tomorrow."
Dia—Spanish for "day."
Bindu—The center of the mandala.
Abracadabra—Commonly used magical term.
Spirit—spirit.

Spiritual values associated with the Land

Kupiri—Corruption of Huichal Indian word "kupuri," meaning the force of life embodied in the peyote plant.
Cybelle—Greek goddess of life.
Kali—Hindu goddess of life and death.

Place names or aspects of the Land

Obvious: *Rainbo, South, Sunshine, Sunny Day, River, Rain, Dawnflower, Sky, Sun, Watershed, Tall Trees, Sun Man, Wind, Hummingbird, Autumn Wind, Flower, Tree, Star, Weasal, Sunsong, Otter, Deerhawk.*

Not Obvious:

Gimli—Elf from the books of J. R. Tolkien. Elves are land spirits.
Acadia—Early flowering local plant.
Osha—Form of ocean (?)
Mateo—After San Mateo River area.
Joaquin—After San Joaquin River area.
Rio—Spanish for "river."
Trilium—Early flowering local flower.
Cedar—After the cedar tree.
Joshua—After the Joshua tree.
Heather—Wildflower.
Panama—After the country, from which comes the strain of marijuana, "Panama Red."
Thane—Danish keeper of the Land.
Utahblue—After the state, which is a form of Ute, meaning "hill dweller," reference to the blue of the ice and sky in winter.
Solar—Pertaining to the sun.
Khola—The ripe marijuana flower.
Sierra—After the Sierra Nevada Mountains.
Douglas Fir—After the dominant local variety of fir.
Iris—Common local wildflower.

Notes

Introduction

1 Harris, Marvin. 1968. *The Rise of Anthropological Theory: A History of Theories of Culture.* New York: Harper and Row.
2 Harris, Marvin. 1980. *Cultural Materialism.* New York: Random House.
3 Harris, Marvin. 1978. *Cows, Pigs, Wars and Witches.* New York: Vintage Press. p. 222.
4 Berger, Bennett. 1981. *Survival of a Counter-Culture: Ideological Work and Everyday Life among Rural Communards.* Berkeley: University of California Press.
5 Castaneda, Carlos. 1968. *The Teachings of Don Juan: A Yaqui Way of Knowledge.* New York: Ballentine Books.
6 Bateson, Gregory. 1980. *Mind and Nature: a Necessary Unity.* New York: Ballantine. Bateson does not specify how much later a secondary change may occur in response to a primary change to be considered to have been caused by the primary change. It is obvious that some changes will be so slight as to be undetectable, while others will cause immediate changes elsewhere in the system. Some causes are clearly bigger than others, in the sense that the secondary change happens sooner rather than later. This fact does not alter the idea of circular cause, it merely requires that one prioritize primary causes in order of importance.

Chapter One

1 Bennett, John. 1976. *The Ecological Transition.* New York: Pergamon Press.
2 *Ibid.*
3 Bodley, John H. 1976. *Anthropology and Contemporary Human Problems.* Menlo Park: Cummings.
4 Roszak, Theodore. 1969. *The Making of a Counter-Culture.* Garden City: Anchor Press.
5 Catton, William R. 1980. *Overshoot: The Ecological Basis of Revolutionary Change.* Urbana: University of Illinois Press.
6 Bodley. 1976. p. 214.

7 Catton. 1980. p. 5. Because I personally am convinced that the generic use of the word "man" to describe the human species is linguistic *hubris* which tends to perpetuate the philosophical basis of the ecological crisis, I feel compelled to state that I am only repeating this usage in quotations because of the current requirements of scholarship, which, in spite of two decades of female input, has not budged. I myself strenuously avoid this arrogant and sexist language, but do not feel justified in attempting to correct the past errors of scholars whom I deeply respect by substituting other forms. The best I can do is to here make a blanket statement that any quote which contains the generic use of the word "man" is considered a necessary evil and used in spite of my reservations about such usage.
8 Bennett. 1976. pp. 5-7.
9 *Ibid*. pp. 2, 11.
10 Rappaport, Roy. 1967. Ritual Regulation of Environmental Relations Among a New Guinea People. *Ethnology* 6 (1): 17-30. 12 Reichel-Dolmatoff, G. 1976. Cosmology as Ecological Analysis: A View from the Rain Forest. *Man* 2 (3): 307-318. Birdsell, Joseph. 1977. *Population Control by Social Behavior. Symposia of the Institute of Biology* 23. F. J. Ebling and D. M. Stoddart, eds; and 1979. "Ecological Influences on Australian Aborigine Social Organization," in *Primate Ecology and Human Origins: Ecological Influences on Social Organization*. Irwin S. Bernstein and Euclid O. Smith, eds. New York: Garland STPM Press. Bodley. 1976. p. 49.
11 Bodley. 1976. p. 3.
12 Rifkin, Jeremy. 1980. *Entropy: A New Worldview*. New York: Bantam.
13 Catton. 1963. p. 3.
14 Bennett. 1963. p. 285.
15 Bodley. 1976. p. 214.
16 Schumacher, E. F. 1973. *Small is Beautiful: Economics as if People Mattered*. New York: Harper and Row.
17 Toffler, Alvin. 1980. *The Third Wave*. New York: Bantam Books.
18 San Francisco *Chronicle*, July 18, 1979.
19 However, see Fritjof Capra and Charlene Spretnak, *Green Politics: the Global Promise*, describing the West German "Green Party," which is attempting with some success to politically implement Ecotopian ideas.
20 Goldsmith, Edward,*et al*. 1972. *Blueprint for Survival*. Boston: Houghton Mifflin Co. Perelman, Lewis. 1976. *The Global Mind: Beyond the Limits to Growth*. New York: Mason-Charter. Taylor, Gorden Rattray. 1972. *Rethink: a Paraprimitive Solution*. London: Secker and Warburg. Ehrlich, Paul and Richard L. Harriman. 1971. *How to be a Survivor: a Plan to Save Spaceship Earth*. New York: Ballantine. Bodley. 1976. pp. 226-227. Anderson, E. N. 1974. Life and Culture of Ecotopia. In *Reinventing Anthropology*. Dell Hymes, ed. New York: Random House. Callenbach, Ernest. 1975. *Ecotopia*. New York: Bantam and 1981 *Ecotopia Emerging*. New York: Bantam.
21 Taylor. 1972. p. 8.
22 Revitalization movements were originally defined by A. F. C. Wallace as "deliberate, organized, conscious effort[s] to construct a more satisfying culture." Wallace, A.F.C. 1956. Revitalization Movements. *American Anthropologist* 58: 264-281. Wallace described them as 1) typical of societies under stress from rapid change, usually as a result of contact between primitive and industrial cultures and; 2) expressing a collective desire to return to the past. The potential of a revitalization movement to create social change "despite apparently irrational elements" and "in a surprisingly short time" is recognized in anthropology. Bock, Philip. 1975. *Modern Cultural Anthropology*. New York: Knopf. Wallace, A. F. C. 1958. Mazeway Resynthesis: a biocultural theory of religious inspiration. *Transactions of the New York Academy of Sciences*. Series 2 Vol. 18 No. 7. pp. 15-30.
23 Toffler. 1980. pp. 137, 167.
24 *Ibid*. p. 153.
25. *Ibid*.

26 *Ibid.*
27 *Ibid.* Unfortunately Toffler describes prosumers only in terms of his First Wave, in which most people were slaves, rather than in terms of pre-First Wave, or primitive, in which economic inequality was less pronounced or absent.
28 Roger Herrick, owner. Personal communication.
29 Mumford, Lewis. 1962. *The Story of Utopias.* New York: Viking.
30 Bodley. 1963. p. 16.
31 The media are unable to grasp or describe more than isolated traits because they are, unlike social science or history, not equipped to do more than report events as they happen, often in an excessively narrow context. The best of journalism is still a long way from good history or anthropology. It is therefore essential to the understanding of this ethnography that the media-produced concept of the counterculture is passé.
32 Gardner. 1963. p. 11.
33 This attitude is depicted in the 1960s film *Little Big Man* and is discussed more fully in Arnold, Barbara. 1985. Death and Ecology in Mateel: The Meaning of Hoka Hey. *Northwest Anthropological Research Notes.* Vol. 20. No. 1. Barbara Arnold began publishing under the name Jentri Anders in 1987.
34 Bodley. 1976. pp. 226-227.
35 Perelman. 1963. p. 163.
36 Osmond, Humphrey. 1964. A Review of the Clinical Effects of Psychomimetic Agents. In *LSD: The Consciousness-Expanding Drug.* David Soloman, ed. New York: G. P. Putnam's Sons.
37 Gardner, Hugh. 1978. *The Children of Prosperity: Thirteen Modern American Communes.* New York: St. Martin's Press. It should be noted that both Osmond and Gardener are referring to the effect of these substances on individuals within a modern industrial cultural context. In cultures where their use is traditional these statements may or may not apply.
38 Wallace. 1956. pp. 264-281.
39 Slater, Phillip. 1974. *Earthwalk.* Garden City: Doubleday/Anchor Press. Goffman, Erving. 1956. The Nature of Deference and Demeanor. *American Anthropologist* 58: 473-502.

Chapter Two

1 Deerhawk. 1984. A Song of Twelve. *Briceland Ecologian* 1 (4): 4-5. (See Appendix 2)
2 As of this writing, the new community center has still not been built because of ongoing resistance from local mainstream entities, governmental and business. Various strategies have periodically been tried to reduce this resistance by re-organizing the MCC in ways which would dilute the power of the hill people in the organization. Each time these attempts have included suggestions that the name be changed. Each time the moves have been defeated.
3 Roszak. 1976.
4 U. S. Census Bureau. 1980.
5 It is interesting that Goldsmith, *et al.* (1972) envision communities of approximately 5,000, broken into sub-units of 500 each. Mateel thus approximates this ecological ideal if one considers the watersheds which are tributaries of the Eel and Mattole as sub-units.
6 Raphael, Ray. 1975. *An Everyday History of Somewhere.* Mendocino, California: Ridge Times Press. pp. 115-136.
7 That there would occur a "land boom" as the result of marijuana cultivation, making this land suddenly very valuable, was apparent to no one at that point. Whether the "land boom" will just bust as quickly as it appeared or continue remains to be seen.
8 *Cf.* Raphael, Ray. 1985. *Cash Crop: An American Dream.* Mendocino, California: Ridge Times Press. As of 1989, the activity of CAMP and the growing recognition, on the part of Mateelians, of the negative effects of marijuana growing has inspired many Mateelian

growers to curtail or abandon that economic strategy. The reduced income has given renewed impetus to efforts to establish small businesses and to bring appropriate industries to the area. Small-scale capitalism is on the rise, along with volunteer efforts, organized by Mateelians, to feed the homeless and unemployed.

9 NORML vs CAMP. 1984. Judge Robert Aguilar, Ninth Circuit Court of Appeals.
10 Bodley, John H. 1975. *Victims of Progress.* Menlo Park: Cummings. It is the circumstance of rapid destruction of traditional cultures by contact with modern ones, in fact, that led to the convention of the "ethnographic present" in which the time of the study is the present tense of the written ethnography and the data is presented as being true at that time.
11 Bateson, Gregory and Jurgen Ruesch. 1968. *Communication: the Social Matrix of Psychiatry.* New York: Norton.
12 The ethnographic present of this study is designated as the years 1968 through 1989. However, the focus of the study changed during that time in response to the marijuana boom. The cultural system described may be seen as hitting a peak in the year 1976, and as then beginning to be submerged, basically intact, under layers of new immigrants brought in by the marijuana industry. After the year 1980, the study focused on institutions created by Mateelians before then, on the assumption that they were now the least diluted expression of Mateelian culture. This methodology avoids contamination of the sample, which may come from later residence in the six core watersheds of persons who are there only to grow marijuana.
13 *Cf.* Berreman, Gerald. 1972. Social Categories and Social Interaction in a North Indian City. *American Anthropologist* 74: 567-586 for a study of a pluralistic culture using this methodology.

Chapter Three

1 Callenbach. 1975. See also: 1981. The history of the Ecotopian revolution in which may be found the roots of Ecotopian social institutions is discussed here. The etymology of the word "ecotopia" is explained in E. N. Anderson as follows: "eco," from the Greek "oikos," means household; "topia," means "place" with the connotation of good. Since "eco" is also the prefix in "ecology," "ecotopia" refers to a good place created with ecological principles in mind. See, Anderson. 1969. p. 275.
2 It is unlikely that any of the sources cited in this chapter influenced Mateelians, except insofar as their ideas may have appeared in such publications as *Mother Earth News* and *Co-evolution Quarterly*. This is not only because the discontinuity experience had rendered most of the college dropouts, who would be capable of understanding these sources, incapable of regarding such dry material without nausea, but also because the immediate demands of survival left little time for reading all but the most practical of handbooks. Mateelian culture does bear many resemblances to the Ecotopian model presented here. However, the resemblance, for the most part, should be ascribed more to unconscious evolutionary processes, with the reading of a few individuals as a small input, than to direct emulation.
3 Wynne-Edwards, V. C. 1969. Self-Regulating Systems in Populations of Animals. *In The Subversive Science.* Paul Shepard and Daniel McKinley, eds. Boston: Houghton-Mifflin. Callenbach. 1981.
4 Harris. 1978.
5 Anderson. 1963. p. 275. Forrester, Jay. 1973a Counter-Intuitive Behavior of Social Systems. In *Toward Global Equilibrium: Collected Papers.* Dennis L. Meadows and Donella H. Meadows, eds. Cambridge: Wright-Allen Press. pp. 26-27.
6 Anderson. 1964. p. 278.
7 Taylor. 1972. p. 154.
8 Taylor. 1972. p. 153.

9 Taylor. 1972. p. 250.
10 *Ibid*. p. 231. Feminists may interpret this whole discussion as resting on outdated, sexist assumptions about male and female characteristics. However, when the male/female question is taken out of it and the values themselves are considered, Taylor's observations are less offensive and not out of line with numerous others on the subject of the Ecotopian personality.
11 Goldsmith. 1972. pp. 37-38. Taylor. 1972. 37-38.
12 *Ibid*. p. 157.
13 Watt. 1974. pp. 145, 231.
14 Forrester. 1963. p. 29.
15 *Ibid*., p. 30.
16 *Ibid*., p. 157.
17 Slater. 1963. p. 195.
18 Goldsmith, *et al*. p. 77. Slater. p. 199.
19 Taylor. 1963. p. 159.
20 Watt, Kenneth, *et al. The Unsteady State: Environmental Problems, Growth and Culture.* Honolulu: East-West Center, University of Hawaii Press. p. 261.
21 Slater. 1963. p. 195.
22 Taylor. 1963. p. 231. Goldsmith, *et al*. 1963. pp. 34-38.
23 Ehrlich, Paul. 1968. *The Population Bomb.* New York: Ballentine Books. pp. 131-135.
24 Goldsmith, *et al*. 1963. p. 121.
25 Toffler. 1963. pp. 433, 448. Slater. 1963. p. 199.
26 Randers, Jorgen and Donella H. Meadows. 1973. The Carrying Capacity of Our Global Environment: A Look at the Ethical Alternatives. In *Toward Global Equilibrium: Collected Papers.* Dennis L. Meadows and Donella H. Meadows, eds. Cambridge: Wright-Allen. p. 73. Ehrlich and Harriman. 1963. p. 71. Perelman. 1963. p. 178.
27 Toffler. 1963. p. 169.
28 Goldsmith, *et al*. pp. 37-38. Watt, *et al*. 1977, 1963. p. 245.
29 Goldsmith, *et al*. 1963. pp. 37-38.
30 Watt, *et al*. 1977, 1963. p. 245.
31 Randers and Meadows. 1963. p. 331. Watt, *et al*. 1977, 1963. p. 248.
32 *Ibid*.
33 Goldsmith, *et al*. 1963. pp. 21-23.
34 Watt, *et al*. 1974, 1963. p. 95.
35 Anderson. 1963. p. 275.
36 Slater. 1974. 1963. p. 28. Taylor. 1963. p. 160.
37 Watt, *et al*. 1963. p. 245. Anderson. 1963. p. 275. Randers and Meadows. 1963. p. 333.
38 *Ibid*. p. 331.
39 Harris, Marvin. 1981. *America Now: the Anthropology of a Changing Culture.* New York: Simon and Schuster. pp. 29-30.
40 Taylor. 1963. pp. 156-157.
41 Watt, *et al*. 1977, 1963. p. 245. Anderson. 1963. p. 275. Goldsmith, *et al*. 1963. p. 39.
42 Watt, *et al*. 1974, 1963. p. 95.
43 Goldsmith, *et al*. 1963. p. 126. Watt, *et al*. 1977, 1963. p. 248.
44 Toffler. 1980, 1963. pp. 261-272.
45 Watt. *et al*. 1977, 1963. p. 245. Goldsmith, *et al*. 1963. p. 39.
46 *Ibid*. Watt, *et al*. 1977, 1963. p. 245. Callenbach. 1975. p. 30. Odum, Howard. 1971. *Environment, Power and Society.* Taylor. p. 156.
47 Toffler. 1980. p. 100. Interestingly enough, in terms of comparing countercultural history in Ecotopia, Timothy Leary, the 1960s LSD guru is now a home computer salesman and enthusiastic advocate thereof. Anders, Jentri. Trek to the Sixties, Part II. *Country Activist* Vol. 4. No. 3.
48 *Ibid*.

49 *Ibid.* p. 219.
50 *Ibid.* p. 210.
51 Ehrlich, 1968, 1963. p. 141.
52 *Cf.* Slater, Phillip. 1976 *The Pursuit of Loneliness.* Boston: Beacon Press. p. 4. Roszak, 1963. p. 14.
53 Toffler. Alvin. 1975. *The Eco-Spasm Report.* New York: Bantam Books. p. 100.
54 Slater. 1976, 1963. p. 146.
55 Randers and Meadows. 1963. p. 331.
56 Taylor. 1963. p. 114.
57 Toffler. 1975, 1963. p. 100.
58 Taylor. 1963. p. 230.
59 Perelman. 1963. p. 166. Goldsmith, *et al.* 1963. pp. 37-38.
60 Toffler. 1975, 1963. p. 100.
61 Taylor. 1963. p. 214. Perelman. 1963. p. 197. Randers and Meadows. 1963. p. 335.
62 Slater. 1974, 1963. p. 199. Odum, 1963. p. 301. Bateson, Gregory. 1972. *Steps to an Ecology of the Mind.* New York: Ballantine, 1972. p. 172.
63 Watt, *et al.* 1963. p. 245.
64 Goldsmith, *et al.* 1963. pp. 37-38. Forrester. 1963. p. 25. Randers and Meadows. 1963. p. 335. Toffler. 1980, 1963. p. 407.
65 Forrester, Jay. 1973b. Churches at the Transition Between Growth and World Equilibrium. In *Toward Global Equilibrium: Collected Papers.* Dennis L. Meadows and Donella H. Meadows, eds. Cambridge: Wright-Allen Press. p. 346.
66 White, Lynn Jr. 1967. The Historical Roots of Our Ecological Crisis. *Science* 155: 1203-1207.
67 Harris. 1980, 1963. pp. 55-58.
68 Bateson. 1972, 1963. p. 490. Ehrlich. 1968, 1963. p. 171.
69 Anderson. 1963. p. 273.
70 Hall, Edward T. 1983. *The Dance of Life: The Other Dimension of Time.* Garden City, New York: Anchor Press/Doubleday. pp. 89-95.
71 Redfield, Robert. 1963. *The Little Community and Peasant Society and Culture.* Chicago: Phoenix Books. p. 41.
72 Randers and Meadows. Forrester. 1973b, 1963. p. 346.
73 Odum. 1963. p. 125.
74 Forrester. 1973b, 1963. p. 347. Redfield. 1952. p. 30.
75 Slater. 1974, 1963. p. 34. Perelman. 1963. pp. 24-25. Rifkin, 1963. p. 6.
76 Watt, *et al.* 1974, 1963. p. 26. *Ibid.* p. 3.
77 Shepard, Paul. 1969. Introduction: Ecology and Man—A Viewpoint. In *The Subversive Science: Essays Toward an Ecology of Man.* Paul Shepard and Daniel McKinley, eds. Boston: Houghton Mifflin. p. 51.
78 Perelman. 1963. p. 186.
79 Anderson. 1963. p. 279.
80 Watt, *et al.* 1974, 1963. p. 26.
81 Slater. 1974, 1963. p. 27.
82 Hall. 1983, 1963. pp. 159-160.
83 Perelman. 1963. p. 178.

Chapter Four

1 Kafka, Franz. 1962 edition. *Amerika.* New York: New Directions.
2 Ehrlich. 1968, 1963. p. 24. Deevey, Edward S., Jr. 1969. The Human Population. In *The Subversive Science: Essays Toward an Ecology of Man.* Paul Shepard and Daniel McKinley, eds. Boston: Houghton Mifflin. p. 43.

3 Bodley. 1963. pp. 163-164.
4 Ehrlich. 1968, 1963. p. 24.
5 Catten. 1963. p. 32.
6 Bodley. 1963. p. 215. Randers and Meadows. 1963. pp. 317-321. Watt, *et al.* 1974. p. 11.
7 Watt, *et al., ibid.* Taylor. 1963. pp. 156-157.
8 Bodley. 1963. pp. 9-10.
9 Slater. 1976, 1963. p. 56.
10 Bateson. 1972, 1963. p. 426.
11 Bodley. 1963. p. 216.
12 *Ibid.* pp. 174, 184.
13 Berreman. 1981. Social Inequality: a Cross-cultural Analysis. In *Social Inequality: Comparative and Developmental Approaches.* Gerald Berreman, ed. New York: Academic Press. p. 35.
14 *Ibid.* p. 4.
15 *Ibid.*
16 Toffler. 1980, 1963. p. 32.
17 *Ibid.* p. 30.
18 Harris. 1980, 1963. pp. 31-33.
19 Anderson. 1963. p. 270-272.
20 Bodley. 1963. p. 182.
21 Goldsmith, *et al.* 1963. pp. 89-90.
22 Bodley. 1963. p. 182.
23 *Ibid.* p. 216
24 *Ibid.*
25 Marx, Karl. 1962. Alienated Labor. In *Man Alone: Alienation in Modern Society.* Mary and Eric Josephson, eds. New York: Dell. pp. 93-105.
26 Watt, *et al.* 1974, 1963. p. 86.
27 Toffler. 1975, 1963. p. 100.
28 Feiffer, Jules, San Francisco *Chronicle*, "This Week," August 2, 1984. Taylor. 1963. p. 240.
29 Goldsmith, *et al.* 1963. p. 82. Perelman. 1963. p. 23. Pettitt, George. 1970. *Prisoners of Culture.* New York: Charles Scribner's Sons. p. 162. Slater. 1974, 1963. p. 55. Watt, *et al.* 1977, 1963. p. 45. Bodley. 1963. p. 175. Goldsmith, *et al.* 1963. p. 94.
30 Pettitt. 1963. p. 127.
31 *Ibid.* p. 128.
32 Slater. 1974, 1963. pp. 62-64.
33 Slater. 1976. p. 131. Slater. 1974, p. 11.
34 Goldsmith, *et al.* 1963. p. 94.
35 San Francisco *Chronicle*, December 18, 1983.
36 Bodley. 1963. pp. 63-64.
37 Berreman, Gerald. 1978. Scale and Social Relations. *Current Anthropology.* 19: 2. p. 237. Slater. 1974, 1963. p. 11. Pettitt. 1963. p. 137.
38 Bodley. 1963. p. 185.
39 Slater. 1974, 1963. p. 11. Snow, John H. 1979. Fear of Death and the Need to Accumulate. In *Ecology: Crisis and New Vision.* Richard E. Sherrell, ed. Richmond: John Knows.
40 *Cf.* Bateson. 1972. p. 490.
41 Kuhn, Thomas S. 1970. *The Structure of Scientific Revolutions.* Chicago: University of Chicago Press. p. 168
42 White. pp. 2-9
43 Bateson. 1972, 1963. p. 492.
44 Mead, 1963. pp. 27-53.
45 Potter, David M. 1954. *People of Plenty: Economic Abundance and the American Character.* Chicago: Phoenix Books. p. 142.
46 The question remains, why is the United States especially an example of the scientific, rational worldview in contrast to Latin America, which also appeared to have unlimited

resources? One obvious answer is that it was populated first by Protestants rather than Catholics and Northern Europeans rather than Southern Europeans. The relationship between Protestantism and the Enlightenment and the related fact that Northern Europe was the source of the scientific worldview would account for this difference. This is by no means an argument that Latin America was not also influenced by the perception of abundance, only that the worldview of Latin countries would resist the orientation to newness, change and scientism more than that of the United States because of the restraining, traditional influence of the Catholic church.

47 The fact that the starship is called the Enterprise reinforces the program's status as a myth codifying frontier mentality and sanctioning the growth/consumption value.
48 Harris. 1981. p. 29.
49 San Francisco *Chronicle*. May 22, 1980.
50 Mead. 1963. p. 8.
51 Hsu, Francis L.K. 1961. American Core Values and National Character. In *Psychological Anthropology: Approaches to Culture and Personality*. Francis L.K. Hsu, ed. Homewood, Illinois: Dorsey Press, Inc. p. 217. Slater. 1976, 1963. p. 33.
52 Kearney, Michael. 1984. *Worldview*. Novato, California: Chandler and Sharp. p. 76.
53 Bateson. 1972, 1963. pp. 95-97.
54 Harris. 1980.
55 Bodley. 1963. pp. 137-138.
56 Marine, Gene. 1969. *America, the Raped*. New York: Simon and Schuster.
57 It may well be asked whether this model of Amerika is not more applicable to the America of the 1960s than the 1980s, since the trends begun by the counter-culture, such as the sexual revolution, and "new age" psychology have presumably had an effect on American culture and since the economic picture is at present so different. If the counter-culture was reaction to America, it was the America of the fifties and sixties, not to the contemporary one. My response to this is that one need only examine the reign of Ronald Reagan and his conservative colleagues to see that the eighties may well be more like the fifties than the fifties were. In terms of values and foreign policy, there is little to distinguish the America of the 1980s from the America of the 1960s except those legislative artifacts of Carter's time which the Reagan forces were not able to abolish. If it were not so, why was Reagan elected for a second term? In any case, the model presented here is an attempt to demonstrate general trends which are true in spite of the constant cycling back and forth of the Amerikan political and economic picture. Short term fluctuations are more and more characteristic of Amerika.

Chapter Five

1 Bodley. 1963. p. 14.
2 Bateson. 1972, 1963. p. 495.
3 Bennett. 1963. pp. 11-12.
4 Birdsell. 1979, 1963. p. 119.
5 Bodley. 1963. p. 14.
6 *Ibid*. p. 104.
7 *Ibid*. p. 45.
8 Bennett. 1963. p. 11.
9 Bodley. 1963. p. 15.
10 *Ibid*. p. 47.
11 Kearney, 1963. p. 151.
12 Goldsmith, *et al*. 1963. pp. 82, 89, 91.
13 Slater. 1974, 1963. p. 42.
14 Bennett. 1963. p. 66.

15 Rappaport reports it as a direct relationship in which a particular religious ritual has multiple effects on ecological variables; Harris. 1978. describes it from the opposite perspective, that religious taboos may be explained as adaptations to ecological variables; Reichel-Dolmatoff sees religions as codifications of resource conservation information.
19 Rappaport.
20 Harris. 1978.
21 Reichel-Dolmatoff.

Chapter Six

1 *Cf.* Bodley. p. 225. Ehrlich. 1968. p. 171. Harris. 1978. pp. 208-228.
2 Klein, A. Norman. 1974. Counter-Culture and Cultural Hegemony: Some Notes on the Youth Rebellion of the 1960's. *In Reinventing Anthropology.* Dell Hymes, ed. New York: Random House.
3 Osmond, 1963. pp. 129, 132.
4 Katz, Martin. 1970. The Psychological State Produced by the Hallucinogens. In *Hallucinogenic Drug Research.* James R. Gamage and Edmund Zarkin. eds. Beliot, Wisconsin: Stash Press. pp. 21-22. Hoffer, A. and Humphrey Osmond. 1967. *The Hallucinogens.* New York: Academic Press. pp. 458-459.
5 Il'Yuchenak, R. Yu. 1976. *Pharmacology of Behavior and Memory.* New York: Wiley. p. 73.
6 Kearney. 1963. p. 28. The concept of worldview has been a basic one in anthropology since German philosopher and historian Wilhelm Dilthey associated the idea of *weltanschauung* with the historical idea of *zeitgeist* in 1931.
7 Redfield, Robert. 1952. The Primitive Worldview. *Proceedings of the American Philosophical Society* XCVIL(1):30-36.
8 Mead, George Herbert. 1964. *On Social Psychology: Selected Papers.* Chicago: University of Chicago Press. pp. 228-233.
9 Redfield. 1952, 1963. p. 84.
10 Kearney, 1963. p. 5.
11 Kearney. pp. 52-58. Kearney also sees the interaction of categories with each other and worldview with the environment to produce a "logico-structural integration" as similar to the "mental processes" described by Bateson as characteristic of ecosystems. See: Bateson. 1979.
12 Wallace. 1958. Wallace, Anthony. 1962. *Culture and Personality.* New York: Random House. p. 628.
13 Santeria is a religious system practiced in the Caribbean, which includes an emphasis upon trance possession and drumming. It has a contingent of followers in Mateel, some of whom follow it closely enough to have undergone strict, year-long initiations involving ceremonies and ritual taboos.
14 Yablonsky, Lewis. 1968. *The Hippie Trip.* New York: Pegasus.
15 Jung, Karl. 1955. *Synchronicity: An Acausal Connecting Principle.* In The Interpretation of Nature and the Psyche. Karl Jung and W. W. Pauli, eds.
16 Hall. 1983, 1963. p. 23.
17 *cf.* Roszak. 1969. p. 82.
18 I have, incidentally, seen cars start in just this way.
19 I am not neglecting the motive of maintaining group solidarity as another reason for "playing along." In that case, the value of group solidarity still outweighs the value of maintaining apparent rationality.
20 In any situation in which I use the word "consciousness" in this work, unless otherwise specified, I am referring to the concept as it is defined by Mateelians as part of their worldview.

21 Sensimilla is Spanish, meaning "without seeds." In the counter-culture, it refers to the very strong marijuana produced by separating male from female plants before pollination, resulting in a product without seeds.
22 Pure Shmint. 1982. Growing Pains. Unpublished play.
23 Roberts, Jane. *The Unknown Reality*. 1979. New York: Prentice Hall.
24 The Mateelian relationship to guns varies individually in the extreme and has been greatly influenced by the marijuana boom, which brought in violent criminals from whom many now feel guns are a protection. At the point in history when this story took place, guns were rare in Mateelian households and kept for hunting or killing domestic livestock to eat or rabid animals.
25 Geertz, Clifford. 1973. Person, Time and Conduct in Bali. In *The Interpretation of Cultures*. Clifford Geertz, ed. New York: Basic Books. p. 368.
26 When informants were asked the Biblical meaning of their child's name, they were frequently unable to tell me and were very interested when I told them. Persons of Jewish ancestry may name a child a Biblical name in reference to the ethnic connection, which, again, relates to an originally tribal people who lived on the land.
27 Deerhawk.
28 Katz, Alan. Letter to the Editor, *Star Root*, April 1977.
29 *Ibid.*
30 Schille, Rettie. Letter to the Editor, Redwood *Record*, September 1978.
31 Baba Ram Dass. 1971. *Be Here Now*. Lama Foundation, San Cristobel, New Mexico. Distributed by New York: Crown.
32 Hall. 1983, 1963. pp. 64, 188.
33 Tinklenberg, Jared and Philip A. Berger. 1977. Treatment of Abusers of Non-addictive Drugs. In *Psychopharmacology*. Jack Barchas, ed. New York: Oxford. pp. 386-388. Il'Yuchenek. 1963. p. 73.
34 Hall. 1983. pp. 9, 164.
35 Condon, William. 1978. *An Analysis of Behavioral Organization*. Sign Language Studies 13.
36 Hall. 1983, 1963. p. 166.
37 *Ibid.*
38 *Ibid.* pp. 151, 153, 161, 162, 166, 168.
39 *Ibid.* p. 149.
40 *Ibid.* pp. 154, 162.
41 Casteneda. 1963. p. 19-25.
42 Kearny, 1963. p. 153.
43 Even if a modern urban individual attempts to maintain a direct relationship with Nature, modern architecture precludes it by designing windows that cannot be opened and heating and cooling systems that cannot be controlled at the room level.
44 Kearney. p. 52.
45 *Ibid.* pp. 149-151.
46 Toffler (1980. p. 184) notes an interesting trend among his futuristic "Third Wave" people. Whereas primitive people imparted a spirit or soul to the environment, seeing rocks as having spirits dwelling within them, and "Second Wave" people see the environment as dead, "Third wavers, who deal with computers and systems theory, impart intelligence to the environment. Toffler presents this idea as an evolutionary continuum. One may agree with Toffler that seeing the environment as intelligent is an improvement over seeing it as dead, but many would question whether losing the sense of the environment as being alive and peopled with spirits is an advance. Bateson's (1980) *Mind and Nature* leaves one with the sense that the environment is alive, intelligent and as able to make claim to a soul or souls as are humans.
47 Kearney. 1963. p. 149.
48 Kearney. 1963. p. 52.

49 *Cf.* Tart, Charles T. 1971. *On Being Stoned: A Psychological Study of Marijuana Intoxication.* Palo Alto, California: Science and Behavior. p. 134.
50 Hall. 1983, 1963. pp. 31, 35, 68, 81, 183.
51 *Ibid.* pp. 79-80, 121.
52 *Ibid.* p. 168.
53 Kuhn. 1963. p. 162.
54 *Ibid.* p. 167.
55 *Ibid.* p. 172.
56 My Karok informant. 1984. On World Renewal. *Briceland Ecologian* 1: 5 (November 1). The last living Karok to remember the last Karok World Renewal Ceremony, deadpanned to me, "the last time we did the ceremony was when I was a boy, and you can see the world hasn't been right since!"
57 Kearney. 1963. pp. 159-161.
58 Hall. 1984, 1963. p. 81.
59 Hall. 1983, 1963. p. 31.

Chapter Seven

1 *New Century Dictionary.* 1931.
2 Some Mateelians question how representative Katz really is of them, but the incumbent did not hesitate to identify him as a "newcomer" who had shaved his beard and removed his Birkenstocks.
3 That a group sense of humor is an indispensible part of magical anarchy is indicated by the complete willingness of the group to be "joked" out of a tension filled situation.
4 To be perfectly objective, it is necessary to point out that this was one of the more tension filled gatherings I have witnessed in Mateel which retained any form at all. If it had gotten much more angry, it would have disintegrated completely. Such situations have occurred in the early history of the Mateel community, but I know of them only through the reports of informants with a longer residence in Mateel than mine. It is significant that the person being physical was widely known and had an impeccable reputation for community service. That he is somewhat more likely than others to use his size for emphasis is tolerated more in his case than it would be if he were not known as such a valuable member of the community.
5 It must be said, however, that since the purpose of this organization is to handle money, the central concern of Amerikan culture, the mainstream Amerikan laws governing it are especially stringent. The idea of an alternative credit union may have been unrealistic from the start.
6 Hall. 1984. pp. 55-72.
7 Hall. 1983, 1963. p. 188.
8 If this cannot be arranged, the meeting will very likely be adjourned before it starts. I have seen people choose to sit outside in questionable weather in order to form a circle rather than sit in a nice warm theater where they would have had to be seated in rows facing front. I have even heard it suggested that one meeting held in this theater for lack of an alternative was invalid because people were not able to seat themselves in a circle. If the group is too large for everyone to hear seated this way, a double-circle may be used. It is rare in Mateel that too many are gathered in one spot to discuss an issue to be seated in at least a double-circle.
9 I have never seen a single person successfully block a proposal. I have however, seen potential blockers who felt strongly about something maintain their position for hours under group scrutiny, finally retreating to the position "I pass," which means that the group may proceed with the proposal, but with the knowledge that some member of the group has strong reservations about it.

10 Toffler. 1980, 1963. p. 448.
11 *Cf.* Randers and Meadows. 1963. p. 335.
12 Hall. 1980, 1963. pp. 55-72.
13 Mills, C. Wright. 1958. *The Causes of World War III.* New York: Simon and Schuster. p. 43.
14 *Ibid.* p. 22.
15 *Ibid.* p. 43
16 Bateson. 1972. p. 275, and 1980.
17 Bateson. 1968. pp. 176-177. 1972. p. 432. 1980. p. 35. Kearney discusses this same feedback relationship between values and perception with regard to the influence of worldviews on environment, and Kuhn's "paradigms," with their supposed effect on scientific research, would seem to amount to the same thing.
18 Mills. 1959. p. 22.
19 Slater. 1974. pp. 195-199.
20 Goldsmith. 1963. p. 96. Anderson. 1963. p. 279. Taylor. 1963. pp. 153-154.
21 Hall. 1984, 1963. p. 177.
22 Taylor. 1963. p. 231.
23 *Cf.* Watt, *et al.* 1977. p. 261.
24 Bateson. 1972, 1963. p. 434.
25 Watt, *et al.* 1977. p. 45.
26 Goffman. 1956. Hall. 1980. p. 59.
27 This is the opinion of an anonymous informant in county government.

Chapter Eight

1 Mills. 1963. p. 44.
2 Arnold, Barbara. 1986. Ecology and Death in Mateel: the Meaning of Hoka Hey. In *Northwest Anthropological Research Notes* 20: 1.
3 Kogan, Ted, Ken Kern, and Rob Thallone. 1976. *The Owner-Builder and the Code.* Oakhurst, California: Owner-Builder Publications.
4 This input, along with foodstamps and MediCal, could be construed as parasitism. That analogy, however, would have to assume that mainstream Amerika derives no benefit from the existence of Mateel. Mateelians often consider that they are as useful to Amerika in the long run as any wage-earner since they are engaging in necessary social experimentation it would be difficult to find wage-earners willing to do. Welfare mothers, will also argue that mothers are necessary workers and should be paid. As one informant said, "I consider AFDC to be funding for alternative child-rearing research."
5 Kearney. 1963. p. 96.
6 Chapple, Steve. 1984. *Outlaws in Babylon.* New York: Pocketbooks.

Chapter Nine

1 Castaneda.
2 Hsu, 1963. p. 218, 219. Slater. 1974. p. 55. Slater sees the same relationship between individuality and freedom on the one hand and conformity and submission to authority on the other.
3 Reich, Charles. 1971. *The Greening of America.* New York: Bantam Books. pp. 142-143, 148.
4 Henry, Jules. 1965. *Culture Against Man.* New York: Random House. pp. 148-149 and pp. 291-293.

5 Reich. p. 143.
6 Slater. 1974, 1963. p. 64.
7 *Ibid*. p. 63-64.
8 Henry. 1963. p. 463.
9 Slater. 1974. p. 64.
10 Goffman. 1961. *Stigma: Notes on the Management of Spoiled Identity*. Englewood Cliffs, New Jersey: Prentice-Hall. p. 3.
11 *Ibid*. pp. 7, 13, 41, 106-108, 123.
12 *Ibid*. p. 95.
13 *Ibid*. p. 10.
14 Berreman, Gerald. 1974. *Bringing it All Back Home: Malaise in Anthropology. In Reinventing Anthropology*. Dell Hymes, ed. pp. 83-98. New York: Random House. p. 94.
15 Berreman. 1978. p. 237.
16 Tart.
17 *Ibid*. pp. 47-48. The focus of Tart's study was marijuana, but space was provided to indicate those effects that were also experienced on LSD. Since his sample was similar to the early Mateelians and his results appear to coincide with the experience of my informants, I have relied on Tart's study for this discussion.
18 *Ibid*. p. 132.
19 Hsu. 1963. p. 21.
20 Tart. 1963. p. 212.
21 *Ibid*. p. 116. Goffman. 1961, 1963. p. 138. This is emphasized by Tart and is implied throughout Goffman's discussion of visible stigmas.
22 Tart. 1963. p. 125.
23 *Ibid*. p. 145.
24 Raphael. 1985, 1963. p. 150.
25 Tart. 1963. p. 212.
26 Slater. 1974. p. 18.
27 Goffman. 1961. pp. 2, 105.
28 *Ibid*. p. 57.
29 For only a few was adopting a new name an adjustment to being some kind of a fugitive. Even in these cases the new name had meaning for the individual, rather than simply being a switch to a meaningless alias. Another reason why people change their names is that they have become tired of having a name shared by too many people. It is a statement against conformity and for uniqueness, reflecting the reaction against mass society.
30 It is not unknown for the third person naming custom to be used as a negative sanction and/or a general warning as to a negative aspect of someone's personality. Thus "Fast Jack" or "Rip-off Annie" may wish to shake the name and the reputation it implies and a major change in behavior would eventually do this. Without that change, however, the name operates as a sanction against antisocial behavior in the absence of other controlling mechanisms. This negative use of the custom is extremely rare. In seventeen years' residence, I have only heard of three examples.
31 Goffman. 1961. pp. 2, 105.
32 Tart. pp. 128-134, 212.
33 Goffman. 1961. p. 95.
34 Bateson. 1972. p. 208.
35 Tart. p. 120.
36 Goffman, Erving. 1957. Alienation from Interaction. *Human Relations*. 10: 47-60.
37 Hall. 1984, 1963. p. 160.
38 Slater, Phillip. 1968. Some Social Consequences of Temporary Systems. *In The Temporary Society*. Phillip Slater and Warren G. Benis, eds. New York: Harper and Row Publishers. pp. 83-86.
39 Tart. 1963. p. 134.

40 *Ibid.* p. 151. *Cf.* Grof, Stanislaus. 1975. *Realms of the Human Unconscious: Observations from LSD Research.* New York: Viking Press. p. 207.
41 Bateson, Gregory. 1958. *Naven.* Stanford: Stanford University Press. The only Amerikan custom which remotely qualifies as the ceremonial releasing of tensions related to self-definition and relationship is Halloween, or perhaps the office Christmas party. How effective either of these might be in releasing such tension would make an interesting study in itself. Certainly, it would be difficult to make a case that they approach the primitive ceremonies in performing this function.
42 Callenbach. 1981. pp. 52-54. See also pp. 27-28.

Chapter Ten

1 *Cf.* Ellul, Jacques. 1964. *The Technological Society.* New York, Vintage. pp. 49-60. *Cf.* Berger, Brigette and Peter L. Berger, 1983. *The War Over the Family: Capturing the Middle Ground.* Garden City, New York: Anchor. pp. 87-104. That kinship, that is, the extended family, was severely affected by the industrial revolution has been a widely accepted hypothesis for generations of sociologists, although there has been recent disagreement as to whether the relationship between modernization and the change from extended to nuclear families is linear or circular in causality.
2 Mead, Margaret. 1978. *Culture and Commitment.* New York: William Morrow. pp.xvii, 97.
3 *Ibid.* p. xix.
4 Slater. 1968, 1963. p. 88-95.
5 *Ibid.* p. 90. One must be careful to note that Western male writers are likely to be biased by the picture of the patriarchal family characteristic of Western society. When laments are made by, for instance, political conservatives about the "destruction of the family," they usually mean the patriarchal family and see the solution as the mandatory return of women to their subservient role in the home. As Marvin Harris (1981, 1963. pp. 76-97), has pointed out, the entry of women into the work force was a result of economic forces more than it was of philosophy. Feminists may justly bristle at this trivialization of their deeply philosophical experiences. Nevertheless, if Harris is correct that the stage for individual female experience was set by economic forces, forcefully returning women to the home would not address these economic forces. Therefore, a family form appropriate to a new, more ecologically oriented, post-industrial economic context would not be a simple return to enforced patriarchy, but would incorporate both complete equality for women and complete security for children through equal access to both parents.
6 Wolf. 1968. *Leonard and Deborah Rothchild, Voices from the Love Generation.* Boston: Little, Brown.
7 Reich. 1963. pp. 271, 272.
8 *Ibid.* p. 273.
9 Why "Sis" was never used by the counter-culture and "Sister" only became commonplace among white women with the women's movement would make an interesting study in itself. A working hypothesis would be the suggestion made here that counter-cultural existentialism was a male philosophy later rejected by women and replaced with a more unifying female conception.
10 U. S. Census. 1980.
11 Wolf and Rothchild.
12 The data presented here is based primarily on my ten year association with Beginnings, Inc. in Briceland. Beginnings is an umbrella non-profit organization which was founded originally for the purpose of obtaining land for a preschool and a community center. It presently includes a preschool, an elementary school, a fire department, a community center and a Tai Kwan Do building and once included, for a period of three years, an experimental

alternative high school. I was a founding member of the Board of Directors of Beginnings and served as a member of the Board twice. I was also an active parent during the time my two children attended Beginnings schools, and a teacher at the high school. The data also includes interviews with parents, teachers and children involved with five other alternative schools located within the six core watersheds, as well as with workers at the Redwoods Rural Health Center in Redway and parents, children and midwives encountered in my general research.
13 Pettitt. 1963. p. 127.
14 Wellish, Pam and Sandra Root. 1986. *Hearts Open Wide*. Berkeley.
15 Anders, Jentri. 1987. Trek to the Sixties, Part I. *Country Activist* 4:3 (April).
16 Bateson, Mary Catherine. 1984. *With a Daughter's Eye*. New York: William Morrow. p. 29.
17 Spock, Benjamin. 1985. *Baby and Child Care*. New York: Pocket Books.
18 Wellish. 1963. p. 167.
19 Neill, A. S. 1962. *Summerhill: A Radical Approach to Child-rearing*. New York: Hart.
20 One interesting observation begs for an explanation which I cannot offer. It is a very common occurance that when Mateelian children reach puberty, in spite of the relatively open attitude of their parents towards sexual matters, they suddenly become modest. At a Mateelian swimming hole in the summertime, the two groups most likely to be wearing bathing suits are the younger Mateelian teenagers and the non-Mateelian visitors.
21 Schneider, David M. 1980. *American Kinship*. Chicago: University of Chicago. p. 67.
22 *Ibid*. p. 38.
23 Mead, Margaret. 1942. p. 41.

Conclusion

1 The arsonist was never caught, but the consensus in both communities at this point is that a young man convicted of one of two similar arsons which occurred about the same time is the most likely suspect. It is widely believed that he was aiming at the fire station located in the MCC building, and that cross-cultural relations were not a factor in the arson. I refrain from mentioning these locations for fear that publicity will disrupt their normal cultural evolution in the same way that publicity has disrupted Mateel.
2 Hays, Dennis, editor. 1970. "Introduction," in *Earth Day—The Beginning, National Staff of Environmental Action*. New York: Arno Press.
3 Hall. 1983. p. 9.
4 Anderson. 1963. p. 279.
5 *Cf.* Bodley. 1974.
6 I refrain from mentioning these locations for fear that publicity will disrupt their normal cultural evolution in the same way that it has disrupted the evolution of Mateel.
7 Harris. 1978, 1963. p. 209.
8 Klein.
9 Bennett. 1963. p. 66.
10 Bateson. 1972, 1963. p. 437.
11 Kearney. 1963. p. 99.
12 Slater. 1968. p. 87.
13 Callenbach. 1975 and 1981.
14 Watt. 1977. p. 45.
15 Bateson. 1972. p. 426.
16 Hall. 1983. Goldsmith, *et al*. 1963. p. 126. Anderson. 1963. p. 275.
17 Taylor. 1963. pp. 156-157. Anderson. 1963. p. 274. Slater. 1974, 1963. p. 157.
18 For a discussion of the direct connection between the realization of personal potential and the rescuing of the global environment, see Roszak, Theodore. 1979. *Person/Planet: The Creative Disintegration of Industrial Society*, Garden City: Doubleday.

19 Slater. p. 175.
20 Skinner, B.F. 1962. *Walden II*. New York: Macmillan Paperbacks.
21 Odum. 1963. p. 248.
22 Perelman. 1963. pp. 196-197.
23 Slater. 1974. 191.

Appendix 2

1 Pure Shmint. 1979. *Vibram Soul*. Unpublished play.
2 Levi-Strauss, Claude. 1966. *The Savage Mind*. Chicago: University of Chicago Press.
3 Hall, Edward T. 1977. *Beyond Culture*. Garden City, New York: Anchor Books. p. 7.
4 *Ibid.*, p. 51.